Praise for

The Manson Women and Me

"A fascinating study of human behavior motivated by evil. . . . deeply poignant and revelatory… Meredith's passionate discussions of psychological influence and cult control are fascinating, and she ties these themes into her own history of growing up Jewish and facing the ever-present specter of anti-Semitism."
—*Kirkus Reviews*

"Meredith delves into the lives of two young women who participated in one of the most infamous murder sprees in American history."
—Susan Kelly, author of *The Boston Stranglers*

"A fully dimensional view of the Manson–led killings that we have not seen before."
—Michael Krasny,
author of *Off Mike: A Memoir of Talk Radio and Literary Life*

"Thought-provoking . . . combines a compassionate memoir with meticulous journalism."
—Julie Smith, author of the Skip Langdon mysteries

"Utterly absorbing and engaging."
—Sue Russell, author of *Lethal Intent*

"A must-read book . . . a disturbing reflection of America today."
—Suzy Spencer, author of *Wasted*

"Meredith asks the questions that have nagged many of us for years—how does this happen? Why them, and why not me?"
—*Shelf Awareness*

"Meredith uses her impressive journalist's skills and narrative powers to give us a fully realized dimensional view of the infamous Manson-led killings that we have not seen before—specifically, helping us to understand who the Manson women followers were and what led them to follow him into the throes of a moral maelstrom. The book is also a wide, illuminating portal to the so-called hippie milieu. Meredith weaves her own story in with a memoirist's certain hand, and it engages us as few memoirs do."
—**Michael Krasny,** award-winning host of *KQED Forum*

"Part memoir, part true crime, *The Manson Women and Me* is a must-read book. By looking back at the Manson crimes and trying to understand how and why Leslie Van Houten and Patricia Krenwinkel fell under the murderous spell of Charles Manson, Nikki Meredith reveals a disturbing reflection of America today. *The Manson Women and Me* is an eye-opening book that I simply could not stop reading."
—**Suzy Spencer,** *New York Times* bestselling author of *Wasted, Wages of Sin* and *Breaking Point*

"Utterly absorbing and engaging, Nikki Meredith's *Manson Women and Me* recounts her long, deeply personal, soul-searching journey toward understanding the roots of the Manson women's heinous violence. Through the intriguing prism of her own turbulent youth in Los Angeles, Meredith melds her decades-long relationships with inmates Leslie Van Houten and Patricia Krenwinkel and insights gained while chasing the elusive psychological truths behind such horrifically incomprehensible brutality. Incredibly, the Manson women took five years even to feel remorse. Almost thirty years later, Meredith's book brings us closer than any other to understanding why."
—**Sue Russell,** author of *Lethal Intent*

"Nikki Meredith has written a unique book. In it, she not only delves into the lives of Patricia Krenwinkel and Leslie Van Houten, two young women who participated, on order from Charles Manson, in one of the most infamous murder sprees in American history, but examines their stories though the lens of her own life."
—**Susan Kelly,** author of *The Boston Stranglers*

"A personal and professional fascination informs this inquiry into members of Charles Manson's family. In 1996, journalist and social worker Meredith wrote letters of interest to murderers Leslie Van Houten and Patricia Krenwinkel, and their responses sparked a twenty-year acquaintanceship that has given the author unprecedented access to these two 'Manson women.' Lively Van Houten, now 68, and a consistently dour, cheerless Krenwinkel, 70, both contributed hours of conversation as the author probed their psyches, hijacked by a cunning Manson, their sinister detachment from the 1969 murders, and their personal methods of deprogramming from their cult affiliation . . . Even more impressive are Meredith's passionate discussions of psychological influence and cult control, and she ties these themes into her own history of growing up Jewish and facing the ever-present specter of anti-Semitism. She also discusses the plight of her brother, who committed armed robbery as a youth and was imprisoned—not far from the women's facility where Van Houten and Krenwinkel remain today. The author also cogently deliberates on the complicated nature of remorse and how organized religion's 'automatic redemption' still prevents Krenwinkel (and many other wrongdoers) from truly acknowledging their culpability and their loss of humanity . . . A fascinating study of human behavior motivated by evil."

—*Kirkus Reviews*

"Meredith asks the questions that have nagged many of us for years: How does this happen? Why them and why not me?"

—Shelf Awareness

"Combining a compassionate memoir with meticulous journalism, author Nikki Meredith has produced a thought-provoking meditation on nothing less than the nature of evil. She cares about what causes it, but she doesn't stop there. She asks: once it's entered a person's psyche, can it be banished? Readers of true crime will find much to ponder here."

—Julie Smith, Edgar Award-winning author
of the Skip Langdon, Talba Wallis, and
Rebecca Schwartz mystery series

Monsters, Morality, and Murder

The Manson Women and Me

NIKKI MEREDITH

CITADEL PRESS
Kensington Publishing Corp.
www.kensingtonbooks.com

CITADEL PRESS BOOKS are published by

Kensington Publishing Corp.
119 West 40th Street
New York, NY 10018

All Kensington titles, imprints, and distributed lines are available at special quantity discounts for bulk purchases for sales promotions, premiums, fund-raising, educational, or institutional use.

Special book excerpts or customized printings can also be created to fit specific needs. For details, write or phone the office of the Kensington sales manager: Kensington Publishing Corp., 119 West 40th Street, New York, NY 10018, attn: Sales Department; phone 1-800-221-2647.

PUBLISHER'S NOTE
This is a work of nonfiction. To protect the privacy of certain individuals, their names have been changed or omitted.

ISBN-13: 978-0-8065-3859-4
ISBN-10: 0-8065-3859-7

First Citadel hardcover printing: April 2018
First trade paperback printing: March 2019

10 9 8 7 6 5 4 3 2 1

Printed in the United States of America

Electronic edition:

ISBN-13: 978-0-8065-3860-0 (e-book)
ISBN-10: 0-8065-3860-0 (e-book)

This book is dedicated to:

My son, for being my technology consultant

My daughter, for being my editorial consultant

My husband, for being my everything

Contents

Foreword
BY CAITLIN MEREDITH

I teach a journalism class in the local jail where I live in Austin, Texas. I alternate between the men's and women's sides, as well as the medium- and maximum-security units. Though I receive an enrollment list with each student's full name at the beginning of the term, because of a rule I made for myself, I make a point of only learning the nickname they ask me to call them in class. My rule? Don't Google until after the final projects are handed in. This is to protect my students from the inevitable biases that would emerge if I knew everything about their worst day on the first day I meet them. It's also to protect me from truly testing my beliefs in the power and promise of rehabilitation for all. In this way, I hope to teach the class to the best part of my students, no matter their pasts.

It turns out some of my most interesting, vibrant, and articulate students have been murderers and attempted murderers. They have used fire and knives and cars to injure and kill—sometimes by accident, and sometimes very much on purpose. One, in particular, comes to mind. She came to class each day, glossy dark brown hair in a high-perched ponytail, bubbling with ideas and enthusiasm. Whenever it came time for the students to read their day's work—a jail-related review, op/ed, or profile—and it was her turn, there would be an extra hush as we prepared to smile, sigh, and reflect on her lively prose. Each time, I would ask myself, how is this woman in jail? (Not to say that it was always obvious why my other students were in jail, but she seemed particularly unravaged by the usual: poverty, drugs, or mental illness.)

After the last class, I finally looked her up. The mystery of why she'd been such a class star was solved: she'd been a mommy blogger on the outside and, according to the prosecutor in her case, she wrote with a "witty, engaging, self-deprecating style that cultivated a regular readership." On a rare break from her social media status updates, however, she drove seven hours, broke into her ex-husband's house in the middle of the night, bound his limbs with zip ties, wrapped him in plastic wrap, and beat him over the head with a billy club. For some reason, this had seemed to her the best way to guarantee that she would get full possession of her children in their hotly contested custody battle. Wow. But she sure did write a riveting review of the Thanksgiving dinner at the Travis County Jail!

My mom, in her work with notorious former Manson "Family" members Leslie Van Houten and Patricia Krenwinkel, has done the opposite of my no-Google rule. Instead of protecting herself from the grotesque realities of human behavior at its worst, her meetings with Leslie and Pat were front-loaded with the meticulous descriptions—and even photos—of the heinous cruelty they'd inflicted on their victims on their worst days, acts so evil that most Americans would never want to be in the same room, much less sit down for a chat. Through this process, she had to navigate her own visceral aversion and anger toward human beings who had committed these acts with eyes wide open. In her work, unlike in my classroom, she could never look away from their crimes, but was compelled instead to look right into the deep center of the wounds, asking again and again: Why? How?

My mother's quest to understand what motivated the Manson women to commit their crimes was contagious. As she embarked on her research, spending time at Frontera Prison talking to Leslie and Pat, traveling up and down California to interview relatives, high school friends, and psychologists, I was hearing about it over the phone from my liberal arts college on the East Coast. I was born after the crimes and I'd never read *Helter Skelter*, so I only learned about Manson and his Family legacy through her recounted discussions with Leslie and Pat. When she first got to know them, I was twenty years old, just Leslie's age when she was in thrall with

Charles Manson, so I was susceptible to projecting myself into the
L.A. stoner scene of the late '60s. There was (and is) something deeply
disturbing about the male/female dynamic that played out through
Leslie's relationship with Manson that bled into my subconscious. I
started to have a recurring nightmare that involved an enigmatic
Manson-like figure seizing control of me while I was driving. The
dream took on the characteristic of a warped real-life version of the
video game *Pole Position*, though this game was no fun. At the
man's direction, I started mowing down pedestrians. As the body
count rose, my fear would finally shake me awake. Was the dream a
glimpse of my own capabilities to inflict harm under the influence of
a dark force? Was the message that under the right circumstances,
maybe I was no different from Leslie and Pat?

My mom confronted this same question in the light of day for
twenty years. Her curiosity brought her to some uncomfortable places.
The better she has come to know Leslie and Pat, the harder it has been
to dismiss them, as most of the world would like to, as incomprehensible demons with nothing to teach the rest of us about our own
natures. When confronted by evil acts, we hope for monsters, but
what my mom found instead were two very human humans. Humans
so familiar, in fact, that the comparisons to her own life and choices
became inevitable. Where most of us would look only for differences, my mom sought resonances . . . and found them.

Make no mistake, the murders Leslie and Pat committed on behalf of Charles Manson can and never will fade into the continuum
of "normal" human experience—there was true, permanent harm
done to the victims and their families. But averting our eyes from
what we share with these women serves only to perpetuate the myth
that the rest of us are somehow immune to influences that might corrupt our own characters.

In 1995, my mother started an experiment. Her guiding question
was to understand the far reaches of the human psyche. Though she
spent hours plumbing the depths of Leslie's and Pat's lives and ex-

periences to help her understand how these particular women could find themselves wielding a murderous knife, she also spent considerable time examining the ways in which the pushes and pulls in her own background both protected her but, at times, didn't protect her in her weakest moments. Few of us want to know how close to the edge we might veer. How lucky we are to be invited along on this fascinating investigation.

April 2017

THE MANSON WOMEN
AND ME

Introduction

In August 1969, on two consecutive nights, a group of young people entered two homes in Los Angeles and systematically murdered everyone present—a total of seven people. It's impossible to overstate the fear that gripped the city that summer. Initially, the lack of an apparent motive served to heighten the panic. There was no evidence of a connection between the victims and their murderers, and though the victims were wealthy, except for incidentals, they were not robbed. Creating terror seemed to be the only motive, and it worked.

From the Westside to South Central, from the beaches of the Pacific to the San Fernando Valley, the panic was palpable. The murders left an indelible stain on the psyche of our culture; it would later be said that the boundless, creative spirit of the 1960s died along with the victims those two nights in August.

When the guilty people were ultimately identified—Charles Manson, Tex Watson, Susan Atkins, Patricia Krenwinkel, and Leslie Van Houten—the dread only intensified. Manson, the mastermind of the carnage, was scary but he was scary in predictable ways. There was much in his life to explain his twisted psyche. The young people he controlled, especially the women, didn't look like anyone's idea of frightening. They looked like our sisters, our daughters, our friends—

ourselves—and yet their bloodthirsty behavior was like something out of a horror movie.

The murders were bad enough. The behavior of the murderers during their trial was unbearable; they mocked the grief of their victims' families and thumbed their collective noses at society's fears and outrage.

Twenty years ago, I started visiting two of these women in prison—Leslie Van Houten and Patricia Krenwinkel—in an attempt to discover whether they were radically different from the young women who carried out Charles Manson's barbaric orders in 1969. If they were different, from their perch of middle age, how did they understand what happened?

In the course of my inquiry, because I more or less share the same demographic as the women, I was lured into exploring the ways in which my own life had been affected by some of the same influences. In doing so I recognized that there were times when had I zigged instead of zagged, my life might also have veered dramatically off course.

I was high school friends with two of the people involved in the case: Catherine Share, Manson's chief recruiter of young women; and Stephen Kay, the deputy district attorney who was second chair to Vincent Bugliosi in the Tate-LaBianca murder trial. As I traced Catherine Share's story and my relationship to that story, I realized how, for a variety of reasons, my connection to her at the age of fifteen was pivotal in my own moral development. Stephen Kay helped me understand the machinations of the justice system; by his side, I observed the parts that are just and the parts that are decidedly unjust.

The journey to find answers has been bumpy, with deep potholes, wide-ranging detours, and frequent dead ends. Many times, I gave up, stowed the ugly, battered baggage, and took off for more scenic and straightforward jaunts.

From the beginning I encountered many roadblocks—so many that they contributed to a recurring fear that the project was doomed.

The first was that as soon as I decided to interview the women, I learned that the California legislature had recently passed a law preventing journalists from doing so. I could visit as a friend but I couldn't take notes or record.

At the time, the new law seemed like an omen—so did losing a man whose expertise I had counted on to help me understand essential aspects of the case. Early on I had sought out Dr. Chris Hatcher, a world-renowned forensic psychologist and an authority on violence who had been involved in many high-profile cases such as David Koresh (Waco) and Jim Jones (Jonestown). For years I had followed his work, reading his articles and attending rounds he conducted at U.C. Medical Center in San Francisco. For weeks we kept missing each other by phone, but when we finally connected, he not only agreed to meet with me, he was enthusiastic about the project and about helping me make sense of the material I was collecting. I was thrilled. Two days before our scheduled appointment, he died of a brain aneurysm at the age of fifty-three.

Some days my superstitious nature got the best of me and I started to suspect that somebody or something didn't want me to write this book. Essential tools of the trade started to malfunction at an alarming rate. Hard drives crashed, monitors failed, keys on my keyboard stuck. My right arm started to ache, my fingers got numb, and at one point I was in too much pain to use the keyboard or write longhand. I couldn't shake the belief that it was not meant to be.

Many of the problems I encountered were of my own making. In the first few years of the venture, I ignored my better judgment and instead of maintaining a sharp focus, I adopted a shotgun approach. Every journalist knows the danger of spending too much time with subjects of questionable value or endlessly chasing down material that is likely to be peripheral. I talked to anyone and everyone who would talk to me, scouted locations far and wide where the band of reprobates left its mark, and compiled my own little Manson Family library. But the quest for "color" and context can take you just so far. This insatiable yearning to acquire even the tiniest clue was sustained by the hope that once assembled with all of the other tiny clues, I might discern a pattern of human behavior that made sense to me. One particularly low-yield example comes to mind: I tracked down a guy who knew a guy whose best friend's grandmother had been a friend of Manson's in the 1960s. That's several hours of my life I'll never get back.

My interest in the two women was the primary draw, but there was also a personal angle. When my brother was the same age as Leslie, he committed a felony home invasion that involved an older couple. No one died, but he did go to prison; in fact he went to the men's prison just a few miles from where Leslie and Pat are incarcerated. I knew how that experience affected my family. I knew that my brother wasn't a psychopath, but I also knew that something enabled him to detach emotionally from the terror of his victims. My unanswered questions about this detachment, in part, fueled my interest in Patricia and Leslie.

In addition to the universe acting as a real or imagined opponent, my progress or lack thereof was influenced by major news events. I completely stopped working on it for a long time post-9/11. After that cataclysmic event, the loss of seven people in the Tate-LaBianca murders seemed almost trivial. Abu Ghraib had the opposite effect. In 2004, the photos of the smiling Lynndie England humiliating prisoners reminded me of the smirking mockery displayed by Leslie and Pat after the murders. On the other side of the cultural divide, as information about young women jihadists started to trickle in, I noticed many parallels with Pat and Leslie: more or less educated, middle class, and under the influence or control of a malevolent "spiritual" leader.

Paradoxically, the main draw to violence for most of these women (and it was true of both Pat and Leslie) is ideological—the desire to right wrongs—and an overwhelming hunger to be part of something larger than their little lives. The most chilling similarity, however, is a complete lack of compassion for victims or potential victims. I also noticed a parallel in the way the media focuses on a particular kind of woman who commits a particular kind of violence.

When the shooting in San Bernardino occurred in 2015, there was universal bewilderment that the mother of a six-month-old baby, Tashfeen Malik, was involved (*Times* of London: "Hatred More Powerful Than a Mother's Love"). I believe we have a special place in our chamber of fears for violent women—especially violent women who look like prom princesses, as did Leslie Van Houten, or who are mothers of babies, as was Tashfeen Malik. The male shooter was the father of the same baby, but that was rarely mentioned in the media's coverage of him.

Even during periods when I set aside the project, I maintained my relationship with the women—corresponding with them and visiting when I could. My wish to understand the discrepancy between who they are now and who they were then never abated, but had I wanted to forget, the culture wouldn't let me. It's no exaggeration to say that almost every day since I embarked on this path, in a multitude of contexts, from jokes to metaphors, to serious references to evil, both Manson and the Manson Family have been mentioned in the media.

The question that kept me returning to the project: If the women weren't psychopaths or whatever term is now used to signify the absence of a conscience—sociopaths, borderline, narcissistic personality disorder—what happened to their humanity on those two nights? In the following pages you will read Patricia's and Leslie's descriptions of the horrible suffering of their victims. The brutality was very up close and very personal. They not only heard the cries, they felt bones and organs crushing at their own hands. What prevented them from responding to such horrible suffering? Why was it that it took a full five years after the murders for them to have any feelings for their victims?

In my attempt to understand, I scoured research on the violent behavior of ordinary people, behavior that was exhibited in experiments but also real-life situations of mass brutality: Rwanda, Guatemala,

Bosnia, and on a smaller scale, the barbarity at Abu Ghraib. But in my life, the extermination of six million Jews in Nazi Germany was what, early on, planted the need to understand this kind of barbarity in my mind. However, it wasn't until I started to write this book that I realized how much my hybrid Jewishness, the Nazis called it *Mischling*, has informed my life and how much it's baked in to my interest in the Manson women.

When I was a girl I had a favorite knitted scarf; the dominant colors were muted shades of charcoal, pale blue, and lilac. But threaded throughout the fabric was a slender gold lamé strand. When I imagine my Jewishness, I think about that gold thread that looped through the length of the scarf. Though slender, it was always visible, always providing a glint of illumination when the scarf caught the light from the sun.

Once I became aware of how much my Jewish heritage informed my life, it started to seem like an apparition hovering over everyone and everything I encountered along the way. At first, its influence seemed out of proportion. I am, after all, only a quarter breed and Jews make up little more than 2 percent of the population.

How could it be connected to my interest in the Manson women? Here's how: growing up in the shadow of the Holocaust, learning that Jews were killed just because they were Jews and realizing that even my diluted Jewish blood would have put me and my family in very real danger, planted the question "why?" at a pretty early age. Why would ordinary Germans, commanded by Hitler, methodically kill people with Jewish blood—babies, adults, grandpas, grandmas—people who had done nothing wrong?

That question hounded me as a girl, affected my young adulthood in complicated ways, and then, more recently, led to the central question of this book: Why? Why did two ordinary women, at the behest of Charles Manson, brutally murder people they did not know? Consistent with one of the themes of this project (i.e., all roads lead to Jewishness) I had always believed that three of the adult victims—Abigail Folger, Jay Sebring, and Voytek Frykowski—were Jews. I didn't imagine this was the motive but I did believe in a way I can't articulate that it was a factor. I'm not sure where I got this idea of their respective ethnicities, but I have been unable to verify it.

We do know that one victim, Sharon Tate's unborn baby, was half Jewish. The father, Roman Polanski, is not only Jewish, both his mother and his sister were imprisoned at Auschwitz—his sister survived, his mother did not. And on the subject of Jewishness, there's another "why" that plagued me: Why would Catherine Share, an orphan of Hitler's holocaust, throw her lot in with Manson, a man who carved a swastika on his forehead? For a while it seemed as though everywhere I looked in my history there was a Star of David or a swastika, both symbolically or literally. Sometimes these associations seemed excessive, even to me, and I'd think about the way Alvy Singer, the character Woody Allen plays in *Annie Hall*, would see or hear references to Jews no one else could see or hear. One example: He's telling a friend about having lunch with some guys from NBC. Alvy asks, "Did you eat yet or what?" And one of the NBC guys answers: "No, didchoo?"

"Not, 'did you?'" Alvy explains, but, "'didchoo eat? Jew?' No, not 'did you eat,' but 'Jew eat?' Jew. You get it? Jew eat?"

How can I explain that the swastika Manson carved on his forehead was, in a strange way, almost as shocking as the murders? How can it have triggered anything in me even close to the shock that they murdered so many innocent people?

Once you understand that there is something about you that is so hated, you could be killed for it, it colors everything. How can there be something about me, something that has nothing to do with the content of my character, that would shut off even a glimmer of empathy in others? How does it work, this mechanism that shuts off empathy in response to an ethnicity, a culture, the color of skin? What happens to the brains of people who can no longer feel the suffering of fellow human beings?

The Jewish question may seem irrelevant to understanding the Manson women but not to me—never to me.

The result of this journey is a mosaic of associations, some having to do directly with the Manson women, some loosely associated with them, and some tangential but all helping me to make a little more comprehensible the incomprehensible.

Over the past twenty years, I have grappled with the brutality of events on those two nights in the summer of 1969 and the opacity of human nature they revealed. This account describes my efforts to penetrate this mystery by peering through several different prisms. In doing so, I've learned a great deal about human behavior, much of it disheartening but some of it proof of our capacity as humans to transform ourselves, even those of us who have committed unspeakable acts. Nonetheless, all these years later, I'm left with an enduring sadness over the suffering of the victims, the ones whose lives were taken in such a vicious way and the ones who were left behind to grieve their loss.

chapter one
THE FORMOSA CAFÉ

1995

I walked into the Formosa Café, adjusted my eyes to the relative dark, and scanned the bar, looking for George, the man I was scheduled to meet. It was 1995 and I was researching a story about settled gypsies, and George, who was one, wanted to meet in Hollywood, far from the authoritarian eyes of the patriarch of his clan in Northern California. I'd suggested the Formosa Café because it was close to where he was living or said he was living, and it was the only bar I still knew in Hollywood, having left the city, my youth, and the bad food at the Formosa more than thirty years before.

I didn't see him when I arrived, so I sat idly watching a tennis match on the TV above the bar. A fleshy man in his late forties, looking uncomfortable in a starched white shirt and pinstriped suit, took the stool next to me. He ordered an Anchor Steam and asked the bartender if he minded switching the channel to the O.J. trial—a request I found puzzling. Even in L.A., most people were taking a break from the proceedings; criminalist Dennis Fung had been droning on for days and all but the most ardent trial watchers had tuned out.

The bartender, a lean, upright man in a waiter's uniform left over from the same era as most of the movie stars whose autographed black-and-white photos were displayed on the walls, handed him the remote. The man clicked through the channels, stopping when he heard "crime of the century." But Dennis Fung wasn't on the screen. Instead, a pretty woman who resembled Mary Tyler Moore was talking about remorse. In 1969, she and three others were involved in the murder of a couple—a thirty-nine-year-old woman, a wife and mother of two, and her forty-four-year-old husband.

"Who is that?" my bar partner said.

"Leslie Van Houten," I said. "One of the Manson women."

I hadn't seen her face for twenty-five years. Of all the actors in that horror show, she was the most puzzling to me. Maybe it was her wholesomeness, her doe eyes, her fresh face.

She was saying that the older she got, the harder it was to reconcile herself to what happened. "Mrs. LaBianca was younger than I am now. I took away all that life."

We were watching a documentary about Charles Manson called *A Journey to Evil*. There were clips of prison interviews with two of Manson's accomplices: Patricia Krenwinkel and Leslie Van Houten. Both were expressing remorse.

"It's bullshit," the guy on the next stool said. "It's an act. They're sick. The whole lot of them."

Manson's diabolical face then appeared on the screen to proclaim his resolute lack of remorse. "Woman, that doesn't wrinkle my forehead none," he said when the interviewer asked how he felt about Sharon Tate's murder.

He continued with his trademark mumbo jumbo, and the guy at the bar decided he was more interested in the current trial of the century and switched to Dennis Fung. After a half hour I gave up on the gypsy and walked out into the afternoon sun.

It was February and one of those rare L.A. days when the air is cool, the sky the color of cornflowers, and the tops of the palm trees more than an impressionistic blur. The Santa Monica Mountains that bound that end of the city were startlingly clear. I remembered being delighted years before when a man at a dinner party in San Francisco proclaimed that nowhere else on earth was there an uglier juxtaposition of mountain and ocean than in Los Angeles.

I had fled the city because of the usual culprits: the car-choked freeways, the ubiquity of strip malls and asphalt, the lung-bruising air. But I was also fleeing the very thing that drew my grandparents there in the early years of the century: the atmosphere of boundless possibility. Since its inception, L.A. had been a place to experiment, to shed the past. But a place that lends itself so readily to transformation is, by its very nature, ephemeral, and when I was growing up, it all felt a little too impermanent.

But now the city stirred some ineffable longing in me; it was no longer the bad air, but other particulates—the night-blooming jasmine, seedy cocktail lounges, red hibiscus, and bungalow courts—that made it hurt when I breathed. What once seemed so transient had become bedrock.

I walked down Formosa Avenue past the Warner-Hollywood Studios, the costume supply and post-production companies, and stucco garden apartments with bars on the windows. Even in the days when Hollywood could claim some glamour, this neighborhood was the underbelly. I thought about the Manson women and how the guy in the bar declared them "sick" with such certainty. His characterization was kinder than prosecutor Vincent Bugliosi's who, in *Helter Skelter*, the best-selling account of the murders, described them to the jury as "human monsters, mutations without hearts, without souls."

I first read *Helter Skelter* in 1975 when I was at home luxuriating in what were supposed to be deliciously indolent days following the birth of my youngest child. A good friend had given it to me, as he wrote in the inscription, "to entertain you while you nurse your new baby." My husband thought another book for my infant care collection might have been a more appropriate gift, but this friend and I had long shared an interest in the murders.

We'd met working in a residential program for young, first break schizophrenics. At the time, I was the program director and a psychiatric social worker; he was an intern getting his PhD in psychology. We were both interested in looking at disturbed behavior in the context of family systems. The young people in Manson's group had rejected their families of origin and had created a new one—one that redefined family and, in the process, stripped them of their basic humanity.

Jacob, the book giver, knew I had more personal reasons to be interested in the case. I'd attended Hollywood High School where I'd been friends with two key figures in the *Helter Skelter* story— Stephen Kay, the young deputy district attorney who assisted Vincent Bugliosi at the trial; and Catherine Share, aka Gypsy, who had assisted Charles Manson in recruiting young girls into his tribe.

Also, there were issues in my own family of origin that were somewhat parallel, though certainly not as extreme. My brother had served time for a home invasion robbery, and Jacob knew how that had affected me. Like the young people in Manson's group, my brother was the offspring of middle-class parents who had high expectations of him. Like Leslie Van Houten, he was popular, smart, good looking, affable. He, too, dropped out of college, lived both aimlessly and recklessly, saturating his brain with psychedelics. This described thousands of kids in the 1960s, but few of them committed crimes like my brother—a frightening home invasion that involved an older couple. He had been incarcerated at the California Institution for Men in Chino, just a few miles from the prison where the three Manson women ended up.

So, despite my personal reasons to be interested in the case, I had just as many reasons to avoid it, reasons about which Jacob was oblivious. He was not yet a father and had a limited understanding of the psychological vulnerabilities of nursing mothers. While *Helter Skelter* was indeed a page-turner, I was so frightened by the contents, the book itself became a totemic embodiment of evil that I couldn't bear to have in the same room as my freshly minted daughter or my six-year-old son. The idea of random savagery is especially terrifying when your protective hormones are at their peak and safeguarding your baby's every breath is your total preoccupation.

But it wasn't Charles Manson, an old-fashioned psychopath with a New Age angle, who was the source of my terror. Because he looked deranged, he was somehow easier for me to dismiss. It was the women. Their seeming normality coupled with the barbarity of the crimes, their insult-to-injury behavior during the trial, their mocking disdain for the grief of the victims' families— ten families in all—was unfathomable. And because I had known Catherine Share, Manson's chief recruiter, when she was a bright, pretty, and all-around appealing high school student, her devotion to him was even more startling. While she didn't directly participate in the Tate-LaBianca murders, she committed other crimes at his direction.

In my mind, the description of the murdered Sharon Tate, eight months pregnant, curled in a fetal position, her silky blond hair and the pattern of her floral lingerie nearly obscured by a cloak of blood, were superimposed on the photos of Leslie Van Houten, Patricia Krenwinkel, and Susan Atkins at the trial, holding hands, skipping down the courthouse halls singing Manson's songs, looking as though they were on their way to some kind of hippie hoedown. The images of those girls and the brutal murders would float in and out of my consciousness for the next couple of decades.

Since the Tate-LaBianca murders, Charles Manson had achieved almost mythic status in the country. To a subgroup of disaffected European and American youth he was a folk hero, an inspiration, an eternal rebel without a cause. To the rest of us, in his pint-size way, he had become as much a symbol of evil as Hitler. Though Manson didn't personally kill any of those seven people, he was more widely known than any other serial killer.

One of the impenetrable mysteries of Hitler's Holocaust continues to be the unspeakable brutality of ordinary Germans—middle-class people who contributed in direct and intimate ways to the slaughter of Jews. Similarly, the enduring potency of the Manson myth derives not only from his involvement in the murders but from his deft extermination of the humanity of seemingly normal young people who killed at his behest.

After a glimpse of Leslie Van Houten's and Patricia Krenwinkel's apparent penitence, I wanted to find out about their journey, and that of Susan Atkins, the third woman who was convicted with them. I remembered Leslie's attorney, Maxwell Keith, pleading with the jury: "Study her, don't kill her." The jury had decided to kill her anyway—a decision that was later reversed when the California Supreme Court declared the state's death penalty law, as it was then written, unconstitutional. (See chapter 7.)

So had she been studied? Did the women have, as Vincent Bugliosi contended, something "deep in their souls" that would have propelled them to violence even without Manson? Or were they simply forlorn, impressionable youngsters whose minds were rendered useless because of a combination of social turmoil, drugs, and the exquisite manipulative skills of a psychopath? From their perch of middle age, what was their understanding of why on two successive nights in 1969 they participated in the murders of seven people they did not know?

I wrote to Leslie Van Houten and Patricia Krenwinkel at the California Institution for Women at Frontera, requesting interviews. For reasons I will explain later, I decided to hold off on contacting Susan Atkins.

chapter two
ABIGAIL FOLGER'S SMILE

August 1969

The nightmare started on August 8, 1969. Though decades later some of the particulars of the murders are still in question, we do know that Charles Manson instructed Tex Watson (22), Susan Atkins (20), Patricia Krenwinkel (20), and Linda Kasabian (19) to drive to 10050 Cielo Drive—a gated estate at the edge of Benedict Canyon—and rob and kill everyone inside. Manson did not include Leslie Van Houten that first night nor did he go himself. He remained at Spahn Ranch, an old movie set in Chatsworth on the outskirts of Los Angeles, where he and about twenty young people were living, commune style.

Why Manson targeted that house, on that night, and for what reason is still subject to debate, but we do know that his connection to the house involved record producer Terry Melcher, Doris Day's son. Though he had since moved out, Melcher once lived at 10050 Cielo Drive with his then girlfriend Candice Bergen. Manson was obsessed with the idea that Melcher, with whom he was acquainted, would help him become a recording star. When Melcher reneged on producing a long-promised record, Manson, according to Susan Atkins's subsequent grand jury testimony, decided to scare the hell out of him.

Once they got to the estate, the four—armed with bolt cutters, a gun, ropes, and knives—severed the phone lines and scaled the fence. Walking toward the house, they encountered an old Nash Rambler driven by Steven Parent, an eighteen-year-old friend of William Garretson, the estate's caretaker, who lived in the guest cottage at the back of the property. Parent was on his way home. Tex Watson shot and killed him.

While Kasabian stood guard outside, the other three went into the house where they found four people. The best known was Sharon Tate. Tate was a veteran of more than ten films, mostly of the B variety, but she hadn't gained public attention until 1967 when she starred in *Valley of the Dolls* with Patty Duke and Barbara Parkins. Lovely, luminous, sweet, sexy are the words her family and friends still use when they talk about her. One of those friends, Mia Farrow, described Tate in her memoir, *What Falls Away*, as a fairy princess, "as sweet and good as she was beautiful."

Tate met Roman Polanski in 1967 when he cast her as the female lead in *The Fearless Vampire Killers,* a horror spoof, and they were married a year later. In August 1969 she was eight months pregnant with their child.

At the time of the murders, Polanski was in London writing the script for his next film. He was still riding high from the previous year's success of *Rosemary's Baby*—a film starring Mia Farrow about a young woman who is forced by her husband into an alliance with a group of devil worshippers. After the murders, of course, the film would come to seem mysteriously prophetic.

In the first frenzied weeks after the murders, there were rumors that Polanski had been involved. To some, his preoccupation with violence and the occult as reflected in his films made him suspect. Any connection was soon disproved. His preoccupation with violence was a logical consequence of his childhood during World War II. Polanski, who is Jewish, was consigned with his family to live in the Krakow ghetto. When his mother was four months pregnant, she was captured by storm troopers and sent to Auschwitz, where she was gassed.

Also in the house that night was hairstylist Jay Sebring, thirty-five, whose clients included Frank Sinatra, Steve McQueen, George Peppard, and Paul Newman. Sebring and Sharon Tate had once been lovers, but now he was a family friend.

Abigail Folger, twenty-five, an heiress to the Folger Coffee fortune, was also there that night. In spite of her pedigree—she grew up on Nob Hill in San Francisco; boarded at the Santa Catalina school in Monterey (as would Patty Hearst ten years later); held her debutante ball at the St. Francis Hotel; graduated from Radcliff—she veered away from the high society path after moving to Los Angeles. She worked in the inner city for the L.A. County Welfare Department as a volunteer social worker and in the months before she was murdered she had joined Tom Bradley's 1969 campaign to become the first black mayor of Los Angeles. When Bradley was defeated by Sam Yorty, Folger, according to her friends, was incensed by the racist tactics used by Yorty's campaign staff.

The fourth person in the house that night was Abigail Folger's thirty-two-year-old lover, Voytek Frykowski—a bon vivant, and a sometime writer. As a youth, he'd been friends with Polanski in Poland, but Abigail met him in 1968 through Polish novelist Jerzy Kosinski.

The victims, who were located in various rooms, were apparently not immediately alarmed by the presence of strangers. According to subsequent testimony by the murderers, the victims must have believed that they were connected to someone in the household. Susan Atkins, who had slipped into the house through a back window, walked down the hall and poked her head into a bedroom where she saw Abigail Folger lying on the bed reading. Sensing someone at the door, Abigail looked up from her book and smiled.

She would have smiled. On the surface at least, it was still a casual, open time in L.A. There were serial parties, parties with ample drugs—cocaine, hashish, LSD—and where the music was loud and ever-present as were the hangers-on. This was the kind of house where people were always dropping in—a place where someone's friend's cousin would stop by, smoke a joint, listen to a record, take a swim, and end up staying for a month. It would later be said that what happened that night was inevitable, that the drugs had gotten too hard, the sex too easy, that a deranged tension had been building. The party had gone on too long. But that night, Abigail Folger looked up from her book and simply smiled at the girl with the bright brown eyes and long dark hair.

It would also be said later that the hope and promise of the 1960s was vanquished forever that night when Atkins, Krenwinkel, and Watson killed eighteen-year-old Steven Parent, rounded up the four occupants of the house, and then clubbed, stabbed, and shot them to death.

Accounts of the bloody tableau found by the housekeeper the next day stunned the country, but even more horrifying were the details we later learned about the terror the victims had suffered. Sharon Tate begged Susan Atkins not to kill her. "I want to have my baby," she cried. In recounting this exchange to the grand jury, Atkins recalled her reply: "I have no mercy for you, woman."

We learned that Steven Parent, a kid from the San Gabriel Valley whose family priest described him as a "stereo bug," a kid who knew everything about phonographs and radios, had been at Cielo Drive only to see if he could sell his clock radio to William Garretson, the caretaker. According to Linda Kasabian's account, Steven also begged for his life. Just before Tex Watson shot him in the head, he cried, "I promise I won't tell anyone."

From Los Angeles County Coroner Thomas Noguchi, we learned that in his entire experience as a medical examiner he had never before seen evidence of the kind of savagery that was applied to Voytek Frykowski, a man who fought fiercely for his life. According to

Noguchi's report, Frykowski was struck over the head thirteen times with a blunt object, stabbed fifty-one times, and shot twice.

The first suspect was William Garretson whom police found sleeping in the guest cottage when they arrived at the crime scene the next morning. But twenty-four hours later, with Garretson still in custody, a second night of terror took place ten miles from Benedict Canyon.

chapter three
"HEALTER SKELTER"

1969

On August 9, 1969, Manson and the crew from the night before—Atkins, Kasabian, Watson, and Krenwinkel—set out in search of another house of victims. This time, however, Leslie Van Houten joined them. Earlier in the day at Spahn Ranch, Manson had asked Leslie if she believed enough in what he said to kill for him. Leslie replied, "Yes." She didn't know the details of the previous night's mayhem, but she did know people had died. She was upset that she'd been excluded. There was a buzz at the ranch, nothing specific, but enough to make her feel left out, the way you do when friends have been to a party to which you weren't invited.

After wandering through L.A. for a couple of hours, Manson directed Kasabian, who was at the wheel, to drive to 3301 Waverly Drive in Los Feliz. Once again, why he targeted this house is still in dispute, but he did know the neighborhood because Harold True, a friend and occasional drug dealer, had once lived across the street.

Inside the house, Leno and Rosemary LaBianca were getting ready for bed. That day they had been to Lake Isabella, a resort

150 miles northeast of L.A., with Rosemary's children from a previous marriage—Frank, (15), and Suzan (21). Frank had been staying at the lake with friends of the LaBiancas but planned to return home with his mother and stepfather at the end of the outing. Before they left, however, he persuaded his parents to let him stay behind with his friend for one more night. The LaBiancas returned to L.A. with the boat and dropped Suzan off at her apartment.

Leno, a heavyset Italian-American, was a wealthy man. He owned real estate in California and Nevada, a small collection of thoroughbred racehorses, and he was chief stockholder of the State Wholesale Grocery Company, which operated a chain of food markets. He had met Rosemary, a pretty dark-haired woman, at the Los Feliz Inn where she was working as a hostess. From all accounts, her life had been difficult before she met Leno. Abandoned by her biological parents at an early age, she'd lived in an orphanage until she was adopted by a family at the age of twelve. After graduating from high school, she got a job as a carhop at the Brown Derby where she met her first husband. They were married in 1948, when she was eighteen, and divorced in 1958. Suzan and Frank were the result of that marriage.

After marrying Leno, she was able to buy her own business, Boutique-Carriage, a women's dress shop in downtown L.A. According to family and friends, Rosemary and Leno, who'd been married for eleven years, were still very much in love when they were killed.

When the Manson group arrived at the LaBiancas', Manson snuck into the house while the others remained in the car. Once inside, he brandished a knife and told the family that he was there to rob them and if they cooperated they wouldn't be hurt. Using leather thongs, he tied the two together back to back and returned to the car, instructing Tex, Pat, and Leslie to go in and kill the couple and then to hitchhike back to the ranch. Then he, Atkins, and Kasabian drove away.

When the three got into the house, they went to the kitchen and found a ten-inch carving fork and an eight-inch serrated wood-handled knife. Patricia and Leslie untied Rosemary LaBianca and took her into the bedroom, where they placed her facedown on the bed. They put a pillowcase over her head and wrapped the cord from a bedside lamp around her neck.

In the living room, Tex pushed Leno back onto the couch and began stabbing him. Leno screamed in terror and tried to free his hands, which were still tied behind his back. Tex stabbed him four times in the abdomen and then slashed his throat with the serrated knife, which he left in his throat.

In the bedroom, Mrs. LaBianca started to fight back and, in the struggle, fell to the floor and pulled the lamp down with her. Both Leslie and Patricia tried to stab her but they weren't strong enough, so they called Tex from the living room, who came in and did the actual killing. He then ordered Leslie to stab her, which she did. Before they left, Tex carved the word "war" on Mr. LaBianca's chest. Patricia took the carving fork and plunged it into Mr. LaBianca's abdomen fourteen times.

After killing the couple, they removed a tapestry from the wall and in its place, with a towel dipped in Mr. LaBianca's blood, wrote "death to pigs." In the living room, they wrote "rise" and then Patricia wrote "Healter [sic] Skelter" on the refrigerator. Before leaving they had a snack and petted and fed the LaBiancas' three dogs.

The following night, Sunday, Frank was dropped off at his house by his friend's parents. As he lugged his suitcase and camping equipment up the driveway, he was puzzled by the fact that the boat was still hitched to the car. Leno never left the boat out overnight. When he went to the back door, he noticed that the window shades, usually up, were all pulled down. When he knocked on the door and there was no response, he became frightened and walked to a pay phone a few blocks away. He called his house and then his sister. She and her boyfriend met Frank at the pay phone and the three of them drove to the house. Inside they found the bodies.

chapter four
BANNED—TOOLS OF THE TRADE

1996

When I first wrote to the women, I was reluctant to use my home address. Every few years one of Manson's true believers on the outside would appear in the news, usually for making threats against people they perceived as Manson's enemies or, in the case of Lynette Squeaky Fromme, for acting on those threats. On September 5, 1975, Fromme was arrested for attempting to kill President Gerald Ford. ("'Squeaky' Fromme unrepentant, still devoted to Manson," David Casstevens, September 26, 2005, *Fort Worth Star-Telegram*).

I decided to send the women copies of articles I'd written and during the few days it took for me to organize them, I woke up with the same terror I'd felt when I first read *Helter Skelter*. I didn't know enough about Pat and Leslie to know whether they still had ties to some of Manson's followers on the outside. Every once in a while, Manson groupie Sandra Good would utter some outrageous threat to make everyone think she was dangerous.

I got permission from a former editor to use the address of a newspaper where I once worked.

I heard from Pat first. She sent me a letter agreeing to an interview. A few weeks later, I got a letter from Leslie, who also agreed to an interview. And then I got a surprise. I met a filmmaker who was planning to make a documentary on the three women. Or, rather, she had planned to until the California Department of Corrections instituted a policy banning the media from conducting one-on-one interviews in prisons. This was unprecedented and occurred at a time when there were an increasing number of reports of abuse of prisoners. Without the press having access, there was no other way for the public to know about the treatment or mistreatment of prisoners. Prison reform depended on that kind of access. I had a hard time believing it was true. I called a reporter who covered criminal justice issues.

"Yep. It's true," he said. "You can go in and do a piece on a topic, say, the variety of food served in the prison. Anyone you can buttonhole while you're in there you can talk to, but you can't arrange an interview with a specific prisoner ahead of time. It's not all bad news," he said. "You can visit specific prisoners, if they agree, but only as a friend."

When we talked further he told me that Charles Manson was one of the reasons for the ban. The Department of Corrections officials didn't like that he was doing so many interviews. They believed that the interviews encouraged more followers and were painful for the families of the victims.

"How long has this been in effect?"

"It was just instituted!"

When he said "just" he meant just—two or three days before. I have a slightly superstitious nature. I'm always sure that the person who arrives at the restaurant ten seconds before me will get the last table. And, I swear, it happens 99 percent of the time. Once I have that mind-set, it's difficult to see it any other way. In this case, my superstitious nature led me to the conclusion that there were unseen forces colluding to prevent me from doing this story.

chapter five
UNFATHOMABLE REMORSE

September 1996

The fifty-mile stretch of the Pomona Freeway that connects downtown Los Angeles with the turnoff for Frontera Prison skirts an endless series of arid, suburban towns, all lacking the subtropical sensuality of the rest of L.A. The prison directions recommended taking the Euclid Avenue exit. I know Euclid Avenue. When I was a child, my family often drove to Ontario to have Sunday dinner with my aunt, and that end of Euclid now looked very much the same as it did back then—a broad boulevard with many grand Victorians and a center parkway lined with pepper trees.

As I drove, I could almost smell the traces of the orange groves I remembered from childhood. That part of Euclid Avenue is east of the Pomona Freeway. The prison is west. As soon as I passed the subdivisions that replaced those orange groves, the smell of cow shit permeated the air. It's a scrabbled, disarranged part of the state—a mixture of dairies, horse ranches, strip malls, boxy housing tracts, and refrigeration plants. In a pasture next to the prison, Guernsey cows stood chewing their cud, ankle deep in dung. The smell was dizzying.

The guard towers and the concertina wire around the top of the cyclone fence made it obvious this was a prison. The sprawling complex of one-story, red brick buildings had none of the art deco grandeur or the imposing presence of San Quentin—California's flagship prison and the one where women were once housed.

It was a warm day and the smells from the pasture clung to the low-lying haze surrounding Frontera Prison. Swarms of pasture flies flitted around my face and the faces of the other visitors as we walked from our cars. Outside the front gate, there was a structure that resembled a bus shelter. Inside were request forms and pens. I filled out my form and, along with about twenty other people, waited to be admitted.

The last time I'd been there was to interview women who were serving time for killing their husbands. Battered women's syndrome was a relatively new diagnosis, and lawyers were beginning to use it as a defense in such murders. One of my friends, a forensic psychologist, had been hired to testify in the trials of two of them. Their histories demonstrated that they had been beaten by those husbands over a period of years. They finally reached their respective tipping points. Unfortunately for them, that threshold was reached when their lives were not at that moment in danger, so their pleas of self-defense didn't work. (I interviewed a third woman who claimed to have been battered but her case was less than convincing. There was the fact that she'd hired contract killers; that she bought a new Cadillac with life insurance money; and that there was no corroboration for her claim that she'd been beaten.)

I thought about those women. One of them had told me that everyone she knew at Frontera had committed her crime because of a man. Her cellmate was in prison for embezzling money from her employer to pay off gambling debts—her *husband's* gambling debts. This kind of loyalty does not generally go both ways. I couldn't help comparing that to my observation that husbands are much less likely than wives to stick around after their spouses are incarcerated. (Of course, in the case of wives who kill their husbands, there isn't much of a choice.)

As each of our names was called, we lined up. We rolled up our pant legs, rolled down our socks, and pulled our pockets inside out. I was told that the only items I could bring in with me were my car keys, two packs of unopened cigarettes, and no more than fifty dollars in cash for the vending machines. Most of us had brought along transparent ziplock bags for these items to minimize the delay. Because the inmates wore jeans, visitors could not wear denim of any kind. It was deemed important for guards to easily distinguish between inmates and outsiders.

After we passed through a metal detector, we were buzzed into another holding area: a frigid, overly air-conditioned, glassed-in room that, for some reason, smelled like day-old urine-soaked diapers. After I slipped my request form through a slot, a guard retrieved it and went to find Leslie.

A tall, slender woman waved to me from behind the bulletproof glass, and the guard buzzed me through the door. Leslie was dressed in jeans and a red knit turtleneck. Her long ponytail was pulled gracefully to one side. She looked older than I'd expected. Long gone was the flawless radiance of her twenties, a radiance that was apparent even in the grainy black-and-white newspaper photos. At forty-six she was still girlish with soft brown eyes, amber hair, and an almost perfectly shaped, slightly turned-up nose. There were still faint traces of the X she'd seared onto her forehead with a hot bobby pin during the trial. (Manson carved an X on his forehead to symbolize his removal from society, and then the three women followed suit. He subsequently redesigned his into a swastika.)

It was her winsome, fresh face that made Leslie's involvement in the horrific events of 1969 so discordant. Susan Atkins, who'd packed a pistol long before hooking up with Manson, looked as though she came out of the womb brash and hard-edged. Patricia Krenwinkel was singularly plain with an atmosphere about her that was both terrified and terrifying. It was easy to imagine that there had been something in each of their early years to explain, if not the murders, at least Manson's initial claim on them. But Van Houten had the Southern California wholesomeness of a Disney Mousketeer, the quintessential 1950s daddy's girl. We'd seen her face on TV: Sally Field as Gidget or Robert Young's perky daughter on *Father Knows Best*, the one he called Princess.

Leslie's charm had been noted by every reporter who ever interviewed her, and while winning supporters, her affability had also been used against her. At her parole hearing earlier that year, Deputy District Attorney Stephen Kay warned the board to read between the lines of staff reports highlighting her stellar accomplishments in prison. "Throughout her life she has been outwardly directed, adaptable, very smart, very charming, but she can adapt to evil as well as goodness."

She and I sat side by side on chrome and vinyl chairs at long, low Formica tables. The large square room had linoleum floors and the bland functionality of a high school cafeteria. I had expected her to be reticent, but there was an accessible warmth about her that made it easy to talk. She'd taken advantage of every educational and therapeutic opportunity available since she'd arrived at Frontera. In June 1982, she'd earned her BA from Antioch College in a program, since discontinued, in which half the students were inmates, the other half were from the community and attended classes in the prison. She majored in English literature and minored in psychology, studying with a professor who was a protégé of Lawrence Kohlberg, a psychologist who took up where

Jean Piaget left off in the study of the moral development of children. For reasons both personal and academic, Leslie was captivated by the subject. According to reports, her class participation was excellent, her term papers original, and she eventually became the professor's teaching assistant. At the time of my first visit, she worked as head clerk for a program administrator, a job for which she earned $53 a month. Over the years she'd been involved in a variety of philanthropic enterprises: she started a program called "sharing our stitches," in which the inmates made quilts for homeless people; she tutored inmates who needed remedial work before they could enter a GED preparation program; she also read for a non-profit group that produced audio books for blind adolescent girls.

"You've been busy," I said at one point when she was describing her many activities.

"That's a lifelong pattern," she said, smiling. "When I was in high school, one of my teachers said I was involved in so many extracurricular activities, my photo was on every page of the yearbook."

I struggled with how I could artfully ask her how much of her altruistic activities were motivated by guilt. She anticipated my question.

"I have a lot to atone for but it's always difficult to know exactly what motivates people. I do know that at least some of my motivation comes from wanting to live the most productive life I can possibly live even though I'm in prison." She added that although she feels an unfathomable amount of remorse, she also knows its limitations.

"There is nothing I can do, *nothing,* that can undo the harm that I caused. I don't kid myself about that. There is nothing I can do to fill the holes that were left in people's lives."

As I walked out of the prison, I was flooded with contradictory emotions. Trying to reconcile the brutality of the murders with the human being I had just met was dizzying. I got in my car and sat watching relatives and friends climb into theirs—they all looked stunned and exhausted, too, no doubt a projection on my part. For them, it was probably just another visiting day.

chapter six
WALLET ON THE BEACH

1996

After I left the prison, I drove to a nearby McDonald's to reconstruct the interview. I found a corner booth and as I started to scribble notes, I picked up enough snippets of conversation from surrounding tables to realize that the people around me eating burgers had also been visiting inmates at Frontera. There seemed to be an equal number who'd been visiting the nearby men's prison. But these friends and relatives displayed none of the emotion I thought I saw in the faces and body language in the parking lot. "Betty seemed to be in a good mood today," said one man who, I assumed from his age, was the father of an inmate. That was as intense as it got. But later, as I started to pack up my stuff to leave, I overheard a couple sitting at the next table talk about someone I presumed to be their son. The woman was weeping.

"He's lost so much weight," she said.

"Honey, he's okay. He'll be okay," the man said. "You've got to stop worrying."

This was an echo of long-ago endless conversations between my parents in the early days of my brother's incarceration in the very same prison: my mother's chronic worry and her resulting insomnia; my father's concern for her alternating with his irritation at her fretting; his own worry about my brother mixed with his fury at the crime he had committed.

When I first visited my brother, he was in the maximum-security section. I went there alone because it was midweek and my parents were both working. I was eighteen, a sophomore at the University of California at Berkeley. We sat face-to-face, a heavy glass partition between us, and talked through a telephone. My tall, handsome brother, confident in the eyes of the outside world, seemed diminished, shriveled by the surroundings. He professed to be fine, just fine. In his first letter to me from prison he'd quoted the seventeenth-century poet Richard Lovelace, "Stone walls do not a prison make, Nor iron bars a cage" ("To Althea, From Prison"). But no matter what he claimed, it was clear that the stone walls of this prison were very thick indeed. He'd lost a lot of weight and his fingernails were pitted, eaten up by psoriasis. Before he went to prison, this disease had been mild. Now there was nothing mild about his disfigured fingernails.

I hadn't seen him since the summer before. It had been a rough summer. Actually, his relationship with my parents had been tumultuous since he had dropped out of college a few years before. He'd been living in an apartment in Hollywood with friends and working on and off at a string of low-paying jobs. In short, my parents' dreams for him had not panned out. He had a girlfriend who they didn't think was of his caliber, though at that point no one knew exactly what that caliber was, and whatever it was he seemed determined to click it down as far below their expectations as he could.

My role in our family was to be my brother's advocate, his defender. I loved him steadfastly but anxiously, and every time he got into a brawl with my parents and stormed out of the house I worried that I would never see him again. And then one night, the brawl was so loud and so intense that I was sure I would never see him again. He had come for dinner, and we'd almost made it to dessert when all hell broke loose. I can't remember what the fight was about. I just remember I backed out of the dining room and into my bedroom and put Ray Charles on my record player, turning the volume up to drown out the shouting. Then, the shouting stopped and I heard a knock on my door.

When I opened it, my brother's eyes were fiery with rage, but he was also tearful. "Good-bye, sis," he said, putting his arms around me. There was a finality in his voice that frightened me. I was right to be frightened. He stopped calling home. After a few weeks, my mother, who was ill from sleeplessness, finally called him. His phone had been disconnected. My father drove by his apartment in Hollywood. It was one of those stucco multiplexes with names like Palm Gardens or Bougainvillea Plaza. The manager said that he'd moved out owing rent and had left no forwarding address. My father was a special agent for the Internal Revenue Service and pretty good at finding people, but he couldn't find my brother.

That was June. Then, one Saturday in August, I came home to find a Santa Monica police officer in the living room talking to my parents. My brother's wallet had been found on the beach in Santa Monica, miles away from his apartment in Hollywood; my parents' address in Silver Lake was on his driver's license. The next morning, I woke up to the sound of my mother crying. My parents were in the kitchen. My father was cooking scrambled eggs.

"Sweetheart," my father said, "I know he's fine. He probably just lost his wallet." My mother worried out loud that he was dead. I worried, too, but for some reason I felt that expressing it would be disloyal to my brother. I feigned confidence that he was fine and, along with my father, adopted a *you worry too much* attitude with my overwrought mother. By the time I returned to school in Berkeley in the fall, there was still no word.

On my eighteenth birthday at the end of September, girls on my floor at Davidson Hall gathered in my room to eat the German chocolate cake my mother had sent. Just as one of my friends lit the candles the phone rang.

"It's your brother," my roommate said, "he wants to wish you a happy birthday."

chapter seven
MRS. TATE'S FURY

1996

The day before my next visit to the prison, I spent some time at the Ontario Public Library to research the history of women's prisons in California, generally, and Frontera, specifically. I came away with a new appreciation for the Women's Christian Temperance Union. The organization is often maligned because of its part in the establishment of Prohibition, but it turns out the group was also involved in prison reform for women. (Their diligence was also a factor in getting the vote for women in 1919.)

Until 1932, women prisoners lived at San Quentin where they were housed in makeshift quarters called "the bear pit." There were no windows, no source of heat, and the smell was oppressive because the slop buckets were stored in something called a "hopper" inside the pit. The women were never allowed outside to exercise or breathe fresh air for fear they would try to talk with male inmates. Through the work of the WCTU, the women were finally transferred in the 1930s to marginally improved quarters at a prison in the Tehachapi Mountains where they remained until the current prison was built in 1955.

The first name selected for the new prison was Corona after a small nearby town—a fact resolutely opposed by the Corona town fathers who succeeded, ten years later, in persuading the Department of Corrections to change it. The prison was rechristened Frontera, the Spanish word for frontier. According to a prison pamphlet, the word was selected to convey a new beginning, a fresh start—a reflection of the optimistic spirit that guided the staff in those days.

It would soon become clear to me that the prison's trajectory from that early optimism to abject negativity and the shift in focus from rehabilitation to punishment was connected to the August 1969 Tate-LaBianca murders. The seeds of destruction of prison reform were planted on those two horror-filled nights. The crusade to replace prison reform with the primacy of victims' rights was, in large measure, fueled by the fury and the anguish of Doris Tate, Sharon Tate's mother, and continued by Sharon's sisters Patti and Debra. But in 1971, when Leslie, Susan, and Pat arrived at Frontera, the state was still committed to providing the necessary components of rehabilitation — education, vocational training, psychotherapy, and family unification — even to women facing the death penalty.

According to the local newspaper, the *Ontario Daily Report*, as soon as the warden at Frontera, Mrs. Iverne Carter, learned that the Manson women were sentenced to death, she asked the state to build a new structure to house them. Frontera was ill-equipped to meet their needs. Executions of women were so rare—there had only been four in California since 1893—that only one death penalty cell had been built and it was occupied at the time by Jean Oliver Carver, who was convicted of beating a woman evangelist to death with a rock during a robbery.

The warden's request was denied and instead, a miniature death row was hastily created in an unused wing of the administration building. A crew of workers from the nearby men's prison at Chino were brought in to build three tiny cells—each one seven and a half by nine feet and placed side by side—that were sealed off from the rest of the building by heavy steel doors. They also installed strong bars on the doors and windows and mesh between the bars to prevent the women from reaching through.

On April 19, 1971, in an interview in the *Ontario Daily Report*, Mrs. Carter, described as an energetic, sixty-seven-year-old grandmother, confessed that she was troubled by the grimness of the quarters. But she said each cell would be equipped with a nine-inch black-and-white television set, and, if the women behaved themselves, they would be allowed to spend some time each day in the hundred-foot-long exercise yard that was built next to the cells. The yard was concrete except for a tiny patch of grass where, according to Mrs. Carter, the women could sit or meditate.

The warden said she was determined to keep the three alive and well while they awaited the gas chamber. After all, she told the reporter, circumstances could change and it was possible that the women would some day be useful to society. (And, indeed, circumstances did change in 1972 when the U.S. Supreme Court ruled that the death penalty as it was then written and carried out in most states constituted cruel and unusual punishment in violation of the Eighth and Fourteenth Amendments.)

chapter eight
LIVING WITHOUT HOPE

September 1996

The first time I met Pat Krenwinkel we only had a few minutes to talk. For some reason, my application to visit was approved just ten minutes before the end of visiting hours. It was an awkward ten minutes. Unlike the welcoming tone of her letters, she was not initially friendly and there was no time for ice breaking to ease us into conversation. I blurted a clumsy "What's it like to live here?"

She didn't pause to think about her reply. "I live every day knowing that I will leave nothing behind when I die that isn't ugly." Her answer took my breath away. "The worst thing about being here is living every day of my life without hope. They might as well have executed me."

The next time I saw her, a month later, I was again struck by her cheerlessness but also by how unadorned she was. Unadorned in her appearance, her language, her outlook. I associate my early impressions of Pat with the color gray. Grayness seemed to envelop her. Some of it was actual—she often wore a stone-gray sweatshirt almost the same color as her short, neatly trimmed hair—but there was an atmosphere of unrelenting bleakness surrounding her.

When I'd first written to her requesting an interview, I received a response a month later consenting to the interview and thanking me for sending her copies of my articles, articles she said she'd read carefully. She referred specifically to a series I'd done on Werner Erhard, founder of EST, in which many former followers accused him of operating a cult. Patricia wrote that there were similarities between the techniques used by Erhard, Charles Manson, and "many more power-seeking individuals." (Both men had been influenced by the methods of Scientology.)

I hadn't given much thought to the articles I'd sent (my purpose was just to show her that I was a serious journalist concerned with serious issues), but after receiving her letter, I reread the Erhard series. In one of the articles, two of Erhard's daughters described a family dinner when they were teenagers in which their father's staff beat up their mother, Ellen Erhard, knocking her down, pulling her hair. They claimed that their father, after ordering the assault, sat and watched, his own hands unsullied. He had accused her of infidelity and wanted his staff to coerce her into confessing.

After hearing the daughters' account of the incident, I'd called a former member of Erhard's staff, a physician named Bob Larzelere. He not only acknowledged that he'd been present when she'd been assaulted, he told me that he was the one who choked her, who felt her body go limp as he cut off the air to her windpipe. "I knew then that I would do anything that Werner asked. I would do anything for his love and approval . . . this is how low I had sunk." (Erhard's wife may have collapsed but she did not die from the attack.)

In the initial letter I received from Pat, she wrote that through therapy she had discovered that Manson was not exceptional or interesting. "He used the same techniques as any abuser to control and manipulate his victims, coercing others through mental, emotional, or physical attacks." She added that she had always wondered why the public finds him so titillating—"this angry, spiteful, vicious little man."

In our second meeting, she talked about the process of breaking Manson's hold on her. "There were no epiphanies, just a gradual awakening." An awakening, she said, that took a very long time. "I do embroidery, and I think of the years in prison as parallel to what happens when you have the task of sorting a big tangle of different-colored threads. One at a time, you pick out a strand and carefully try to pull it out. That's what I've been doing all these years—sorting it all out, a strand at a time."

During the trial, in an effort to portray her as sympathetic to the jury, her lawyer had made much of the fact that she was tormented as a child because of a surplus of body hair. The only evidence of this I observed was the down on her forearms. Though dark, it wasn't freakishly excessive and if I hadn't been looking for it, I wouldn't have noticed it.

When I asked her about it, she said she was teased mercilessly as a child and it contributed to her feeling that she was ugly, something Manson later used to his advantage. In the beginning of their relationship, he told her she was beautiful. He made her feel attractive for the first time.

She mentioned that she'd read that there are now lasers that can remove excess hair. "When I heard about that it made me so happy to think that young girls don't have to suffer the way I did." And she did look happy when she said it. She so rarely smiled that when she did the effect was electric; the intensity of her close-set blue eyes penetrated her austere grayness.

In our first extended conversation, she talked about her life without self-pity; though the content was dramatic, her manner of conveying it was not. "During the trial there was a rumor that Colonel Tate, Sharon's father, was carrying a gun and was going to try and kill one or all of us. I've often thought how much better it would have been if he had killed me. As it is, I will leave nothing positive behind. No family, no career, no possibility of contributing to the world."

What she said was so resolute, there was no room for an atta girl platitude.

"I know what I'm saying makes people uncomfortable. When new women come in here, everyone is aghast when I talk like this. But I'm not going to sit around and talk about hope when there isn't any."

She'd also refused to talk about hope the last time she appeared before the parole board. She declined to ask friends and family to write letters pleading for her release because she knew there was no chance. (She later changed her mind and did ask for letters of support.) Her well-founded pessimism about release was based on the fact that, unlike Leslie, who was only present on the second night, Pat had participated both nights. Though she actually killed one person—Abigail Folger—she is legally guilty, and most would argue morally as well, of killing all seven of the people who died.

Later, eating lunch at what was becoming my regular booth at McDonald's, I thought about Pat's pessimism, her lack of hope, her dour, bordering-on-sour disposition. There was something about her brutal candor that I admired. There was also something about it that made me uncomfortable, though I wasn't sure precisely why. I once again reflected on the discrepancy between the tone of her letters, which was always warm, and her in-person demeanor. It would not be the last time this discrepancy puzzled me.

chapter nine
ORPHANED BY THE HOLOCAUST

1960

Catherine Share was an appealing dark-haired beauty in high school, and if I had voted on what she was most likely *not* to become, it would have been chief recruiter for a psychopathic serial killer. We were in the same social club at Hollywood High, and years later when I first heard her name associated with Manson, I assumed it was a different Catherine Share. When it proved to be the same person, I was sure she was on the periphery and if not on the periphery, then a reluctant participant in the activities of the so-called Family.

Leslie set me straight: there was nothing peripheral or reluctant about her involvement. She was an aggressive recruiter for Manson. Her primary quarry: pretty girls who could be used as bait to attract men into the fold and girls who had access to their parents' credit cards. Although she was in the inner circle of the group at the time of the murders, Manson had not included her in his plan either night. She's quoted on a website (manson2jesus.com) as saying she wouldn't have participated in the murders even if Manson had asked her to, but there's ample reason to doubt the validity of that claim.

What is not in doubt: after Manson was in prison, Catherine

was a major aider and abettor on the outside, working assiduously and violently under his direction. Among her activities: an attempt to kill a witness and an attempt to rob a surplus store to steal guns. The most chilling, however, occurred in 1971 when she and several cohorts planned to highjack a Boeing 747 and kill one passenger every hour until Charles Manson, Tex Watson, and the three women were released from prison.

When I think of her at Hollywood High, I remember a quiet, restrained girl with ink-black hair and a distracted air about her. She was smart and talented with a pure singing voice, a violin virtuoso, and a beauty—though not the kind of conventional beauty for which Hollywood High was known. There was something slightly off kilter about her angular features, and that lack of symmetry only contributed to her beauty. Her name when she was with Manson was Gypsy—a name she acquired, I assume, because of her exotic looks.

How could that girl, a Jewish girl whose biological parents had died under Hitler's reign, dedicate her life to a man who carved a swastika on his forehead? How could that same girl later marry a member of a white supremacist prison gang? This was not the behavior of a rebellious kid. She was a twenty-seven-year-old woman when she attached herself to Manson and a thirty-three-year-old woman when she married Kenneth Como, a member of the Aryan Brotherhood whom Manson met in San Quentin.

When Catherine Share and Leslie Van Houten were teenagers, though eight years apart, they shared many attributes—smart, pretty, popular—but when I ponder Leslie's transformation from "prom queen to murderer," I have to rely on my imagination to recreate who she was in high school. Catherine's transformation was more astonishing and more upsetting for me personally because I did know her before. I wouldn't have known the earlier version as well as I did, though, if it hadn't been for our club's slumber party when I was a senior and she was a junior.

There were many elements that came together to make that night remarkable for me. The house—a house so spectacular it could have been a movie set—was definitely one of those elements. It was located off of Mulholland Drive, a wealthy, wild area emblematic of Los Angeles, often used as a backdrop to movies. Also, it marked a time in my life when connecting with people who were different from my usual friends held a particular excitement. Unlike previous slumber parties, there were no crank calls, no lemon squeezes, no Ouija boards, no charades. We just talked, and Catherine and I talked a lot.

There was one more ingredient that made the night special. As I looked around at the girls in attendance, a small group of eight or ten, I realized that the narrow-minded culture of our club that had been a torment to me—a culture created by the older, all-white, Protestant girls—had changed. My class was the first to rush and accept girls who were not WASPs. For me, that night reflected, if not celebrated, the shedding of what had been bad about the 1950s and embraced what was good about the 1960s.

When I discovered that Catherine was a kindred spirit—and when I say that, I mean when I discovered that she was Jewish—it was the first time I felt comfortable about my membership in the club. Until that moment, I had lived like a secret agent. The clubs at Hollywood High were patterned after college sororities and were so elitist and exclusionary the administrators were in a pitched battle to get rid of them.

I'll admit the possibility that I projected more onto Catherine than was there, but that night she seemed to embody a depth and complexity that I admired and felt had been missing in my life, certainly in the club. Or maybe the intensity of my feelings was simply the result of having gotten lost on my way there. By the time I arrived safely I was so relieved, I loved everyone at that damn party and this certainly engendered an intimate connection with her. At least it did for me. I have no idea whether it was mutual. When we got together decades later in Dallas, Texas, I noticed a flicker of recognition when she first saw me. Was that flicker an acknowledgment of what we shared that night or simply an acknowledgment of the familiarity you feel with friends from high school? Either way, it was clear that whatever had existed between us was no longer there.

Mulholland Drive is a narrow, winding, country road snaking fifty miles along the crest of the Santa Monica Mountains from Hollywood to the beach in Leo Carrillo State Park in Malibu. The slumber party was scheduled to start in the late afternoon on a Saturday, but I couldn't go until the evening. I had a standing date with my father to go sailing every Saturday, and because my parents didn't approve of the club, though they didn't forbid me to participate, I decided life at home would be easier if I didn't cancel sailing. Arriving late, however, meant that I had to drive up there alone in the dark.

I wasn't crazy about that plan. Mulholland Drive was legendary for being a place where rich people lived and, because of its isolation, a place where scary people lurked. When I was in high school, there was a stretch that served as lover's lane, and every time anyone parked there, the story of the man with a hook for a hand was retold. In various versions, a man had escaped an insane asylum or was a serial killer or both. A couple making out in a car sees a man walking toward them in the dark. The boyfriend frantically starts the car and speeds off. When the couple arrives at the girl's house and the guy gets out to open the car door for her, there's a hook dangling from the door handle.

Film critic David Thompson describes Mulholland Drive as both civilization and a dangerous wilderness—"an idealized spectacle and a place from which to survey the classic city of visibility even as you drive, the paranoia turns into a model for both grace and dread."

Dread precisely describes my feeling as I took wrong turn after wrong turn in my father's old 1949 Cadillac. There were no people walking on the road, no phone booths, no streetlights. At one point, I was so lost on a side road that I couldn't even figure out how to give up and drive home.

Finally, I stopped the car in front of a house that looked like it would be friendly to a young girl and unwelcoming to men with hooks. There was no high fence around it. No security gate. In fact, as I recall, few of the houses I passed had either of those accessories. I got out and knocked on the door. A middle-aged man in a silky robe over striped pajamas let me use his phone and stood there while I relayed information between him and the mother of the hostess of the slumber party. Between the two of them, I was able to find my destination.

None of the above has anything directly to do with Catherine, but in my mind it's always been connected. Here's what I think: if the Tate-LaBianca murders had taken place a decade earlier, I might still be lost on Mulholland Drive. The fear that was generated by the blood bath at Sharon Tate's house—a house in another wealthy, isolated area of L.A.—meant that houses would no longer be unsecured. No house would be standing there naked without a major security apparatus protecting it and if, by some miracle, I had gained access to a front door, no one would have let me in at night to use the phone. I may have been a young girl, but that would no longer signify safety. Leslie, Susan, and Pat were young women. Before Tate-LaBianca, people were frightened of urban legends with hooks for hands. After Tate-LaBianca, they were frightened of everything.

When I finally arrived at the house, in spite of my tense drive, I was awestruck. Not before or since has a house made such an impression on me. I remember that the angled glass walls, luminescent, glowing, gorgeous, reminded me of my aunt's engagement ring, an emerald-cut diamond. The windows were lighted in such a way as to create an airborne effect, as though, with the flick of a switch or the loosening of a tether, the whole house could float away.

Sometime later I saw a black-and-white photo in *Life* magazine that at first glance reminded me so much of the house, I thought maybe it was that house until I looked at the Hollywood Hills location. I cut it out and taped it into my scrapbook. As it turned out, it was a photo of Case Study House No. 22, the most photographed house in the world and considered the iconic photo of modern architecture. It's certainly iconic in my life. When I look at that photo, I remember Mulholland Drive. I remember that slumber party. I remember that night. I remember Catherine. I think of Charles Manson.

Once inside, I saw pillows, duvets, sleeping bags, and clothing strewn around the otherwise pristine living room—a living room that could have been and probably was at some point featured in *Architectural Digest.* The jumble of clutter on the expanse of plush, cream-colored carpeting was comically incompatible with the manicured setting. I remember girls smoking. I remember the array of sleepwear—half the girls wearing Lanz flannel nightgowns with rows of tiny hearts and flowers, vestiges of our girlhood, and the other half wearing baby doll pajamas that foretold our upcoming womanhood. This lacy diaphanous sleepwear was new on the scene—sexier than flannel nightgowns but not yet as erotic as Victoria's Secret lingerie. (I think of that slumber party every time I read the account of Sharon Tate's murder, ten years later, and picture the baby doll pajamas she was wearing.) There was an empty space on the carpet next to Catherine, so I threw down my overnight case and sleeping bag. I remember she didn't smile or even look at me initially. I sat down on the floor and leaned my back against the wall, still feeling a little breathless from my scary drive on Mulholland.

After I calmed down, Catherine and I started to talk. At first her reserve continued but as the night progressed, she got more expressive. I'm pretty sure we discussed a Hollywood High student who had chopped down trees on campus (see chapter 49). Maybe I told her my plan to go to Cal after graduating, or she told me her plans, though hers would come a year later. I was younger but graduated first because I had skipped a grade in elementary school. I doubt that we talked about the flag twirlers, the booster club, or the Red Cross Club, all of which, according to the HHS yearbook, she was a member. I'm sure we talked about boyfriends. Hers was in my class, a smart, good-looking musician. The two of them played folk music together. I remember we mostly talked about family; her boyfriend's mother and my mother, both social workers, had been colleagues at one time. But it was Catherine's family situation that I found compelling and that I thought about for years afterward.

She told me she was adopted, which I hadn't known. She told me that life at home was hard, which I hadn't suspected. She lived alone with her father, a psychologist, who was blind. I was captivated by elements in her story. For one thing, I had a cousin I adored who was adopted—the only adopted person I knew until I met Catherine—and, for me, there had always been a mystique surrounding her very existence. Also, I'd recently started volunteering at the Foundation for the Junior Blind and was learning about those challenges. (Later, when I was in college, I worked as a counselor at Camp Bloomfield, the camp for blind kids a few miles away at the very end of Mulholland Drive.) It felt like more than a coincidence. These details, along with the fact of her Jewishness, which I discuss later, contributed to a feeling that our connection was somehow preordained.

I was touched by how tough her life seemed. Certainly more difficult than my life or the easy, privileged lives of the other girls in our club. These particulars made her seem vulnerable and appealing and translated to complexity, to character; to my adolescent eyes, her father's blindness cast him in a sympathetic light.

The truth was more complicated, but I didn't discover that until later.

As the others dropped off to sleep, we kept on talking. When the sun started to lighten the sky we dragged our bedding out to the swimming pool, laying it down on chaise longues. The air was cool and steam was rising from the pool; we could hear the high-pitched chorus of coyotes. The pool was cantilevered out from the house and, from our perch on the deck, we could see the bejeweled grid outlining the blocks of the city below. Or I think we could. Over the years, I have stared at the photo of Case Study House No. 22 so many times, I'm not entirely sure I didn't, in my imagination, superimpose the grid portrayed in that photo onto the view from the pool that morning.

What I learned directly from Catherine and what I subsequently learned about her life from other sources have merged, like the Case Study House No. 22 and the actual view from the slumber party swimming pool. All of the versions contain elements of the following: She was born in Paris in 1942. Her biological father, who was Hungarian, was a member of the French Resistance. Her mother, who was German, may or may not have also been part of the Resistance. Her maternal grandmother died in a Jewish ghetto in Eastern Europe, and both of her paternal grandparents died in concentration camps during World War II. Some accounts have her parents committing suicide in Paris when she was two years old.

I was stunned. In my mind, Catherine was Anne Frank, an Anne Frank who survived. My heart hurt for her and with that hurt came enormous respect.

On the manson2jesus.com website, where Catherine, along with other former Manson acolytes, has written a short bio of herself, she doesn't mention her parents' suicide but states simply that they died during World War II. She says she was hidden from the Nazis, presumably in France, and that she remembers the "fear, loneliness, and confusion" of that time. In any case, her father commissioned a French lawyer to arrange for the French underground to get her out of France where the Vichy government had helped the Germans deport and/or kill most of the French Jews. It's not clear where she was or precisely when it was that the French lawyer found a woman Catherine has described as "wonderful" to adopt her. She remembers her family life after that as being enviable, rich, and happy. And then her adoptive mother died of cancer when Catherine was sixteen and her world collapsed.

The night when she told me her life was difficult, I assumed she meant having her father dependent on her was hard. And it was. But according to her boyfriend at the time, "difficult" is an understatement. After her mother died, the relationship with her adoptive father deteriorated. Some of this was because of his disability. Tasks that had been her mother's now fell to Catherine. The house had to be kept in perfect order so he could find his possessions; if the house wasn't orderly, he could trip on a stray chair or bang his head on an open cabinet door. Most young girls would find it difficult to take this on, but a girl who was grieving for her mother found it unbearable. When she failed to perform perfectly, her father would become enraged.

At one point, Dr. Share developed a relationship with a former patient who moved into the house with her twin boys, displacing Catherine. But according to her former boyfriend, her father did more than neglect her. He verbally abused her—he called her a slut when he suspected she was having sex with her boyfriend. When she graduated from high school at the age of seventeen, he kicked her out of the house. (One of Manson's gifts was exploiting young women who had histories of difficult relationships with their fathers.)

Instead of going off to college with the rest of her friends, she supported herself working as a cashier at Akron in Hollywood—a cross between a Navy surplus store and Cost Plus—and she attended a few classes at Los Angeles City College.

She had a short, doomed marriage during which she lived in Connecticut. After that relationship fell apart, she moved back to Hollywood where she worked as a musician on movie sets and where she met Bobby Beausoleil, soon to be a member of Manson's tribe. The two of them acted in a soft-core porn film titled *Ramrodder.*

1997, Dallas

In 1997 I flew to Dallas, visited the Kennedy assassination exhibit in the book depository building, and had lunch with Catherine. It wasn't easy to arrange. By that time she had been out of prison for quite a few years and was living under an assumed name. When I tracked her down she referred me to a friend of hers who was acting as her agent.

Catherine had every reason to distrust journalists. I later found out that she'd recently been stalked by photographers who ambushed her at a Sunday morning church service. Because of that, she did not want me to know where she lived. Her friend/agent invited me to meet at her house and then we drove together to a local café. When I saw Catherine come through the door she was easily recognizable though she had gained a lot of weight since I'd last seen her. (She mentions overeating as a problem on the website.) She was still very pretty. The meeting did not yield much in the way of information. Catherine said she was writing her own account of her years with Manson—her friend/agent would be representing her to Christian publishers—and wanted the material to be fresh for her own book. I had wondered if any of the spark would be there between us. There was no spark, only vigilance on her part. How could it be otherwise, given what she'd lived through?

Writer Eve Babitz had a different take than mine in high school. In a February 3, 1972, *Rolling Stone* article about attending Hollywood High, Eve wrote about sitting next to Catherine in her chemistry class. "On my other side was this nice girl named Cathy whose only flaw was that she was kind of gullible and that kept me from being too shocked when I saw her in *Life* magazine crouched under a rock as one of the 'Manson Family' and called Gypsy."

chapter ten
MONDO VIDEO A-GO-GO

October 1996

Because I planned to spend time at the L.A. County Courthouse in search of transcripts and at the Los Angeles Public Library looking at old newspaper articles on the case, I decided I would camp out in Santa Monica at the house my brother and I had inherited from our parents. I had my evenings free so I phoned my parents' oldest friends, a couple I'll call Ruth and Sid, and arranged to meet them for dinner at a bar and grill on Vermont Avenue in Los Feliz Village. I had always been grateful to them for their friendship to my parents during my brother's troubles. The couple was now in their nineties and no longer able to drive, but they lived only a few miles from the restaurant and insisted on taking a cab though I had offered to pick them up.

When I arrived they were already seated, but Sid, always courtly, struggled to stand to pull a chair out for me. They were a decade younger than my parents, so when I was growing up, I always thought of them as my parents' young friends. Even in their nineties they had a youthful air. Sid was lean but his face was plump with high, apple cheeks and a rosy complexion. His dark hair was accented with silver at the temples. Ruth was still a strawberry blonde and wore her hair, as she always had, in a pageboy. She had a tailored Nancy Reagan quality. She was more reserved than her husband, but under that reserve was a deep reservoir of kindness and warmth. It was that warmth that had helped buoy my parents emotionally as they dealt with my brother's situation. In addition to providing emotional support, Sid, who had been a judge in Los Angeles, helped my parents navigate the court system.

After dinner, he asked me what I was working on. I should have been prepared for the question, but I wasn't sure I wanted to talk about Leslie and Pat. I was beginning to discover that even though the Manson murders had occurred thirty years before, the feelings were still fresh and the anger near the surface for people who were around at the time. Ruth and Sid were liberal Democrats, but political leanings seemed irrelevant when it came to discussing anyone connected to these murders. Liberals and conservatives alike tended to find the Manson women, or anyone associated with the women, contemptible. But because Ruth and Sid had always been so unconditionally loving and parental with me, I decided to risk talking about Pat and Leslie.

I told them about the television documentary I'd seen, my visits to the prison, and my quest to find out if the two women were as transformed as they seemed. At first, neither of them said anything, but Ruth had a quizzical expression on her face.

"Are you surprised?" I asked.

"Not really," she said, smiling. "It's familiar territory for you."

What territory was she referring to? My brother's history? Criminal justice issues about which I'd written? Prisons I'd visited while doing stories? All were true. Before I could ask what she meant, she said, "That poor woman."

Which woman? There were so many involved who could be described that way. Sharon Tate? Sharon Tate's mother? Abigail Folger? Her mother? Mrs. LaBianca? Ruth may have been kindhearted, but I doubted that she was referring to either Pat or

Leslie. The most logical would be Mrs. LaBianca because she'd been a neighbor of Ruth's. Perhaps she'd even known her. "I agree," I said. "It was a horrible way to die."

"Oh, I don't mean the murder victim. Of course that was terrible, but I was actually talking about Leslie Van Houten's mother. We had the same employer, though I didn't know her. I couldn't help feeling bad for her."

Ruth had been an administrator for the Los Angeles Board of Education for more than thirty years; Leslie's mother worked in the same system as a teacher for high-risk youth. It's a massive school district, but Ruth explained that once the murderers were identified, the gossip quickly spread through the bureaucracy. "The word through the grapevine was that she was very proud. I don't mean that in a mean way. She didn't try to hide who her daughter was, but she made it clear she did not want to talk about it . . . but who would?"

Though Sid had been a superior court judge at the time, he said he didn't have any special knowledge of the case. "But anyone who worked anywhere near the courthouse knew what a circus the trial was." Actually, anyone who lived in L.A. or anyone who had a television set knew what a circus it was. Every morning during the trial, Manson groupies conducted a vigil, sitting on the sidewalk outside the Hall of Justice, holding up photos of Manson.

Ruth talked about how frightened everyone was in their Los Feliz neighborhood before the police had a suspect. "At night, the streets were empty. People were afraid to leave their houses," she said. "I remember thinking that wasn't entirely logical since the LaBiancas were killed in their house."

Ruth said she wished they could provide me with some sort of scoop about Manson or the murders, but whatever they knew was already public knowledge. I said as much as I liked scoops, that wasn't what I was after. I was primarily interested in the women, their lives before, during, and after the murders.

I'm not sure she heard me because she said, her face brighten-
ing, "Oh, I just remembered a bit of trivia. Do you know who
once lived in the LaBianca house?"

"No."

"Walt Disney."

"Really?" I said. "I've seen photos and it didn't look grand."

"Oh, it's not. It's a fine house but modest for someone like Disney. He lived in it in the 1930s while he was building a house a
few blocks away. The one he was building was his version of
Hansel and Gretel's cottage."

After we ordered dessert, Sid mentioned a case he'd had the
year before he retired. "One of the defendants was a Manson nut.
I don't think he was an official follower; well maybe he was, I'm
not sure, but before that I didn't realize Manson had any kind of
following. Apparently he's a genuine cult anti-hero." He shrugged
and shook his head, a *go figure* gesture. "The guy worked in a store
that specializes in cult novelties. Or, now that I think of it, maybe
he stole merchandise from the store." He laughed. "You'd think
I'd remember that. In any case, I'm only mentioning it because
the store is in this neighborhood." He said he used to drive by on
his way home from work and was tempted to peek in but never
did. "My hunch is they have quite a bit of Manson memorabilia."

I thought, once again, that I should clarify my lack of interest in
Manson himself, but in light of their eagerness to help me, it seemed
churlish to keep harping on that so I said I would check it out.

After dinner, Sid and Ruth offered to escort me to the store.
"It's only a few blocks," Sid said. "I don't think you should go
alone."

"Don't worry," I said, holding up my cell phone. "I'll be fine."

I was touched. No matter how old I was or how old and frail
they were, they would always act in *loco parentis*.

After they left, I realized that though I wasn't interested in Manson memorabilia, I was interested in people who were. I walked a few blocks down Vermont until I got to Mondo Video A-Go-Go.

I was instantly transported into a world I had only imagined. At first glance I couldn't help feeling that someone had lifted an enormous rock and the inventory of Mondo Video A-Go-Go came to life and crawled out. I thought of the survivalist guy who owned the Army and Navy surplus store in *Falling Down* with Michael Douglas. That guy wore a black watch cap and a black leather vest that revealed his tattooed biceps. I think he might have worked at Mondo Video A-Go-Go. He certainly shopped there. That's not entirely fair. There were no guns on display and, unlike the survivalist guy's hate speech in *Falling Down*, no obvious homophobic material. The store's tag line, however, could be: If it's offensive, we've got it. The walls were festooned with posters, buttons, bumper stickers, magnets, much of which looked to have been designed by Hitler or his disciples.

I saw swastikas, whips, Ku Klux Klan hoods. There was a dizzying array of cult and specialty films clearly labeled and well organized. A sampling: UFO documentaries, serial killer flicks, amputee porn, midget porn, all manner of S & M, black exploitation films, lost episodes of *The Twilight Zone*. I didn't ask but my guess was that tucked away somewhere were snuff films. I was grateful, needless to say, that I was not accompanied by the judge and his wife.

There was a group of men gathered at the counter and, out of the corner of my eye, I was pretty sure I could make out a photo of a disembodied penis and its adjoining testicles taped to the cash register. I was feeling way too shy to call attention to myself by asking a question. I spotted a guy set apart from the crowd who was reading liner notes on a CD. He had a hank of coal-black hair sprouting out of an otherwise shaved head and was wearing a black leather jacket. If he wasn't a card-carrying member, then perhaps he was an employee. *Sotto voce* I asked if there were any Manson videos. "Oh, let me see, I think I can find one or two," he said, smiling. He led me down the crowded aisles to a massive section of Manson-related material.

There were dozens and dozens of videos—almost three decades' worth of TV interviews, parole hearings, snippets from Court TV of Manson, Tex Watson, and the three women—all obviously recorded on someone's home VCR. I braved the crowd at the register and purchased a lifetime membership for $10. I could now rent videos during the week for only $1.50 a night, on the weekend for $2.50. I rented my first ten, bought some microwave popcorn, drove back to Santa Monica, and started watching.

chapter eleven
DISORDERED THOUGHTS AND
DEMENTED MACHINATIONS

*I*n the decades after the murders, before the California legislature put an end to it, Charles Manson appeared on a wide array of network and cable tabloid shows from all over North America as well as Europe. Among the interviews in my stack were those by Geraldo Rivera, Tom Snyder, and Ron Reagan Jr. The shows were inevitably billed as containing never-before-heard answers to never-before-asked questions, but, in fact, the interviews were interchangeable. Manson was playful, he was maniacal, he was nuts. He alternated between the nonsensical and the almost astute, and it was always difficult to discern how much he was intentionally disordering his thoughts or how much his thoughts were disordering him.

Each interviewer became confused by his neologisms, charmed by his antics, and then, inevitably, horrified at being seduced. The realization was a reminder of what the creep actually did, so the interviewer then felt compelled to express outrage at the murders. Manson would then get angry and slightly menacing. A favorite trick: he coiled the microphone cord around his hand in a way to suggest that any minute he might decide to leap forward and wrap it around the interviewer's neck.

His responses were tangential, and most of his conversations consisted of word play based on loose associations.

"Are you a criminal, Mr. Manson?"

"There's no such thing as a criminal. If I be in my will, if I will be, I'll shoot you, I'll beat you, too."

"Do you have any children, Charlie?"

"I have lots of children. I don't know how many children I have, sometimes I think you are a child."

And always, grandiose, delusional ideas. "I don't operate on a local level. When you're with me you've got to think much, much bigger than that."

The spectacle of interviewers such as Tom Snyder and the exceedingly young and earnest Ron Reagan Jr., probing Manson's philosophy of life, is comical. (Ron Reagan: "What would you do if you were released?" Manson: "If I'm paroled I'll run for president.") Each interaction further reinforced Manson's grandiosity.

His trickery and quixotic use of language made a precise diagnosis problematic. Because his thoughts often seemed chaotic, some experts concluded that he was a latent schizophrenic. His actions, however, were controlled and calculating. Whatever else he was, there was general agreement that he was a psychopath. In *Helter Skelter*, Roger Smith, who had been his parole officer when he lived in San Francisco, was quoted as calling him "a manipulative little anti-social."

I made sure to watch the videos in the morning. I needed many hours to pass between my viewing and my sleep. Each interaction captured what Hannah Arendt called "the banality of evil," and I didn't need Manson's demented machinations invading my dreams.

When I wasn't watching the videos, I was either at the library reading the *L.A. Times* coverage of the original trial on microfiche or checking out magazines and books about Manson or members of the Family. I soon realized that my initial plan to avoid material on him was self-defeating. I couldn't understand the women without having some understanding of him. Since the initial trial, a cottage industry of Manson material had been published, so I soon amassed a little library of books written by people claiming to know the real person.

According to many accounts of his childhood, including a biography written by his former cellmate, Nuel Emmons (*Manson in His Own Words: The Shocking Confessions of the Most Dangerous Man Alive*) and, more recently, *Manson* by Jeff Guin, there is much about his early life that's in dispute. Manson has offered an array of stories, some of them contradictory, to interviewers over the years. But there is some agreement about the following: there was a teenage mother, Kathleen Maddox, and a biological father, Colonel Scott, a married con man who took off before the baby was born. There was a stepfather, William Manson, who hung around long enough to have his name affixed to his stepson's birth certificate.

At fifteen, Kathleen Maddox was not an ideal mother. She hung out at bars, leaving the boy with a variety of unsuitable sitters. Manson himself told the story that she had so little attachment to her infant son that she once offered him to a barmaid in exchange for a pitcher of beer. When the boy was four years old, Kathleen was sentenced to five years in prison for robbing a service station with her brother. So Manson's youth was spent bouncing between religiously fanatic grandparents and state institutions where he was routinely abused by staff and other inmates. Given his childhood, it would have been a wonder had he turned out to be anything but a user and abuser of people. But the young people he attracted were a different story. Though none had had picture-perfect childhoods, most of them were raised by parents who appeared to give them the basics: love, protection, opportunities, and more than a modicum of material comfort.

Nikki Meredith

The contrast between his history and theirs is striking. As a little boy, Charles Manson had no father who claimed him; as a little girl, Patricia Krenwinkel's father was taking her on Saturday morning walks in their Westchester neighborhood to watch the new LAX being constructed. When Charles Manson was eight years old, his mother was serving time for armed robbery at Moundsville State Prison in West Virginia; when Leslie Van Houten was eight years old, her mother was timing her daily batch of brownies so that her children would smell them baking when they walked in the front door from school. Tex Watson, described by his mother as the family's "pride and joy," was raised in an intact family, a member of the 4-H Club and the Boy Scouts. At his Farmerville, Texas, high school he was an honor student, a track star, a halfback on the football team.

Most of the other young people in Manson's inner circle—Mary Brunner, Sandra Good, Lynette Fromme—came from similar backgrounds. Susan Atkins, whose family had more than its share of drinking problems and financial woes, was an exception. As indicated above, Catherine Share's childhood, after her mother died, left her vulnerable to a man who was skilled at preying on weaknesses.

So how was this "angry, spiteful, and vicious little man" able to seize such absolute control over these kids? Clearly, when it came to manipulating people, he had some natural gifts, but prison provided an effective educational opportunity in this regard. On the cell block he learned the tricks of the pimp trade and acquired basic Scientology coercive techniques; his most influential teacher, however, was Dale Carnegie, the author of the bestselling, *How to Win Friends and Influence People.* Not only did Manson read the book, he took the course that was then offered by the prison. Manson enrolled and for the first time in his life, excelled as a student. Most of the tenets of Carnegie's approach are fundamental sales techniques—make other people feel important, use showmanship to dramatize your ideas—but the combination of those techniques with Manson's instinctive manipulative skills proved to be successful and lethal when applied to young people whose lives were unanchored and who were desperately looking for something to believe in.

chapter twelve
"I FELT LIKE A PREDATOR"

October 1996

Among the second batch of Mondo Video A-Go-Go videos that I rented was a recording of Leslie Van Houten's most recent parole hearing (at the time)—May 12, 1996. It was her eleventh appearance before the California Board of Prison Terms and, thanks to Mondo Video, I had the previous ones to compare it to. Over the years, the composition of the panel had changed, but the pattern of the questioning had not. These members seemed as bewildered by the killings as those assembled for each of the previous hearings. Though technically, their only purpose was to evaluate her suitability for parole, they couldn't resist one more attempt to comprehend the incomprehensible. Parole Board Commissioner Thomas Giaquinto asked Leslie to describe what happened at the LaBianca house. I find Leslie's answers to these questions astonishing, and it hasn't gotten less astonishing with every reading. There's nothing else she or anyone else has said to me that has saddened me, haunted me, puzzled me as much.

> LESLIE: I had Mrs. LaBianca lay down on the bed. I don't
> remember putting the pillowcase over her head but

I'm sure that I did. I wrapped a lamp cord around her
and she began struggling as she heard her husband
dying in the living room. When Mrs. LaBianca heard
him dying she came forward and I was trying to hold
her down and Pat attempted to stab her . . . and she hit
her collarbone and the knife bent and I went out of the
room and I called for Tex and Tex came into the room
and killed her.

GIAQUINTO: You stabbed her also, right?

LESLIE: After that . . . Tex handed me a knife and said
"do something" and I stabbed Mrs. LaBianca in the
lower torso . . . I think sixteen times.

GIAQUINTO: If you knew Mrs. LaBianca was already
dead, why did you stab her sixteen times?

LESLIE: I . . . I . . . I . . . couldn't . . . it was such a violent
act once I started I wasn't able to stop . . . it was a
horrible thing to do and while I was doing it I think I
was fighting with myself . . . I . . . think back on that
moment and I felt like a predator . . . I felt like a shark
just out of control for that moment.

GIAQUINTO: Surely, after the frenzy was over and you
were calmer, surely then you felt some regret.

No, she said, regret is not what she remembered feeling. She
did remember wiping away fingerprints and changing into some
of Mrs. LaBianca's clothing. She remembered Tex taking a
shower in the LaBiancas' bathroom. She remembered drinking
chocolate milk and eating cheese from the LaBiancas' refrigerator. (It was on the door of this refrigerator that Patricia Krenwinkel, using a towel dipped in Mr. LaBianca's blood, wrote,
"Healter Skelter," misspelling the title of one of the Beatles
songs from the *White Album*.) Leslie remembered the three of

them hiding in the bushes until dawn and then hitchhiking back to the Spahn Ranch.

"Surely," Giaquinto asked, "when you got back to the ranch you felt remorse. Horror? Regret?"

She shook her head. "No."

GIAQUINTO: Then what did you feel?
LESLIE: I don't . . . at that point empty and I went back to
   the farmhouse and I had some clothes and some
   change from the LaBianca house and I spoke with
   Dianne Lake and I told her that it had been fun. At least
   that's what she said. I don't remember exactly telling
   her that but it's something I would have said . . . you
   know, everything at the ranch was supposed to be fun,
   no matter what it was.

I have watched this video many times. It never gets less painful to imagine the horror Mr. and Mrs. LaBianca experienced. But each time I'm also struck by Leslie's honesty, by her willingness to accept full responsibility, and by her refusal to rationalize any part of her participation. In my experience these are all rarities among convicted murderers.

chapter thirteen
FOLIE À FAMILLE

1968

When Leslie and Pat describe how they ended up in Manson's lethal orbit, I can't help thinking about the fable of the frog. If a frog is thrown into boiling water, he will leap out of the pot. If he's thrown into a pot of tepid water, he happily burbles away as the heat under the water is ever so slowly increased and will never attempt to escape. He'll just slowly be cooked to death. (Apparently this is an urban legend. If the lid is off the pot, the frog will attempt to escape when the water gets hot, no matter how gradually. But I have always found it so useful as a life lesson that I'm reluctant to part with it.)

Pat and Leslie say that if, when they first met Manson, he had been the malevolent dictator he later became, they would have headed for the hills. But he was a guy talking about God and Oneness and spiritual love, and he seemed in possession of an uncanny knowingness. He not only knew their thoughts and feelings, he seemed to have some special extrasensory connection with all living creatures—babies, dogs, coyotes, lizards. He was wise, he was gentle, he was attentive, but he was also child-like and playful. His spirit of adventure was infectious and best of all, at least in the beginning, there were no rules, and both of them had spent the past few years chafing at rules.

Leslie's attraction to Manson was very different from Pat's. She didn't see him as a romantic figure but as a mystical one, so her attachment was not that of a lover, as it was with Pat, but as a leader, a guru, a God.

To be free of self, to fuse with Charlie and each other, they had to cut loose from their families. He wanted them to be, he said, the way they were before their parents contaminated their souls and twisted their hearts. "Who you are is beautiful," he told them. "It's everyone else—society, school, your parents—who are wrong." Before Charlie came along, Pat had seen herself as a failure in society; Leslie saw herself as a disappointment to her parents. For both of them, Charlie's dismissal of society's expectations was a salve.

"He knew just how to play on our dissatisfactions," Leslie said.

Gradually, his nurturing, supportive message turned into one of criticism, humiliation, and sometimes physical abuse. What had started out as an opportunity for a fresh start became a war against not only their past but their present autonomy. (By that time, it was too late, not only because of their attachment to him, but also because of their attachment to the other women in the group. It felt like a family.)

Both women talked about how important the feeling of sisterhood was. Manson, who'd never genuinely belonged to any family, knew how to engender the feeling of connection and family, something these kids yearned for.

But there was a cost to belonging to that family. The once-free-spirited commune morphed into a totalitarian society, a society without points of reference to the outside world.

Manson allowed no clocks, no calendars, and he micromanaged everything from the music they played (only his songs, and songs by Moody Blues and the Beatles) to when they had sex and with whom. He dictated when they could take drugs and he often orchestrated the "trips" they had. (The most vivid of these, according to Leslie, was the day they dropped acid and, with Manson as both director and star, they reenacted the crucifixion of Christ.) Soon, the boundary between hallucination and reality was hopelessly blurred.

Eventually they came to fear him, but the fear was intertwined with dependency and what felt like intense love. He told them the ultimate test of that love was the willingness to die. "I would die for you, would you die for me?" was his mantra.

One of the psychiatrists who testified at Tex Watson's trial and later at Leslie's second trial postulated that the so-called Manson Family was a *folie à famille*—a psychiatric term that refers to a group of people who share elements of mental illness such as delusions. He explained that in this way, Manson's pathology became the group's pathology.

The power he wielded in his little kingdom fueled a long-held ambition to be a recording star, and he managed to make enough contacts in the music business to bolster this dream. In 1968, Pat and one of the other girls met Beach Boy Dennis Wilson when they were hitchhiking in Malibu. The girls introduced him to Manson and he introduced Manson to rock manager Gregg Jakobson, who had produced The Doors.

Jakobson would later tell Vincent Bugliosi that he'd been drawn to Manson personally and fascinated by the "whole Charlie Manson package." The two men got to know each other over a period of a year and a half. "Charlie loved to rap about his views on life," Jakobson told Bugliosi. I include this here because one of the frustrations Pat and Leslie have had over the years is trying to get people to understand how they could have been attracted to Manson. I have no idea if Jakobson is any measure of normality, but he was certainly more mainstream, to the extent that a music producer can be mainstream, than most of Manson's young followers.

Jakobson introduced him to Doris Day's son Terry Melcher, who had produced The Byrds. This was a critical introduction to Manson. He was counting on Melcher to provide his big break.

Jakobson eventually arranged for Manson to record a demo, with the Family as backup. By the end of 1968, Manson's dream of cutting an album became a dangerous fixation. When he listened to the Beatles' *White Album*, the message he "heard" in their lyrics was that the time for revolution—a revolution between blacks and whites, a revolution with the title of "Helter Skelter"—was nigh and we anoint you, Charlie, to start that revolution with your songs.

There are many pages in the book devoted to Bugliosi's analysis of what Manson took to be directives in the *White Album* lyrics, the how, why, and where of the racial war. (Like everything else associated with Manson's motive, the selection of the title "Helter Skelter" for the revolution is subject to interpretation. In their book, Bugliosi and Gentry write, "'Helter Skelter' is another name for a slide in an amusement park.") The blacks were going to win the battle, and the entire white race, save Manson and Family, would be destroyed. They would be spared because the blacks would recognize that they needed a few whites to lead society. In "Honey Pie," they urged him to sing the truth to the world when they asked Honey Pie to show the "magic of your Hollywood song." In "Revolution," they told him they were waiting for him to sing the word that would trigger the "real solution . . . the plan" they'd "love to see."

Working day and night, Manson wrote an album's worth of new songs incorporating the Beatles' mandate. Melcher agreed to come and listen to the songs and, in preparation, the women cleaned the house, rolled joints, and cooked a special dinner. Melcher never showed up.

The extent to which Manson truly believed in "Helter Skelter" is still debated, but what is not in question is his bitter disappointment and frustration about his album's dead end. One person who believed that his thwarted music career was the motive behind the murders was Roman Polanski, Sharon Tate's husband. "Manson's rage was that of the spurned performer—one who seeks revenge on others for his own lack of talent and recognition," he wrote in his 1984 memoir, *Roman*. In the book, Polanski contends that Manson targeted that house because he believed that Terry Melcher, the man who declined to produce his compositions—compositions Polanski described as mediocre—still lived there. He speculates that the murder of the LaBiancas was an attempt to confuse the issue.

chapter fourteen
FALLING IN LOVE WITH ANNE FRANK

1958

It wasn't until I started re-tracing my interest in Catherine Share that I understood the way the issue of Jewishness hovered in my youth and why the Manson swastika was so significant to me. At some point, Hitler and Manson, the macro and micro of monsters, merged in my imagination, and Catherine was an unwitting participant in that merger.

In high school, my Jewish heritage defined who I was. Not because I talked about it but because I didn't. And I especially never mentioned it to the girls in my immediate social circle.

There is a theory that anti-Semitism is more rampant in Austria because, unlike Germany, after World War II, Austria refused to confront its treatment of Jews so all that poison has lain dormant. For some reason that feels loosely analogous to the effect submerging my Jewish identity, even as diluted as it was, had on me while I was in high school.

Jews are now such an open, vital part of our culture, it's sometimes difficult to remember the pervasiveness of anti-Semitism in the 1950s. There were still quotas in medical and law schools, country clubs and social clubs either had quotas or banned Jews altogether, and more affluent neighborhoods had restrictions. When I was younger I was aware of all this but at a remove. I was, after all, only one-quarter Jewish. As a child, my grandmother emigrated with her family from Russia in the late 1800s. Her family was religious, but as an adult, she wanted nothing to do with religion and they wanted nothing to do with her. She was an atheist, an anarchist, and a vegetarian who had a child out of wedlock and sent her daughter (my mother) to school with a note pinned to her dress, "Do not feed my child meat."

As a kid, I was aware of anti-Semitism. I knew about Hitler. I knew Jews had been imprisoned in concentration camps and executed. And I was vaguely conscious of anti-Semitic chatter but only because my parents discussed it. Given that my mother and grandmother spoke Yiddish to each other, I should have felt more connected but I didn't. And then I fell in love with Anne Frank.

In the spring of 1956, when I was twelve and my brother sixteen, our parents took us out of school to travel through Europe for three months in the spring. This trip could be described as the most wonderful thing a family could do together or a familial catastrophe of epic proportions. It was, in fact, both. It was wonderful in all of the predictable ways—culturally, historically, artistically, architecturally—but it also exposed pathological strains in our family dynamic. From the outset my mother's Jewishness was a factor. A variable? A theme? A hurdle? Or, put another way, she was never as Jewish as she was before and during that trip. It also, eventually, occasioned my own Jewish awakening.

The conflict started when my father brought home a color brochure for the Volkswagen microbus he planned to buy. We'd pick it up in Southampton, England, drive it through thirteen countries, camping whenever possible, then ship it home and sell it. In those days, you could make money doing that. The profit would pay for the use of the car in Europe.

My mother picked up the brochure, leafed through it, handed it back to my father. "I won't travel in a car Hitler invented." My father said she was thinking of the VW Bug and even that, Hitler didn't invent, only promoted. She replied that everyone knew that Volkswagen was a Nazi company and she'd think of Hitler every minute that she was in the car.

And then my father brought home a slick color brochure of the SS *Kungsholm,* the Swedish American passenger ship we would take coming home from Copenhagen to New York. I was thrilled with the brochure. Swimming pools, movie theaters, gift shops, ice cream parlors. "Look," my father said, showing my mother the map of the staterooms. He pointed out that we'd be saving a bundle of money because he had reserved inside staterooms. My mother erupted: "No Goddamn way. My mother came from Russia in steerage," she yelled, her face scarlet, her eyes blazing. "I'm not going anywhere in steerage."

Sometimes these discussions started calmly, even playfully, depending on the issue. It was, after all, a dream of a lifetime (my father's dream, her lifetime, as she repeated, more than once), and then a detail would surface that triggered an outburst. Depending on the detail, she'd either calm down or her anger would mount and the yelling would continue long after we had all gone to our respective bedrooms.

She won the argument about the SS *Kungsholm.* My father booked outside staterooms. He did, however, buy the Volkswagen microbus. The latter was the usual outcome of their *pas de deux*—my mother protesting initially and then ultimately my father prevailing. I think I know why. In spite of the fact that she was assertive in most areas of her life and as a successful career woman she certainly carried her own weight and had a right to have an equal say in decisions, she found it very difficult to insist on anything with my father. When you grow up poor with an eccentric single anarchist mother and a mystery surrounding your paternity, you're lacking in the entitled department.

I also think being Jewish (or as my daughter describes it, Jewish*ish*) was a factor. Had she been part of a big Jewish clan like her mother's family of origin, she might have had a buffer. She only had her crazy mother for support. What I don't know, to this day, is whether my father recognized this vulnerability and exploited it to override her wishes or whether he failed to recognize it at all. He certainly suffered the consequences; she held these unilateral decisions against him for the rest of their lives. (When she would bring up one of many grievances in their later years, his frequent response: "What's the statute of limitations on that one? thirty years? forty years? fifty years?") As a kid, I was not an objective judge. I always took my father's side, if only in my heart.

Before we left for Europe, my English teacher gave my parents a list of books she wanted me to read on the trip. *The Diary of a Young Girl* by Anne Frank was one of them, and my mother suggested that I read it when we were in Amsterdam since that's where Anne Frank was hiding with her family when she wrote it.

In Amsterdam, we stayed in a two-bedroom suite in a small hotel, and my brother and I shared a room. After my parents went to sleep, he would leave the hotel and prowl the streets of the city. I don't know everything he did, although smoking was one of them. Before we left home, he had figured out a way to attach cartons of American cigarettes to the lining of his London Fog raincoat, but he still needed to find times and places when he could smoke without my mother, who had the nose of a bloodhound, finding out.

Every night, after he left for his usual venture, I was paralyzed with fear for him. I distracted myself by reading Anne Frank under the duvet with a flashlight; I was afraid that if my parents saw the light under the door, they'd be suspicious. As I got deeper into the book and as Anne's situation got more perilous, my anxiety about both of them increased. It was difficult for me to sort my fears. Would he be arrested by the Dutch police? (He'd been arrested on Hollywood Boulevard with friends for drinking beer in his car right before we left home.) Would my parents discover that he was gone? Would I get in trouble for not telling them? Would the Gestapo discover Anne's family? And what would happen to them? It's a wonder I slept at all.

Anne's diary entries were addressed to "dear Kitty" so it read more like a collection of letters to a friend than a diary. I immediately identified with Kitty. I was Kitty, Anne's best friend, and I pictured myself reading those letters while sitting on my bed in my bedroom in the Silver Lake District in Los Angeles where we lived. I don't know why, but Kitty seemed like a gentile name and therefore I, as Kitty, was a gentile reading letters from my Jewish best friend. Initially it didn't cause me to identify more with Jews, but it did open my heart to their suffering.

In Anne's early entries, before the family went into hiding, she cataloged the increasing restrictions. Jews could no longer ride streetcars or buses, they could no longer watch movies in the movie theaters, swim in public pools, sit in public gardens, eat in restaurants.

I understood the issue of segregation. When, in 1954, the U.S. Supreme Court ruled that separate was not equal in *Brown v. Board of Education*, my parents used it as a teaching opportunity—discussing it at dinner a few nights in a row. Our country seemed to be getting better. When Anne lived in Hitler-occupied Holland everything, for the Jews, was getting worse.

I must have been a little dim because when I started reading the book, I didn't know that Anne died at the end. I was probably the only kid of my age in the country who thought it had a happy ending. I didn't find out that Anne and her mother died in a concentration camp until I read the afterword. I was heartbroken. Anne Frank's writing was so vivid, so immediate, I felt as though I had truly lost my best friend. How could it be that this funny, smart girl died for no other reason than she was Jewish? Mixed in with my sadness was my sense of outrage. I was heartbroken but, in my mind, it was still about losing my friend. It wasn't about me.

The morning after I finished the book my eyes were red and puffy from crying when I showed up for breakfast. My parents were talking about the town we were going to visit that day, Volendam. My mother kept glancing my way and finally asked what was wrong. "Why are your eyes so swollen? Have you been crying?"

"No," I said. "I think I'm getting a cold." I blew my nose to prove it. I was embarrassed. I changed the subject. I pointed to a photo in one of the travel books. "So people still really dress this way?"

"Yes!" she said. "It will be fun." In 1956 the residents of Volendam wore traditional garb every day—starched white caps, dirndls with aprons, for the women, dark loose pants, red neckerchiefs, and suspenders for the men. Wooden shoes for everyone. (I bought a pair of wooden shoes for my teacher.)

By the following morning I didn't feel as raw. I told my parents I'd finished the book. My father asked me what I thought of it.

"I was so sad," I said. "I can't believe Hitler killed those people just because they were Jewish."

There must have been something about the way I said "those people" that alerted my mother.

She was standing at a side table pouring coffee. As she handed my father his cup, I saw her glance at him with a puzzled look on her face and then turn to me. "What do you mean, 'those' people?"

I was confused by her reaction. What was I missing? Wasn't Anne Frank's family Jewish?

When I thought about this years later, after I was a parent myself, it occurred to me that my mother wasn't sure how to handle this conversation. Was I old enough to digest what she was about to tell me? Maybe it was like sex. She was trying to find out what I already knew. She didn't want to plant frightening images that weren't there already, but she wanted me to know the truth. She decided to rip the bandage off.

She took a sip of her coffee and said, "You do realize that under Hitler, you would have been just as Jewish as Anne Frank." Her tone was matter of fact as though she was talking about membership in the Girl Scouts. "He had rules about that."

"But I'm hardly Jewish at all." The minute I said it, it felt wrong, cowardly or something like cowardly. I nonetheless soldiered on: "But Mama Sarah was the only Jewish person in our family."

"That's true," she said. "But it's also true that the Nazis declared that anyone with a Jewish grandparent had to die. He wanted to get rid of everyone who had any Jewish blood. They had a word for it. *Mischling.* It means a hybrid . . . people who had both Aryan and Jewish blood." (I think my mother might have been wrong about this. The Nazis had a complicated system of labeling. With one Jewish grandparent I would have been labeled a *Mischling* of the second degree. Apparently there wasn't total agreement about what to do with my group. If I looked Jewish or acted Jewish or "felt" Jewish, I would be deported.

There was agreement about one thing: *Mischling* of the second degree would be sterilized. My mother, however, because she had three or more Jewish grandparents, would have been gassed. (To this day, I don't know if my mother knew the truth—that I wouldn't have automatically been eligible for extinction—but didn't want me to distance myself from my heritage. I also don't know how the knowledge would have changed my perception of my place in the world.)

Everything I'd heard—the lampshades, the soap, the ovens, the showers—took on a new meaning.

I must have looked frightened.

"So I would have been gassed in the ovens?"

Is that how I asked? I can't imagine now but that's what I remember.

Again she glanced at my father. "I'm afraid so, sweetie." My hunch was that the sweetie was meant to soften it, but it didn't work. Later I would ask about the rest of the family, but at that moment, I was having trouble integrating my twelve-year-old self being gassed because I had a Jewish grandmother.

Before, when I pictured losing my new best friend Anne Frank, my heart hurt. Now, when I realized I was not gentile Kitty, the view of my position in the world was entirely changed.

chapter fifteen
EVERYBODY CAN BE A KILLER

1963, 2003, 2015

After years of researching violence, I thought I would be somewhat desensitized to descriptions of brutality, but then I learned about the work of Father Patrick Desbois. He is a French Catholic priest who, for more than a decade, traveled from village to village in the Ukraine to unearth both the truth and the remains of 1.5 million Jews who were killed in the Holocaust. These murders occurred before Auschwitz, before Birkenau, before Treblinka, before Dachau, before the Nazis completed their methodical plans for the Final Solution. The killing centers that came later were out of public view; the massacres in the Ukraine occurred in plain sight. Unlike Poland and Germany, where reminders of the killings were memorialized after the war, the horror in Ukraine was hidden away, first by the Nazis, then by the Soviets. What attracted me to the story initially was that most of the people involved were simple country folks—not Nazis. Acting on orders from the Germans, they shot fellow villagers and dug the ditches where they threw the bodies and where the truth was buried for seventy-five years.

Since the Holocaust, when so many ordinary Germans tortured and killed Jews, there has been ongoing research and corresponding dialogue about what impels presumably average people to commit "crimes of obedience" under the leadership of malevolent leaders. The most famous of these studies was initiated in 1961 by Stanley Milgram at Yale University. In a fake laboratory the "naive subject," a volunteer who had answered an advertisement in a New Haven newspaper, was instructed to give increasingly painful electric shocks to a person in response to every wrong answer to a test question. The subjects were told they were participating in a study of the effect of punishment on learning and memory, when in fact it was their capacity for cruelty when ordered to do so by an individual in a position of authority. Milgram's idea was to see how average Americans would behave when put in a situation roughly comparable to ordinary Germans who were ordered to participate in the torture and killing of Jews. No real shock was actually administered, but the recipient of the faux shock would scream louder every time the voltage was set higher.

In his 1974 book about the experiment, *Obedience to Authority,* Milgram wrote of his surprise at the large number of ordinary people, from lawyers to day laborers, who were willing to obey orders. Over two-thirds obeyed the experimenter and kept pulling the lever despite hearing the screams from the person receiving the shocks. Most subjects continued giving shock after shock. Milgram speculated that this tendency to obey orders (even immoral, anti-social orders) is rooted in our species' evolutionary struggle for survival. Without this capacity for obedience we would not be able to function in a hierarchical social organization, a social form that insures the survival of the weaker of the species. "When the individual is on his own," he wrote, "conscience is brought into play. But when he functions in an organizational mode, directions that come from the higher level of competence are not assessed against the internal standards of moral judgment."

This seemed like a credible explanation for Pat's and Leslie's behavior. If ordinary people were willing to inflict suffering on orders from an authority they didn't know, it seemed plausible that the women were compelled to follow orders of someone they considered their leader, even if those orders were repugnant. But every time I found an explanation for their behavior, a circumstance was revealed that either invalidated my conclusion or made it problematic. This happened when I watched the films of Milgram's experiments. The degree to which ordinary people obeyed was shocking, but I was struck by something else: it was traumatic for the majority of them to do so. Many tried to resist but were ultimately bullied into submission.

When Milgram varied the conditions of the experiment, he got different results. In the original study, the person administering the shock was in a different room from the recipient, though he could hear the screams. As Milgram moved the subjects closer to each other so the people administering the shocks were better able to witness the expressions of pain, the more frequently they were willing to defy the orders of the experimenters. In the final stage of proximity when the administrators of the shock had to place the victims' hands on the shock plate, a fully 70 percent refused to administer shocks.

While it's true that, like the majority of Milgram's subjects, Pat and Leslie were willing to obey the orders of an authority figure, unlike 70 percent of his subjects, being close, hearing the cries, seeing the pain on their victim's faces had no effect on them. Zero. Does that mean they could be in the same category as the 30 percent in Milgram's experiment or does that mean that something in addition to obedience to Manson's authority was at work?

Over the years, Milgram's obedience-to-authority explanation of the Holocaust has had many challengers—the best known of these is Daniel Goldhagen. In his 1997 book, *Hitler's Willing Executioners: Ordinary Germans and the Holocaust*, he wrote that what fueled the brutality of ordinary Germans who killed Jews in the Holocaust was not the drive to be obedient to authority but centuries-long hatred of Jews embedded in the German culture. Goldhagen also took issue with the findings of American historian Christopher Browning whose 1992 book, *Ordinary Men: Reserve Police Battalion 101 and the Final Solution in Poland* was influenced by Milgram's work.

Battalion 101 consisted of five hundred policemen who, before the war, had worked as businessmen, dockworkers, truck drivers, construction workers, machine operators, waiters, druggists, and teachers as well as some who had been professional policemen. Only a minority were members of the Nazi Party, and only a few belonged to the SS. According to Browning, none of the men were openly anti-Semitic. Battalion 101 participated in the shootings and/or the transport to the Treblinka gas chambers of at least eighty-three thousand Jews.

After the war, many assumed that ordinary Germans were under orders to kill Jews from a brutal regime and therefore had no choice but to obey. Browning's research revealed that the men killed even when not under a direct threat to obey. In one situation, the commander of the unit gave his men the choice of opting out of the massacre if they found it too troubling. Out of five hundred men, only twelve opted out. Chris Browning and Daniel Goldhagen drew opposite conclusions from that behavior. Browning's takeaway: the men in Battalion 101 who did not opt out were acting out of an instinctive drive to obey authority, even when they found what they were ordered to do morally reprehensible. They were not, he asserted, motivated by fear, blood lust, or primal hatred.

Goldhagen, however, believed that so few opted out when given the opportunity because they wanted to kill Jews and to kill them in a way that maximized suffering. He identified what he called "eliminationist anti-Semitism," a mentality that grew out of medieval attitudes and was fundamental to German national identity. "The eliminationist ideology, derived from the German cultural cognitive model of Jews, was at the root of the policies of the 1930s which the German people supported," he wrote. "The genocidal program of the war was grounded in the same ideology."

At the time of these debates, not much was known about the killing of the 1.5 million Jews in the Ukraine. Now, thanks to the interviews Father Desbois and his team started conducting in 2003, we know the murders were coordinated by German special killing squads but with the participation of willing locals. Most of the villagers Father Desbois interviewed had been children and teenagers at the time of the killings, but they remembered witnessing the horror. They remembered that the victims had been primarily women, children, and old people who the willing locals knew as friends, neighbors, or childhood playmates. They remembered that the victims were taken from their homes on foot or by car or truck to pits just outside the villages where they lived. They remembered that these women, children, and old people were often stripped of their clothing, lined up, and shot at close range, face-to-face or in the back. They remembered that many of the victims did not die immediately and were left to suffer in a pile of death. They remembered that the massacres were treated as spectacles—the villagers flocked to watch the people they knew slaughtered.

There are photographs that document these events, and if I thought the photographs of the Tate-LaBianca victims and the photos of the brutality at Abu Ghraib prison would be the ones to haunt me forever, it's only because I hadn't seen these yet.

It now seems clear that the motivation for killing in the Holocaust was not, by any means, binary. Obedience to authority? Yes. Anti-Semitism? Yes. Primal hatred? Yes. Blood lust? Yes.

Which boxes would Pat and Leslie check? They say they were motivated by the wish to obey Manson but even more, the desire to please him. (I would imagine that the desire to please authority figures would have figured prominently in the Nazi bureaucracy,

if only for career advancement.) And it was Manson's primal hatred they were acting out, not their own.

What about blood lust? Blood lust is not a clinical term, though
it crops up in a lot of both fictional and non-fictional accounts of
murderers, usually referring to serial killers. When used in popular culture it seems generic, covering many pathologies, including
sadism. I have the sense that when Browning referred to it in the
context of the Nazis, he was using it synonymously with bloodthirsty. Either way, there's no indication that it pertained to either
Pat or Leslie. Susan Atkins is another story. There is a clinically
recognized blood fetish, *hematolagnia*, which refers to people
who are aroused by the sight, smell, and taste of blood. If I had
been able to interview Susan Atkins before she died, how would
she have explained her boast to her cell mates about tasting Sharon
Tate's blood?

In October 2015, Father Desbois told *60 Minutes* that among
the many disturbing lessons the Ukrainian villagers taught him
about human nature is the universality of our propensity to violence. "I learned everybody can be a killer, anybody can be a victim." Given how hard he's worked on the Ukrainian project and
how committed to humanity he is, what he added was odd and
more than a little disheartening—the fact that he expressed it in
the second person made his conclusion feel more personal, more
pointed and more chilling: "I learned that you like to see other
people dying in front of you, killed by other people, when you are
sure you will not be killed."

chapter sixteen
"Is There Anything Worse Than Dying in Terror?"

1996

*T*he next time I saw Leslie, I mentioned that I had watched several videos of her parole hearings and I asked whether she got tired of having to repeat the details of the murders over and over again, decade after decade. After all, everyone on those panels had heard the description before.

"It's horrible to have to repeat those details," she said, "but I completely understand why they have to keep asking. They have to be sure that I acknowledge what happened . . . all of it. And," she added, "the parole board has to be sure that I not only take responsibility for the consequences, they have to be sure I understand the full extent of those consequences." She talked about the holes that were left in the LaBianca family, pointing out that Frank, who was fifteen, had to grow up without a mother, and his older sister, Suzan, lost the benefit of her mother's love when she was a young adult. "When I was her age, my mother was so important to me and my survival. I don't know if I would have made it without her.

"And it didn't stop there," she said. "Another generation was deprived of having Rosemary as a grandmother and Leno as a grandfather. And so it continues. It's so unfair."

I told her that while I appreciated her honesty—she never backed away from acknowledging how much the LaBiancas have suffered—I had a hard time wrapping my head around the situation. If she claimed that she had amnesia or was so awash in adrenaline it affected her memory, it might be more understandable. But at the time of the murders, she recognized how horrible it was for Mrs. LaBianca to hear her husband being killed in the other room and yet she felt no empathy, no basic human feeling for either of them.

"I know it doesn't make sense," she said, shaking her head. "I wish I understood. I don't. When I was still able to have one-to-one therapy, that's what we were working on. And then the state stopped offering individual therapy so it had to end."

While she doesn't understand her absence of feeling then, she says she feels a deep sadness for the LaBiancas now. "Is there anything worse than that . . . to die in terror?"

At some point we shifted from the topic of the murders to the topic of long-term coping with difficult circumstances. We talked for a while about how important resilience is. Can one acquire it? We agreed that it's probably, like so many things, a little bit of nature, a little bit of nurture.

I said that in the short time I'd known her, her mood generally seemed good, in spite of having been in prison for decades. She said she was an optimist by nature, but acknowledged that she couldn't help occasionally mourning the life she'd never have. It was not a thought she allowed herself to have for long. "When I think about what I did to that family, how can I allow myself the luxury of mourning anything about my life?"

On the drive back to Santa Monica, I thought about the circle of grief that Leslie talked about. Of course, she couldn't help mourning the life she'd never have, the life she apparently had been destined to have. But as soon as she allowed herself those feelings, she was slammed with guilt over being both a survivor and a murderer. Mourning can be cleansing and therapeutic but not if, every time you feel it, you punish yourself for feeling it. I don't think she was asking for sympathy from me; she was simply stating the circular nature of grief in her situation. I also realized that many people, unless they know her, would feel nothing but scorn for this problem.

1991

*I*n recent years, empathy has become a hot topic among researchers. Once considered a bonus, a perk of civilization, empathy is now increasingly viewed as a fundamental requirement for human survival. Primatologist Dr. Frans de Waal maintains that primates, both human and non-human, are hardwired for empathy and that empathy has deep roots in the origin of our species. "It begins in the body, a deep unconscious synchrony between mother and child that sets the tone for so many mammalian interactions," he writes in *The Age of Empathy: Nature's Lessons for a Kinder Society.*

If, as de Waal suggests, empathy is hardwired in the brain, the neurons that are possibly responsible are a relatively new discovery.

On a hot and humid day in the summer of 1991 in Parma, Italy, a macaque monkey sat in a lab waiting for researchers to return from lunch. Wires had been implanted in his brain—the region of the brain that's involved in planning and carrying out movements. Every time the monkey grasped and moved an object, that region of his brain fired and registered a *brrrrrip* sound on the monitor. A graduate student entered the lab with an ice cream cone in his hand. The monkey stared at him. When the student raised the cone to his mouth, the monkey's monitor sounded in the same way it would sound had the monkey raised the cone to his own mouth. He simply watched the student eating the ice cream.

The researchers, led by Giacomo Rizzolatti, a neuroscientist at the University of Parma, had earlier noticed the phenomenon with peanuts. When the monkey watched humans or other monkeys bring peanuts to their mouths, the same region of the monkey's brain fired as though he was bringing the peanut to his own mouth. Likewise, with bananas, raisins, and all kinds of other delicacies.

The cells that were firing in the monkey's brain were mirror neurons—brain cells that fire both when the animal sees or hears an action and when the animal carries out the same action on its own. This was a very big deal. Ice cream cones all around.

The discovery was an enormous breakthrough and, according to Dr. Christian Keysers, a professor at the brain and cognition program, University of Amsterdam, it was analogous to finding out that after years of watching television, your television was also watching you. In his book, *The Empathic Brain* (2011), he explains that mirror neurons allow us to feel the other person's distress or pain as our own.

V. S. Ramachandran, a pioneer in mirror neuron research, calls these neurons "empathy neurons" or "Dalai Lama neurons." In a 2007 article titled "The Neurology of Self-Awareness" in *Edge*, an online publication, he wrote that mirror neurons "dissolve the barrier between self and others."

The theory is that mirror neurons kick in at birth. Studies show that infants a few minutes old will stick out their tongues at adults doing the same thing. Even more than other primates, human children are hardwired for imitation; mirror neurons are involved in observing what others do and then practice doing the same thing.

The research on mirror neurons in humans is still in its early phase and like so many issues in science, there's no consensus. Despite the excitement about the discovery in monkeys, the claims about the role they play in the human brain is premature. For one thing, the kind of measuring that's done on monkeys is too invasive to be performed on people. As of this writing, there's been only one study on humans and that was when brain surgery was performed on people with intractable epilepsy. These patients had electrodes implanted into their brains to identify the loci of their seizures; the search for mirror neurons was incidental to the surgical procedure. According to Christian Jarrett, in a 2013 article in *Science*, that study did find evidence of mirror neurons in the human frontal cortex and temporal lobe but revealed that the term "mirror neurons" actually covers a complex mix of cell types. "This is not to detract from the fascination of mirror neurons. It does show they are not the beginning of a causal path . . . rather they are embedded in a complex network of brain activity" ("A Calm Look at the Most Hyped Concept in Neuroscience—Mirror Neurons," December 12, 2013).

There are those who maintain that mirror neurons are fixed and innate; others, like Cecelia Heyes, a researcher at the Department of Experimental Psychology, University of Oxford, argue that they are affected by cultural practices just as much as they influence them. Her research shows that learning experiences can reverse, nullify, or exaggerate mirror-like properties in motor cells. These findings would seem to support the idea that Manson's influence on Pat and Leslie changed their neural systems, but we are years away from proof of that sort of conjecture.

Much about the development of empathy is still unknown, but according to Frans de Waal, examples of empathy in animals (other than humans) suggest a long evolutionary history. In a UC

Berkeley publication, the *Greater Good*, he argues that empathy is essential to survival. "Without a proper mechanism to understand and respond to the needs of offspring, a species will not survive." He also points out that empathy plays a role in cooperation—another necessity for survival. "Effective cooperation requires being exquisitely in tune with the emotional states and goals of others.

"A lioness needs to notice quickly when other lionesses go into hunting mode, so that she can join them and contribute to the pride's success. A male chimpanzee needs to pay attention to his buddy's rivalries and skirmishes with others so that he can help out whenever needed, thus ensuring the political success of their partnership" (September 1, 2005).

One does not usually associate Rhesus monkeys with empathy. They have a well-deserved reputation for being aggressive and dangerous once they reach sexual maturity. I can attest to this having been tackled and bitten by a Rhesus monkey named Harriet. (A friend had somehow acquired her believing she would make a wonderful pet. Harriet did not make a wonderful pet, and she especially didn't like women.)

Because of the breed's ferocious character and because of my own experience, I was surprised when I came across the results of a Milgram-inspired study conducted on Rhesus monkeys (Masserman, J., S. Wechkin, and W. Terris, *Am. J. Psychiatry* 121:584–585). Several monkeys were trained to pull on one of two chains, in order to receive food. After they had learned this response, another monkey was placed in an adjacent cage and displayed through a one-way mirror; pulling the chain now caused the monkey in the second cage to receive a painful electric shock. Most of the monkeys would not shock another monkey even if it meant they wouldn't be able to eat. Some of them went so far as to go without food for five days rather than shock the other monkey. One of the animals went without food for *twelve days* (italics mine). Further evidence that empathy was involved: monkeys who'd been shocked themselves in previous experiments were even less willing to pull the chain that subjected others to suffering. Clearly Harriet's empathy did not extend to female Homo sapiens.

chapter eighteen
UNFORGETTING RETRIBUTION

1996

I looked across the café table at Steve Kay and realized that in spite of some gray hair and wrinkles, I could still see the lean, clean-cut, kind-of-square boy I knew in high school. I immediately felt comfortable with him. I didn't actually know him anymore but I knew him. There's something about the familiarity that's established in adolescence that can persist years later, even without ongoing or even intermittent contact. In high school, he was a nice guy to girls, so nice that he had much better luck attracting friends who were girls than girlfriends, though he had been the boyfriend of one of my best friends until, that is, she threw him over for a sexy, not-as-nice guy.

After we ordered lunch, we talked about what had happened to the people we knew at Hollywood High and then filled each other in on our families and our careers. I knew from reporters who covered the courts that he had a reputation for being a tough but honest prosecutor; I knew that he'd been awarded deputy prosecutor of the year five years before in 1991. And I knew that he continued to follow all of the people who'd been involved in the Tate-LaBianca murders. I just didn't know how closely. How single-mindedly. How obsessively.

He was a young deputy district attorney, only three years out of law school, when he assisted Vincent Bugliosi at the original trial, and he subsequently represented the state in two retrials after the California Supreme Court overturned Leslie's original conviction. In addition, he'd insisted on representing the district attorney's office in every single parole hearing, not only of Manson, who had no hope of release anyway, but of any and all of the people connected to the case. One *L.A. Times* reporter characterized him as "the leading voice for unforgetting retribution" and likened him to the obsessed prosecutor in *Les Misérables*.

We discussed the fact that since the Tate-LaBianca murders there had been an increasing emphasis on victims' rights—in large part because of the work of Sharon Tate's mother and sisters—that had culminated in the victims' rights bill in 1982, which gave victims and their families a greater role in sentencing and parole hearings. We also argued affably about the Three Strikes sentencing law. Like most prosecutors, he believed it worked. Most other people I knew, judges and defense attorneys, thought it was a terrible law. But when we went back to talking about victims and the families of victims and how important it was that they be given ample opportunity to be heard, there was little he said with which I disagreed. "Moving on with one's life after the trauma is difficult and painful," he said. "Participating in the court process helps families move on."

Steve told me he had been close to Doris Tate, Sharon's mother, before she died in 1992 of a brain tumor; and he continued his relationship with her two remaining daughters, Patti and Debra. He suggested that if I wanted to learn more about the family's involvement with victims' rights, I talk to Patti Tate and he said he would arrange it. He also invited me to attend a trial he would soon be prosecuting. I accepted the invitation.

chapter nineteen

DUES-PAYING MEMBER OF THE LITTLE WILDLIFE SOCIETY

1947–1969

On December 3, 1947, Patricia Krenwinkel was born into what is now called a blended family. Her mother, Dorothy, a young widow with a child from her first marriage, moved from Mobile, Alabama, to Los Angeles where she married Joe Krenwinkel in 1944. When Patricia was born, her half sister Charlene was seven.

The family lived in Westchester, the section of Los Angeles where LAX is located. Pat's mother was a housewife, her father an insurance agent; both parents were active in the community. They organized neighborhood Easter egg hunts, Halloween parades, and Christmas parties; they taught Bible School; her mother was a member of the World Church Women's Council, helped out with the Campfire Girls, and went door to door for the March of Dimes.

Pat remembered being especially close to her father, a man she described as gentle and kind. A cherished memory from her childhood was walking hand-in-hand with him down the street on weekends to survey, in wonder, the progress of the construction of LAX. Her memories of her relationship with her father were marred only by the fact that he was not as involved with her half sister Charlene—a persistent source of pain for Charlene and, hence, for Pat.

Pat described her mother as warmhearted, a woman who was always concerned about society's underdogs. "I remember down-on-their-luck guys coming to our door and asking to work for food. She would always give them something to eat."

As a kid, Pat read the Bible, sang in the church choir, and had a vast collection of pets: dogs, hamsters, goldfish, parakeets, canaries. She was a dues-paying member of the Little Wildlife Society.

During the penalty phase of the trial, her parents testified to what a perfect little girl she'd been. They were clearly still stunned by their daughter's involvement in seven murders, and some of their testimony reads, point by point, like a rebuttal to the standard warning signs of a future serial killer: she was gentle with animals; she was never cruel to other children, in fact never even fought with other children; she belonged to normal childhood organizations; she liked going to the beach; she never lost her temper; she got good grades; she was so cooperative at school, her teacher loved having her in class; she was a good Presbyterian; she read the Bible with enthusiasm; as a teenager, she never got in trouble with police, never even got a traffic ticket.

"Pat," her mother testified, as recounted in *Helter Skelter*, "was one of those babies who would wake up in the morning and play in her crib for hours without crying." And her mother remembered that when she was a little older, she'd spend many uncomplaining hours in an indoor swing.

She may have seemed contented as a baby, but Pat remembers growing up in an atmosphere of "hushed desperation" and loneliness. She always felt loved by her parents, but that acceptance was not matched by her experience at school, where she had few friends. As she entered adolescence, the security at home vanished. There was no yelling, no acrimony, but the tension mounted. Her father started sleeping on the couch in the den. Pat got quieter and withdrew. Meanwhile, her sister Charlene acted out—she was sexually promiscuous and she abused drugs. Pat's parents di-

vorced when she was seventeen and her mother moved back to
Alabama, taking Pat with her. Pat was miserable there. She always had trouble making friends, but it was worse in Alabama.
The kids at the high school she attended were suspicious of Yan-
kees.

Finally she returned to Los Angeles to live with her father and
attend University High. She made a few friends and her grades
were okay, but she described her life at that time as dreary. She
started smoking marijuana. After high school, she moved back to
Alabama, enrolling in a teacher's course at Spring Hill College, a
Jesuit institution in Mobile. After one semester she decided she
didn't want to be a teacher, so she dropped out and returned to
L.A. There she moved in with her sister, who was living in Manhattan Beach, and landed a job as a claims clerk at an insurance
company. It was less than ideal.

Her sister's life was in disarray; she'd had a short turbulent
marriage and she'd started using hard drugs. (Four years later,
Charlene died of an overdose of heroin. One of Pat's painful
memories is the last letter her sister wrote to Pat's father. "She es-
sentially begged for his love.")

While living with her sister, Pat's social life centered around a
group of Marines who were stationed at Camp Pendleton. She
dated a couple of them and was drinking buddies with all of them.
"Sometimes they'd even sneak me onto the base. I loved being
with them. One by one they were shipped off to Vietnam and it
stopped being fun and games—some of them were dying over
there."

I asked her if losing friends to the war made her political. It was,
after all, 1967 and there were many opportunities to organize
against the war. "No," she said. "The only thing political about me
was the music I listened to. I loved folk music—The Weavers, Pete
Seeger, Bob Dylan, Joan Baez."

One night Billy Greene, a friend of her sister's, came by with a prison buddy who played the guitar and sang songs like "The Shadow of Your Smile." His name was Charles Manson. He had a tough-but-wounded James Dean look. Pat swooned. That night, she and Charlie made love and he told her she was beautiful. "He said, 'You should never be ashamed of your body.' I couldn't believe it. I had always been ashamed of my body. No one had ever called me beautiful. I started to cry."

Charlie seemed to know things about her no one else did—secret fears, secret dreams—and she was convinced that he had psychic powers. Much later, much, much later, she learned that his skills weren't supernatural, just super vigilant. "He knew how to pay attention to people's strengths and weaknesses and he knew how to use that information to manipulate people," she said. He'd acquired a bag of tricks in prison—some were literally tricks using playing cards and sleight-of-hand maneuvers—which also caused people to believe he possessed extraordinary powers.

After a couple of days, Manson invited her to travel with him to Northern California. Because she felt adrift, because she wanted something to matter, she said yes. "You can't imagine what a relief it is when you have no idea what to do with your life and then someone comes along and tells you exactly what to do with it."

It's a decision she's replayed in her mind many times over the years. "I was desperate for direction and I wanted so much to have someone I could hold on to and call my own."

Though she didn't know it immediately, she couldn't, in fact, call Charlie her own. By the time they got to Santa Barbara, she discovered that he already had two other women—Mary Brunner and Lynette Fromme.

When Manson was first released from prison, he started hanging out in Berkeley. One day when he was sitting on the grass on the U.C. campus strumming his guitar, he met Mary, a serious, twenty-year-old blonde from Eau Claire, Wisconsin. After graduation from the University of Wisconsin with a BA in history, she'd gotten a job as an assistant librarian at U.C. When he told her he had no place to live, she invited him to stay with her while he looked for housing on the condition that there was to be no sex. But her Midwestern values were useless against Manson's allure. She not only had sex with him, she tolerated his having sex with other women in her apartment while she was at work.

Mary soon quit her job and the two took off in a VW bus that Manson had somehow acquired, driving up and down the coast, stopping for a while and then moving on. On one foray to Los Angeles, he met Lynette Fromme at Venice Beach. According to Pat, Lynette was a feisty nineteen-year-old with red hair and freckles. She was from a comfortable middle-class family and, as a little girl, was close to her father but that fractured when she reached adolescence. She had attempted suicide twice after arguments with him, cutting her wrists on one occasion, taking barbiturates on another. It was after another serious argument with him that she met Manson.

"I really liked Mary and Lynette," Pat said. "In many ways my attachment to them, and later to the other women, was as important to me as my relationship with Charlie."

They continued to shuttle up and down the coast, alighting in the Haight, in Berkeley, and in Santa Cruz. "It was an exciting adventure for me. We'd stop into coffee houses and Charlie would play the guitar and sing pretty Spanish love songs. Everyone loved him. We'd meet more people. He'd collect more girls."

There was a pattern to Manson's recruitment. "Charlie had his front street girls, pretty girls who he used to lure men into the family, and his backstreet girls who were useful for their work and their loyalty to him. I was a backstreet girl. I was the designated mother. I cooked, I did the laundry and ironing, and I took care of the children, though I didn't have a child of my own."

(Several of the young women in the group did have young children, including Mary Brunner, who had a son with Manson.)

On September 25, 1967, Pat sent her father a letter from San Francisco. "'For the very first time in my life, I've found contentment and inner peace. I love you very much. Take good care of yourself.'"

chapter twenty
"THEY WERE ON A TEAR"

July 2001, Coeur d'Alene, Idaho

*P*at's father lived in an assisted living facility in Coeur d'Alene, Idaho. The town is named after an Indian tribe indigenous to the area. (Coeur d'Alene was the French name for the tribe, and it literally means "awl heart." The speculation is that perhaps the tribesmen were sharp traders.) It's a pretty little town with a lake in the center. In 2001, the year I visited, most people had heard more about neighboring Sand Point, home of the recently relocated Mark Fuhrman, one of the investigating police officers in the O.J. Simpson trial.

The facility where Mr. Krenwinkel lived had a fresh, well-scrubbed atmosphere: the hallway carpet was periwinkle and gave off a new, slightly chemical odor; the walls were papered in a cheerful, sky-blue floral pattern. I stopped at a reception desk and there was a woman, presumably a nurse, scribbling in what I assumed was a chart. I said, "Hello" and stood waiting to be acknowledged. She didn't look up or ask if she could help me. Finally, I cleared my throat. Still no response.

"I'm looking for Mr. Joseph Krenwinkel," I said, raising my voice.

At the mention of his name, she not only looked up, her face brightened into a broad, welcoming smile.

"Oh, he is such a sweet gentleman," she said. "They don't make them like him anymore. I wish I could escort you to his room but I can't leave the nurses' station unattended . . . wait, I'll call someone to help you."

"Thank you, but I'm sure I can find it."

"Please wait," she said firmly. "I'll get someone."

Finally a nurse's aide arrived and asked me to follow her. As we walked down the hall, she said, "Mr. Krenwinkel is such a gentleman, so well-mannered."

On each resident's door there was an object meant to personalize the occupant—athletic team banners, teddy bears, Raggedy Ann dolls. On Mr. Krenwinkel's door, there was a straw wreath studded with brightly colored papier-mâché flowers.

When I had asked Pat about visiting him, she was enthusiastic. She hadn't seen him much since he had moved away from California several years before. She'd explained that he was too old to travel, but they corresponded and talked on the phone regularly. When I wrote to ask him for an interview, he responded quickly with a note inviting me to visit.

I knew from Pat that after she went to prison, he had no other family. Neighbors had taken him under their wing and had served as his family since. When they moved to Idaho from Southern California, he moved also.

One of Pat's cousins similarly looked after her mother, who I briefly met when she was living with that cousin in Pacifica. She kept in touch with Pat but was not eager to talk to me and had very little to say about Pat in the past or the present. I wasn't sure if she'd been talked out years ago or simply didn't like the intrusion.

When Mr. Krenwinkel opened his door, he extended his hand. I'd say he was in his early eighties. His handshake was steady, as was his smile. He had clearly prepared for my visit; though it was summer, he was dressed in a starched white shirt, a dark tie, and a blazer. As soon as I sat down and we started to talk, however, it was also clear that I was too late. Perhaps a year or so too late. I don't think Pat knew that he had dementia. I imagine their phone conversations had long ago become routine and ritualized. I'm sure they talked about the easy things: the weather, the meals at their respective institutions, his surrogate family. He easily managed the niceties with me. It was only when I gingerly approached the topic of Pat's arrest that it became clear he could only manage conversations he'd had many times before.

"Yes, those kids went on a tear," he said. "There wasn't much her mother or I could do."

He repeated that expression—on a tear—many more times before I left. It stayed with me for a long time. Not only because it was ludicrously understated, or because he repeated it so often, but also because it seemed to summarize a way a dad might explain his only child's behavior to himself, to the outside world. Also, the expression was evocative of a bygone era. I hadn't heard it since I was a little girl.

I'm not sure what I'd been hoping would be revealed by our interview, and there wasn't much, if anything, in the way of content, but even in his slightly addled state, what came through was his love for his daughter. It was clear he would have done anything for the little girl she'd been, the girl she became, and the young woman who was in a place where there was very little he could do for her. He may not have understood her or why she went on a tear that resulted in many murders, but in his eyes you could see that it hadn't changed the feelings he'd had for the baby who played quietly by herself in her crib or the little girl he took on walks in Westchester to see LAX being built. She was still that little girl.

A few months after that visit, I got a letter from his surrogate daughter who had found my note among his belongings. "I knew you would want to know that he passed away on September 3rd. Joe is at peace now. He was a dear man."

chapter twenty-one
DREAMING OF HITLER

*D*uring the trip to Europe with my parents in 1956 I started having dreams about Hitler, dreams that appeared fairly regularly for about a year. They weren't all nightmares, though some certainly qualified. The setting and circumstances varied. Sometimes Hitler was sitting at a podium the way a judge does, or in the really scary ones, he was actually about to plunge a knife into me. The constant was that I begged him not to kill me. "Please don't kill me. I'm only a little girl." (Sometimes I would say, "I know I'm tall but I'm actually a little girl.")

I always woke up before he killed me. For a long time, even after I learned the particulars of the Holocaust, I believed that such an appeal would work with any killer, if I were the one who made it in my most sincere, tearful, and heartfelt way. It was as though I thought no one else ever thought of that strategy. When I was older I learned how often murder victims plead for their lives and how, in reality, it almost never makes a difference. Later, when I read in *Helter Skelter* that Sharon Tate pleaded with Susan Atkins not to kill her or her unborn child, it rekindled the terror I had in those Hitler dreams.

This ushered in an era in my life when I was confused about my

Jewishness, a confusion that continued the following year when I entered high school. I didn't have a Jewish name and, though I had dark hair and dark eyes, no one identified me as Jewish. (Probably for the same reason I didn't think Catherine was Jewish. She, too, had dark hair and dark eyes, but her last name was Share, which didn't sound Jewish to me.) Because no one detected my Jewish heritage, people didn't bother to hold back anti-Semitic comments.

My mother once said, half-kidding, or maybe not: "You scratch the surface of any gentile, and you'll find an anti-Semite." Keep in mind, she was married to a gentile. My father, in fact, was more sensitive to anti-Semitism than she. Between the two of them, my antenna for bigotry was sturdily constructed. Perhaps some of what my parents labeled anti-Semitic was benign and born out of ignorance — to me there's a difference between an artless joke involving a Jew with a long nose and a mean-spirited observation about Jews being greedy, dishonest and conniving. But when I was in high school I didn't see the difference and sometimes, especially among the older girls in my club, I felt I was in hostile territory.

I don't want to be melodramatic about it. I didn't suffer the way young gays did (and do). Not even close. What weighed heavily on me in high school was not the anti-Semitic remarks; it was my lack of courage in challenging them. It wasn't until college when I was open about my Jewish heritage that I experienced actual hatred against Jews in a very personal way.

chapter twenty-two
THE NEED FOR A SCAPEGOAT

One day when I was with Leslie in the visiting room, Susan Atkins stopped by our table to say hello. She was startlingly manicured—she had the look of someone who just walked out of a beauty parlor. Her coordinated clothing ensemble, her well-coiffed hair, and her jewelry all combined to give her the put-together persona of a real estate agent who shops at Nordstrom. This was a stark contrast to both Pat and Leslie. Pat had given up on adornment; Leslie was still allowed to dye her hair but had a natural, wholesome look.

Maybe Susan's attention to her appearance had something to do with being married. Every time I saw her in the visiting area, she was with her husband. Leslie introduced me, indicating that I was a writer. I explained that my focus was still undetermined but that I would very much like to interview her. She was pleasant and said she'd be happy to meet with me, adding, "Write me a letter and remind me of this conversation." In my career as a journalist, this was a request I'd heard countless times but always from busy politicians or celebrities, never from an inmate in prison.

I wrote to her later that week and, as I had with Pat and Leslie, sent her copies of articles I'd written. She wrote back, sending me what looked very much like a public relations press packet. It contained generic letters to her supporters that were filled with born-again Christian rhetoric. She attached a personal note indicating that she was sorry but she would have to decline my request to meet because she had promised a filmmaker that she would not talk to anyone else, adding, "I take giving my word very seriously."

It seemed odd that she hadn't mentioned that at the time Leslie introduced us and she invited me to write to her. Since I knew the filmmaker to whom she referred, I called and asked if she had required Susan to make such a promise. She was surprised. She said she had only asked that she not be interviewed by another filmmaker until she'd completed the documentary she'd was working on. (That project had been stalled indefinitely because of the prison's new restrictions.)

I suppose it's possible that Susan misunderstood the filmmaker's request, but I doubt it because of her initial enthusiasm. I believe she changed her mind and, for some reason, didn't want to acknowledge it. I can't say exactly why, but Susan's duplicity didn't surprise me; it only reinforced my negative feelings about her. Since the first time I'd read accounts of the murders, there was something about Susan that inspired in me more anger than any of the other women. She wasn't any more guilty than Pat, who'd also participated both nights, but forty years later, it was still hard to get some of her declarations out of my head. Not only did she brag about tasting Sharon Tate's blood to her cell mates, she told the grand jury that when Sharon begged for her life, for her baby's life, Susan replied, "I have no mercy for you, woman!" Almost all of her quotes had an element of braggadocio about them. And she was a liar. She kept changing her story. Even what she bragged about kept changing. In his 1979 memoir, Tex Watson referred to Susan's need for attention.

When she wrote that she was a person who took her promises

seriously, it seemed to be in the context of her born-again Christianity—a prevalent conversion in prisons. It may be a perfectly fine route for redemption of a kind, but it's not necessarily a path to self-examination. My experience is anecdotal, not scientific, but I have interviewed enough born-again child molesters, rapists, and murderers to conclude that this conversion does not automatically lead to insight.

There's something else about my feelings regarding Susan that bears parsing. It's a phenomenon that has surfaced repeatedly over the years and that I have observed in myself and others. I believe I was actually relieved when Susan ultimately declined the interview because, by continuing to be at a remove, she served as a scapegoat, a scapegoat that was useful in helping me integrate some of the horror of the crimes. I explore this further in a subsequent chapter, but suffice it to say, my problem with Susan wasn't all Susan's fault.

The day Leslie introduced me to Susan, she also introduced me to Susan's husband, James Whitehouse. I'd seen him in the parking lot driving a turquoise car that seemed, if not exactly a lowrider's vehicle, first cousin to one. His appearance—very long stringy dirty-blond hair and a goatee—was at odds with Susan's put-together look. A goatee can give a man a slightly menacing look, but on Mr. Whitehouse, it made him look more anemic than sinister. I was curious about the origins of their relationship. My gender is notorious for being attracted to violent men in prison. (Over the years, while on death row, serial killer Richard Ramirez, aka the Night Stalker, has had dozens of women competing for his attention.) But men, generally, do not seek out paramours who are serving life sentences for murder.

One day, Mr. Whitehouse and I were leaving the visiting room at the same time. Our timing was bad. The security door behind us locked as did the gate in front of us, trapping us together for about twenty minutes while the guards did a count and performed various other security checks. Since there were only two of us there with nothing else to do, I seized the opportunity to get some information. I asked him how he'd met Susan. He told me that after he'd read *Helter Skelter* about ten years before, he started writing to her. (I couldn't imagine what part of Susan's story enticed him. Surely not her dialogue with the dying Sharon Tate. I didn't ask. He was wearing what appeared to be religious medals around his neck, so maybe that was the source of her allure.)

"Do you attend Harvard Law School?" I asked, pointing to the front of his gray sweatshirt that had that emblazoned on the chest. It seemed so improbable that I expected he would tell me it had been a gift from a relative or friend.

"Yes," he said. "I'm going there now." My next assumption was that it had to be a different Harvard Law School—a knockoff perhaps? Harvard Law School of Anaheim? "Oh," I said, "and where is that located?" He looked puzzled, the kind of puzzled one looks when someone you think is of average intelligence turns out to be dim-witted.

"Cambridge," he said. I must have looked confused and evidently it showed. "You know, in Massachusetts."

"Oh, yes," I said. "Of course. How did you happen to get interested in the law?" I expected that he'd answer something about Susan's legal situation.

"I was a biochemist," he said, "and one day decided, just for the hell of it, to take the law school admission test."

(He was knocking over each of my assumptions, one by one, like so many dominoes. If ever there was an example of the journalist's warning—to assume makes an ass out of you and me—this dialogue was it. My assumptions, however, were making a total ass out of me alone. He was fine.)

Mr. Whitehouse told me that he'd scored so well on the LSAT he decided to apply to Harvard. (I couldn't help myself. The next day I called Harvard Law School to verify. Yes, he indeed was in his second year.)

"What kind of law do you plan to practice?" I asked.

"Patent law," he answered.

A subtle version of my next question—how in the hell are you going to help Susan get out of prison with patent law?—was forming in my head when he said, "You know, one of the reasons I don't like coming here is that people in the visiting room constantly ask me legal questions."

"Well," I said, smiling, "I guess it's not surprising that people in prison have legal questions."

"Yes, I know," he said stiffly, "but I get tired of telling them that A, I don't know very much about criminal law and B, I'm not familiar with California law, because I go to school in Massachusetts." He didn't bother hiding the exasperation in his voice.

I was so very tempted to suggest that perhaps he should rethink his choice of sweatshirts when visiting his wife. I did not.

chapter twenty-three
AN ABIDING FRIEND TO
FAMILIES OF VICTIMS

October 1996

Courtrooms divide much the way weddings do—family and friends of the accused on one side, family and friends of the victim on the other. Since I was there to observe the prosecutor, Stephen Kay, I sat on the victim side, in the row behind the victim's parents.

Whenever I saw Steve in those days the word (or, rather, nonword) "erectitude" came to mind—someone even taller and straighter than the word "rectitude" conveys. Not quite the farmer in *American Gothic*, but if I were looking for a guy to help me portray the deacon of a Presbyterian church in Iowa in the 1950s, I'd pick Steve. If I'd been on the jury that day, I would have trusted his honesty.

The victim was Linda Sobek, a twenty-seven-year-old model and former Oakland Raider cheerleader; the accused was Charles Rathbun, a thirty-nine-year-old freelance Hollywood photographer being tried for the brutal sexual assault and murder of Sobek during a photo shoot in November 1995 on a dry lakebed near Palmdale, California.

Mr. and Mrs. Sobek sat calmly as the judge dispensed with what is generally known as housekeeping. I was struck, as I always am at trials like these, at the coexistence of a dramatic brutal murder and the inevitable backdrop of the quotidian details of everyday life. No matter that the issue at hand is a violent death, meals must be arranged, parking laws must be enforced, pleasantries are still exchanged. Life does go on.

After the housekeeping came the horror. The session opened with a dramatic reenactment of the prosecution's version of the murder. (Rathbun claimed that the victim died in an accident and that he panicked and left the body in the desert because he didn't think anyone would believe his version. In fact, no one did, at least no one who counted.)

Steve had arranged for a young woman with long blond hair—a staff member from the district attorney's office—to play the part of the victim; the medical examiner played the part of the accused. The young woman arranged herself facedown in the area of the floor right in front of the jury. The medical examiner grabbed her long hair, yanked her head back to expose the creamy skin on her throat, and then simulated choking her. It was horribly realistic and dreadful to witness and clearly an unbearable moment for Linda's mother, who was now hunched over, her head buried in her arms, her shoulders heaving as she wept.

Of course I thought of the Tate family and what they had endured: photos of their daughter's butchered body; Susan Atkins's account of Sharon begging for her life and the life of her unborn child. As a parent, how do you bear it? The sounds? The sights? The ones that are captured by the camera? The ones that are captured in your head?

As an unequivocal friend to the families of victims, Steve Kay is a man who thinks solely in terms of good and evil, black and white. He is not interested in psychological causes, except as they relate to constructing a motive by which to convict the accused. And that day, observing Linda Sobek's mother's most palpable pain, watching the simulated murder and imagining the photos of Linda Sobek's body parts, I was grateful for the Steve Kays of our criminal justice system. Linda Sobek's family depended on his advocacy, and I have to believe it provided comfort. Rathbun, the man Steve Kay called a "human monster," needed to answer for the torture, the terrible pain he had caused. During the adjudication of the crime, there was no room for putting him, his needs, or his history into a human context. "Monster" isn't a term I would use, but I could certainly understand why the Sobek family might agree with Steve's use of it.

(Note: Rathbun was convicted of first-degree murder and sentenced to life in prison.)

chapter twenty-four
THE AGONY OF MOTHERS

1996

A s I sat watching Mrs. Sobek struggle to control her sobbing, I thought about the agony suffered by Doris Tate as well as the pain of mothers of murdered children I'd interviewed over the years. One mother in particular had taught me about the enduring nature of that category of grief. I spent time with the mother of a ten-year-old little girl who was kidnapped and murdered by a man who worked as a janitor in her church. I interviewed her several years after the fact, and she was still trying to claim a scrap of a normal life for herself. She told me that in the first few years after the murder, she compulsively talked about her daughter and the crime, repeating over and over and over again the details to her friends and family. And when she had exhausted them, when the people who loved her said they couldn't listen anymore, she took her case to strangers, showing her daughter's photos to people she met on buses, in parks, in bars.

She eventually found her way to a therapist; actually, the therapist found her. After reading an article in the local newspaper in which the mother expressed her anguish and talked about the difficulty of moving on, the therapist called her and offered to provide her with therapy free of charge for as long as she needed it. (I am overwhelmed with hope for humanity whenever I think about that therapist. I believe she saved that woman's life.) When the mother told the therapist that her family and friends had warned that her obsessive talking about her daughter wasn't helping, the therapist said that though the retelling was hard on the listener, it could, in fact, help the talker—one person's spinning of wheels is another person's healing process. People respond to tragedy in as many ways as there are people, she said.

It's impossible to overstate the pain suffered by parents who have lost a child to violence. For most parents in that situation, the need to bear witness to that pain is so compelling and, according to the experts, such a necessary part of the healing process that it's shocking that it took the Tate-LaBianca murders to shake the system into creating a place for it in criminal proceedings.

In the first years after her daughter was murdered, Doris Tate's way was to suffer in silence. Her way was not to obsessively retell the story of the murder. She did not show strangers photos of her daughter or recount anecdotes from her daughter's life. She did not roam shopping malls in hopes of buttonholing sympathetic listeners. Her pain was locked away and so was she. In the years after the murders, she virtually checked out of her life. Her two remaining daughters—Patti and Debra—not only lost a big sister, they lost a mother.

What I know about this I learned from her daughter, Patti Tate, who I interviewed four years before she died; it was a meeting Steve Kay helped arrange. At the time she was undergoing treatment for breast cancer. She was wearing a scarf because she had lost her hair to chemotherapy, but even without the blond tresses I had seen in photos, her resemblance to Sharon was unmistakable. She had the same luminous blue eyes, peachy complexion, and sweet, open face—a face, however, that clouded over when she talked about her memories of the painful years after Sharon's murder.

She said that she and her younger sister Debra were in desperate need of a mother's strength and support at a time when her mother was unable to give it. "Murders have a ripple effect on a family," she said. "It's not one loss." She likened it to a stone dropped in a lake. "The ripples keep going and going and going."

As we sat talking in her den, her son, a boy about eleven with the same blue eyes and peachy complexion, brought her a glass of water so she could take a mound of pills she had in a small glass bowl. How hard this illness must be for you, I thought. Her boy was about the same age she was when her own mother suffered a kind of death that made her unavailable emotionally for years.

Doris Tate did return to the land of the living, a return Patti credited to Steve Kay. In 1982 he called her with a proposal. A group called Friends of Leslie had presented parole officials with nine hundred signatures urging Leslie's release. He pleaded with Doris Tate to get involved. And get involved she did. With the help of the *National Enquirer*, which printed coupons for people to sign and send, she collected 352,000 signatures opposing parole for not only Leslie but for all of the Tate-LaBianca killers.

This kicked off Doris Tate's decade-long involvement in all manner of victims' rights. She joined the Los Angeles chapter of Parents of Murdered Children, a group that worked on Proposition 8, the 1982 Victims' Rights Bill, which allowed families of victims to address the judge and/or the jury during the penalty phase of trials and at the parole hearings of their victimizers. Doris Tate became the first Californian to take advantage of the provision when she spoke at the parole hearings of Susan Atkins and then Tex Watson. (At that point, she was not allowed to speak at Leslie's parole hearing because Leslie wasn't involved in the murder of Sharon Tate. Tate's other daughter, Debra, recently got around that restriction by getting herself appointed a spokesperson for the LaBianca relatives.)

For the rest of her life—Doris died of a brain tumor in 1992—she became a powerful influence on the California legislature.

When she talked, lawmakers listened because she was able to mobilize thousands of constituents. Steve Kay and Doris Tate were pioneers together: she was the first relative and he was the first prosecutor the state allowed to participate in parole hearings.

Mrs. Tate subsequently got involved with the Victim Offender Reconciliation and Justice for Homicide Victims groups. The program, which still exists, brings offenders face-to-face with victims of their crimes or with victims of other people's crimes. The goal is to demonstrate to criminals the human consequences of their actions with the hope that such exposure will deter them from further violence. For victims, the hope is that the opportunity to express their anguish will help with the healing process.

I never met Doris Tate, but I saw video of her talking to prisoners as part of that program. She was impressive. She had a Barbara Bush no bullshit bearing, but it was softened by a quasi-nurturing demeanor. I say "quasi" because she seemed like someone who would offer a shoulder for you to cry on, but after helping you dry your tears, she might deliver a lecture on how you brought the troubles on yourself. The way she connected with those men was powerful. She got them to take responsibility for the harm they had caused and did so in a way that also exposed their basic humanity. But as the years went by, she focused more and more on punishment and less and less on reconciliation. She amped up her advocacy for capital punishment and her emphasis on stripping prisoners of their rights.

The current family website, presumably now run by Debra Tate, the youngest sister, refers to these activities as prison reform. Their prison reform, which was the result of a letter writing and phone call campaign, included legislation to rescind overnight family visits for violent offenders. Again, this effort was successful. On the one hand, it's understandable why the family was enraged that Tex Watson could father four children in prison. On the other, depriving Pat and Leslie of visits with their parents is quite another thing.

Overnight visits, also known as Extended Family Visits, were originally instituted in California because studies showed that behavior improved in prisons after adopting the practice. (This privilege is a powerful incentive to follow the rules.) These visits also strengthen family bonds, an important factor when and if an inmate is paroled. The practice was suspended for a few years and then reinstated but not for inmates serving time for violent crimes. As of this writing, the Department of Corrections has not stated a clear policy for that population.

Since I first started visiting Pat and Leslie, victim rights groups have succeeded in stripping prisoners of rights and services, many of which were hard won over the past thirty years and accepted as standard practice in enlightened prison systems. Some of what's been taken away may seem trivial—Leslie can no longer dye her hair—and some not so trivial, such as individual therapy.

chapter twenty-five
HOMECOMING PRINCESS

December 1997

The visiting room was crowded and Leslie wanted to smoke, the one addiction she hadn't yet managed to shake, so we sat outside. (She has since quit.) It was mild but breezy and there were lots of kids buzzing around the picnic tables. If you blurred your eyes a bit, you could imagine that we were in a suburban park. Well, blurred your eyes and held your nose. The breeze, though light, was blowing the smell of cow shit right into our faces and, I feared, cow shit particulates into our noses. I briefly considered taking up smoking myself.

Every once in a while an inmate would stop to say hello or to introduce Leslie to a visitor. Her reaction was always animated, her eyes eager and bright. There was something poignant about her lively cordiality even under those bleak circumstances. She acknowledged that she had periods of depression, especially in connection to the endless cycle of parole hearings, but clearly her temperament's set point is one of good spirits.

When I asked her about her childhood before her parents' divorce, she described a picture-perfect suburban family: a community-minded, churchgoing mom and dad; well-adjusted, healthy kids living in a comfortable house with a swimming pool. At some point, Leslie's parents wanted to share their good fortune and adopted two children from Korea. And then, when Leslie was fourteen, the carefully constructed life crumbled. Her father left the family. There was, of course, another woman.

Before the divorce, Leslie was active, high-achieving, and socially successful. She'd been a Bluebird, a Campfire Girl, and later a Job's Daughter. She sang in the church choir. She was a talented seamstress and started designing and sewing her own clothes when she was in junior high school. In high school she was elected Homecoming Princess and student body secretary.

Once her father left, her mother, who had been a stay-at-home mom, went back to work and could no longer greet her kids when they arrived home from school. One day, instead of her mother greeting her with brownies fresh from the oven, Leslie came home and found her older brother and his friend drying marijuana leaves in the oven. She said she wanted to try it. He said no. "I blackmailed him. I said if he didn't let me try it, I'd tell Mom he was smoking dope. He relented.

"From almost the first hit, I was a goner. I loved getting high. I didn't have a take-it-or-leave-it response. I now know better than anyone the terrible toll drugs can take but as a teenager, fun was my priority."

At school, she'd always been part of the college-bound elite, but her newly acquired drug use separated her from the friends with whom she'd grown up. While they governed the student body, rallied at football games, and studied for their SATs, Leslie got stoned. Another factor separating her from her old friends was a boy named Bobby Mackey, who transferred from another school. Bobby, a bit of a bad boy, was just enough of an outlaw to appeal to the newly discovered thrill-seeking part of her. She and Bobby smoked grass, they took LSD, they had sex, and they soon decided that they had outgrown the boring blocks of Monrovia.

They managed to borrow a car and ran away to the Haight-Ashbury. This adventure only lasted a week. They had no money, no place to live, and they knew no one. Sobered, Leslie returned home to face her parents; though they were no longer married, they presented her with a united front. Sometime during the recriminations, the family talks, the beginning of a new plan for Leslie to get her life back on track, she discovered that she was pregnant. The news was traumatic. "I was really upset. I was crying. I reached for my mother. I wanted her to hold me."

What happened next, Leslie recalls, was a pivotal moment in their relationship. "My mother recoiled. She physically withdrew from me and said, 'Don't touch me.' The look on her face reflected how contaminated she thought I was."

Her mother arranged an abortion and this, too, was traumatic. As a result of all this anguish, she and Bobby decided they were through with drugs. They got involved with a group called the Self-Realization Network, a semi-religious, philosophical organization whose members acquire discipline through Yoga and meditation. Bobby would be a monk, Leslie a nun. Both required abstention from sex and drugs, which is perhaps why she was able to complete high school during this period.

The discipline finally proved to be too much for her, and though it meant breaking up with Bobby, who was still a disciple, she left the fellowship. At home, the tension between Leslie and her mother continued to intensify, so she moved in with her father and his wife in their Manhattan Beach duplex. They gave her the lower unit and a car, and she took a secretarial course at Sawyer Business School. She learned shorthand by day and took drugs at night.

Meanwhile, her brother Paul, after reading *On the Road* by

Jack Kerouac, took off for parts unknown on his motorcycle. Inspired by his example, Leslie and a friend drove to San Francisco in the friend's VW Bug, eventually ending up, once again, in Haight-Ashbury.

She called her mother. "'Good-bye, Mom. I'm never coming back.'" She believed that her mother's reaction to her pregnancy justified cutting her out of her life.

chapter twenty-six
A GOOD SOLDIER

*W*hen I was a young girl, the movie that had the most enduring influence on me was *The Bridge on the River Kwai*—one scene in particular. It takes place in World War II and our soldiers are in a Southeast Asian jungle fighting the Japanese. A young American soldier comes face-to-face with a young Japanese soldier. It was kill or be killed. For an instant, they both freeze—two fresh-faced, young men, boys really, with no desire to kill each other—and then a shot rings out and the young Japanese soldier drops. An older American soldier witnessing the scene has killed him. When the young man falls to the ground, his wallet falls out of his pocket and opens. We see a photo of his wife and young children. The scene is too "on the nose" for my taste now, but at the time I believed, I wanted to believe, that all soldiers in all wars had initial flashes in which they connected to each other's humanity.

Leslie's participation in the murders of Mr. and Mrs. LaBianca has been likened to a soldier's slavish obedience to a despotic leader, at least among her supporters. The good soldier following orders is a frequent explanation for people committing heinous crimes against their fellow human beings, and it's usually offered to diminish culpability.

In May 2000, Christie Webb, Leslie's lawyer at the time, commissioned Dr. Margaret Singer—the now-deceased psychologist and expert on cults and thought reform—and her associate Dr. Patrick O'Reilly to interview Leslie and report their findings to the parole board. Singer compared Leslie to a young, peaceful, and inexperienced soldier who may hesitate when first confronted with the need to do his duty (in this case killing), but ultimately does it, even after a lifetime of being told that killing is wrong.

Singer didn't make up the soldier analogy. Leslie did think of herself as a soldier for Manson. In 1996 she told the parole board, "I was disappointed that I hadn't been selected to go the first night. The day after the first murders, Manson met me on the boardwalk (part of the old movie set at Spahn Ranch) and asked if I believed in him enough to kill. And I said, 'Yes.' I wanted to do it for Manson or for Manson's approval. To let him know I was a good soldier and to let him know I was willing to lay my life on the line for him."

I do, however, take issue with Singer's claim that Leslie killed in spite of her initial deep resistance to killing. My belief as a young girl watching *The Bridge on the River Kwai* was, as it turns out, not entirely naive. Contrary to popular belief, the great majority of combat soldiers have the kind of strong resistance to killing that Singer cites in her report, and in spite of specific training to overcome that resistance, most of them never do.

In his critically acclaimed book, *On Killing,* Lt. Col. Dave Grossman asserts that in WWII only one out of five U.S. soldiers actually fired at the enemy. Most men, including combatants, find it very difficult to kill and, he claims, within most men their intense resistance to killing is so strong that, in many circumstances, soldiers on the battlefield will die before they can overcome it. According to Grossman, this resistance to killing is the result of a powerful combination of instinctive, rational, environmental, hereditary, cultural, and social factors. "It is there, it is strong, and it gives us cause to believe that there may just be hope for mankind after all."

Even military people killing from a remote location thousands of miles away are not immune and many suffer from PTSD. "I felt like I was haunted by a legion of the dead," Brandon Bryant, a former drone operator, said in an interview on KNPR in Nevada in 2015. "I was in so much pain I was ready to eat a bullet myself."

Dr. Singer's explanation for Leslie's willingness to overcome her resistance to kill was Manson's shrewd methods. He employed "an absolutely horrendous process of thought reform" that destroyed Leslie's self-confidence, alienated her completely from her past life, suppressed her critical thinking skills, and taught her that he was a divine being whose directives were those of God.

Singer believes that both LSD and marijuana played an important part in Manson's gaining control. The role drugs may have played in the commission of these crimes was discussed extensively at the time of the trial. There's no evidence that any of the killers were on LSD on the night of the murders, but they all had taken it during the previous months. In her report, Singer wrote that much more is now known about the cumulative effects of LSD and marijuana. "Marijuana can induce stupor, which makes it prohibitively difficult to think clearly. With heavy usage, and the Manson cult members were heavy users, there is frequently a splitting of consciousness and a marked decrease in short-term memory." She goes on to list other symptoms: "spatial and temporal distortion and depersonalization; passivity; apathy; loss of inhibitions; increase in fantasy ideation; toxic psychosis; perceptual distortion; bewilderment; illusions; and disorientation."

Singer maintains that Manson used hallucinogens to heighten belief in him as Jesus Christ. "While his followers were under the influence of LSD, Charles Manson tore down their personal values and replaced these values with his own perverse worldview.

He hammered away at the evils of the outside world and preached his visions of doom and subservience." At one point, according to Leslie, Manson directed the group to reenact the crucifixion of Christ while they were on LSD.

"How do you turn your back on Christ when he's telling you that something needs to be done?" Singer wrote. "Leslie said she felt morally obligated for the good of mankind to hang around and see this through."

But in her report, Singer also asserts that Leslie was conflicted about what Manson was ordering her to do. "A part of Leslie Van Houten did not want to obey Manson when confronted with a directive that she had known was wrong even though she had been indoctrinated into believing that she was prepared."

There are two problems with Singer's characterization of Leslie's behavior that night—at least two. By her own admission, at the time, there wasn't any part of her that believed what she did was wrong. "After the murders, when I was watching the reports about them on TV, I didn't understand the horror of it," she told the parole board in 1996. "I remember feeling sad that the world had put itself into a position where these kinds of things would happen, but I didn't understand the idea of personal responsibility. If I heard something like that on the news today I would be devastated. But at that time I wasn't able to connect to the personal tragedy of it."

The only thing she was upset about was that Manson hadn't chosen her to go to the blood bath the first night at the Tate house.

Leslie may have wanted to be a good soldier for Manson, but unlike most soldiers she had no feelings for her victims. She did not have the natural inner resistance to killing that Grossman describes in his book. Neither Leslie nor Pat had it. It was the complete absence of that resistance that makes their behavior so extraordinary (and a missed opportunity for Dr. Singer to explain when she was evaluating Leslie). While the report details the process by which she was seduced by Manson, we're left with no explanation of how it was possible to completely and absolutely erase all human compassion for Mr. and Mrs. LaBianca.

This question would not be of interest to me if I believed that these women were "human monsters"—the way Bugliosi characterized them at the first trial and Steve Kay echoed in subsequent parole hearings. But after getting to know them, I believe they had the requisite equipment to be compassionate human beings before they became entangled with Manson.

To counter the many times the district attorney's office has contended that Leslie's psychiatric status continues to pose a threat to society, Singer details the reasons Leslie does not meet the criteria for a psychiatric disorder. She has minimal violence potential; she is able to form her own objective judgments of people independently; she is not repressing hostility or anger; she sees her cognitive abilities favorably and does not meet the criteria for an eating disorder. Other than finding that she has addictive potential that she monitors and controls by participating in 12-step programs, she is an intelligent, emotionally well-adjusted person, with no known pathology.

In spite of the district attorney's explanation for Leslie's criminal behavior, there is no evidence that she harbored inborn pathology, was "a monster without a heart and soul," then or ever. If she'd been a psychopath in 1969 she would have been one in 2001 when Singer evaluated her. And she'd be one now. Something else was wrong with her. Very, very wrong.

2001

NIKKI MEREDITH: Dr. Singer, I've read your report on
    Leslie Van Houten. I understand the process you de-
    scribe but there's one thing I don't understand.
DR. SINGER: What's that?
NM: I understand your explanation of the process by

which Manson took control of Leslie's psyche, but this was a woman who committed brutal murders. She not only inflicted pain, she witnessed it in the most intimate way possible. She not only didn't have any feeling about it when it took place, she didn't feel even a twinge of empathy for her victims for another five years. Can you explain what psychological mechanism would be responsible for suppressing empathy to that degree and for that long?

Long pause.

DR. SINGER: My daughter is a surgeon . . . she has to cut into people daily and in order to do that, she has to be detached, that is, suppress her empathy, while she's operating.

NM: I don't think that's analogous. For one thing, the patient is anesthetized so the surgeon is not witnessing suffering. And even in the old days when surgeons had only whiskey to numb the pain and consequently they observed suffering, they knew that what they were doing, in the long run, would alleviate suffering. I fail to see the similarity.

DR. SINGER: Obviously, I disagree. In both situations, we're talking about detachment.

Yes, we are talking about detachment in physicians and the issue has been studied. Dr. Singer has science on her side, but only partially, in my opinion. An experiment by Jean Decety and colleagues at the University of Chicago examined the basis of pain empathy in physicians. Physicians who practiced acupuncture underwent functional magnetic resonance imaging (fMRI) while watching videos of needles being inserted into another person's hands, feet, and areas around their mouth as well as videos of the same areas being touched by a cotton bud. Compared to controls, the physicians showed significantly less response in brain regions involved in empathy for pain. In addition, the physicians showed significantly greater activation of areas involved in executive control, self-regulation, and thinking about the mental states of others. The physicians appeared to show less empathy and more of a higher-level cognitive response.

While the study may point to the ability of surgeons to suppress empathy to some degree, I'm not yet willing to agree with Singer that it's analogous to the empathy suppression that Leslie experienced. Furthermore, I have a problem with the design of the experiment. Acupuncture is not particularly painful and doctors who administer it know that. I won't be satisfied that this is a measure of the empathy gap among surgeons until either the photos are different or the fMRI is hooked up while the doctor is performing surgery.

chapter twenty-seven
SEARCHING FOR A CESSNA

October 1958

On a warm fall day in my first year at Hollywood High, a month or so into the semester, my father picked me up from school right after lunch. The night before, he'd told me he needed my help with a case he was working on . . . did I mind missing my last classes?

He needed my help? This was puzzling. My father was an IRS special agent whose caseload consisted primarily of the so-called L.A. Jewish mafia, Mickey Cohen and friends. How could he need my help? He explained that he was looking for a Cessna airplane that was probably parked at one of the general aviation airports in the L.A. area. The airplane was owned by a guy who owed the government thousands of dollars (I assume millions in today's dollars). The goal was to take possession of it—one of the ways the government got what it was owed.

In fact, the car my father was driving that day, the company car as it were, was a late-model Thunderbird. When they seized expensive cars in those days, they didn't auction them off, they used them for IRS business. My father, who skewed tweedy and looked more like an academic than a special agent for anything, never looked quite right driving Thunderbirds, Coupe de Villes, or Corvettes, the crop of cars they had seized that year. He said the practice saved money. Maybe so but it must have been a public relations problem because I'm pretty sure they stopped doing it by the time my father retired in 1966.

He needed my help, he said, because he was in a hurry. If the guy got wind of the IRS search, he'd hide the plane. "If you come with me we can cover twice the territory in half the time." I remained puzzled. Surely they had staff to enlist. Maybe he thought I wanted to go into law enforcement when I finished school. I had recently asked if he would come to career day at the school to talk about his work. Whatever the reason, there was nothing about his proposal I didn't like. My dad was a G-man; I'd be a G-man's assistant! I just hoped the kids filing out of class that day saw me riding down Highland Avenue with my father in a red Thunderbird convertible.

For a long time, I thought it was weird that my father, who was a revolutionary at heart, a Trotskyite with a small t, worked for the government. It was only later that it made sense to me. My father believed in publically funded services and institutions—quality schools, government-supported medical care, sturdy, well-funded safety nets—and hence, he believed that people should pay taxes. He was at a high enough pay grade to entitle him to go after the big tax evaders, not waiters or hairdressers who failed to report tips.

The IRS might not have agreed that his Marxist principles were consistent with government work (this was, after all, the era of red baiting, blacklisting, and loyalty oaths), but he once told me he wasn't a joiner so was never a member of any organization that Uncle Sam deemed seditious. Besides, he detested the American Communist Party, a group he referred to as Stalinists, and blamed Communists for various crimes and misdemeanors, from union busting in the United States to the defeat of the Republicans who'd fought against Franco in the Spanish Civil War.

We took Olympic Boulevard through the heart of the still-inchoate Century City, cutting over to the Santa Monica Municipal Airport before Olympic reached the beach. When we got out of the car, he showed me a color photo of the Cessna, a red and white airplane with the wings on top. I had never taken much notice of small airplanes before. This one was beautiful. I was already loving the detective work.

"I guess we need to split up," I said, remembering his reason for wanting me along. "We can't," he said, shaking his head. "I forgot that I only have one photo so we'll have to stick together." Fishy.

We walked down the first aisle. I had always been a little afraid of airplanes, but lined up that day they looked innocent, safe, tethered like big docile land animals. In the second row, there was a guy polishing the wing of a biplane the color of a yellow rain slicker, the kind I'd seen in World War II movies. My father introduced himself to the man and showed him the photo. The guy whistled. "That's a beauty."

"Have you seen it here?"

"No," the man said, shaking his head. "I would have remembered it."

As we walked away, I asked my father why he didn't show him his badge. I'd been disappointed. "Special agents don't usually bring their daughters along on investigations," he said, putting his arm around me.

We walked down two more aisles. There were Cessnas but not the one we were looking for. By that time, the heat of the day had been absorbed by the tarmac and heat waves were pulsating up from the blacktop. "There's a snack bar inside. Let's go get something to drink."

We sat at the fountain in the air-conditioned café. My father ordered me an all around chocolate malt (chocolate milk and chocolate ice cream), a drink he had introduced me to as a little girl. As

I sucked the thick milky mixture through the straw, he said, "You have an important decision to make. I want us to talk about it."

I assumed he was referring to the decision about which social club to join—two had accepted me.

"I've already made that decision," I said. "I like the Gammas."

"That's not exactly what I'm talking about. Have you considered not joining any club?"

"Not really," I said. "I think I want to be in a club." I was dissembling. There was no "think" about it. I had no doubts. As soon as I got to high school, scoped out the scene, as soon as I'd received my first invitation to a Coke session—the first step in rushing—I'd made that decision.

Later, I wondered why he hadn't delivered this lecture when I was first rushed. Maybe my parents didn't think I'd get in so why stir the pot for nothing?

He didn't say anything right away and then asked if I remembered Polly, my best friend in grammar school. "Of course I remember her."

"Do you remember what happened to her?"

"Did something happen to her?" I said, alarmed. So this was what this much-needed "help" was about. He didn't need my help on a case, he needed to tell me my friend was dead. We had been best friends when we were younger but had grown apart when we went to different high schools. I went to Hollywood High; she went to John Marshall. There were gangs at Marshall. Though it was in our district, my mother didn't want me to go there because she had so many foster kids on her caseload who attended. She never said it, but I think she was worried that I wouldn't be safe there.

"No, sweetheart," he said, patting the top of my head. "I'm sure she's fine. I'm talking about what happened to her when you were kids." When we were in the third grade, a vicious little twerp named Jimmy started teasing her about being biracial. Her father was Chinese and her mother was Caucasian. He didn't know the difference between Chinese and Japanese so kept referring to her "Jap" father and white mother. (There was still intense hatred of the Japanese in California, a leftover from WWII.) Every day at lunch this kid with a group of his creepy friends would taunt her. Sometimes Jimmy would yank her black silky hair and ask her why her hair wasn't half white. Or he'd pull down the side of one of his eyes to simulate the epicanthic fold and ask why she didn't have one round eye and one slanted.

Polly would cry and I would stand helplessly by, screaming names at him. It was the first time I remember feeling pure hatred. He had a group of boys supporting him. We had no one—girls or boys. I don't know how long we put up with it, but he started getting more aggressive. One day, he pushed her and knocked her down. That night I told my parents. My mother called the principal, who called Jimmy and his parents into her office. He stopped teasing Polly overtly but whenever he could catch her eye without the teacher noticing, he'd pull a menacing face.

"Daddy, Jimmy wasn't in a club," I said. He laughed but then explained that not accepting people who are different originates from the same mind-set. It's all about making some people feel special while making sure everyone else feels left out. The clubs are worse, he said, because they make it official. He asked me how many Asians were in the club. How many Mexicans? How many Negroes? I lied and said I didn't know. I did know and so did he. There were none. He wasn't finished with the lesson of the day.

"Do you remember how you felt when you saw those signs in New Orleans?" He was referring to our stop in New Orleans on our way back from Europe in 1956. It was one year after Rosa Parks refused to go to the back of the bus in Montgomery, Alabama. Nothing had yet changed in Louisiana. The signs said WHITES ONLY and COLORED at the drinking fountains, the bathrooms, and in the train station. I nodded. I remembered having a stomachache the whole time we were there. "Do you really want to be a part of a system that excludes people?"

My parents had told my brother and me to ignore the signs. No one seemed to notice when we drank at the colored fountain and sat in the colored section. I was surprised and maybe a little disappointed that our efforts at solidarity passed unnoticed.

His little guided tour down memory lane changed nothing. At that point in my life, I wanted to be part of a system that excluded people as long as I wasn't the one being excluded.

In junior high I wasn't exactly a misfit; my identity wasn't even that defined. I was a nobody. At twelve years old I was five-foot-seven, towering over everyone, in particular the boys. I skipped a grade in elementary school and I was convinced, though no one said it, that I was advanced because I was tall. Even then, though I was a year younger than everyone else in my class, I was still the tallest.

The first dance I attended, I was the girl for whom the term "wallflower" was invented. I stood against the gym wall while the boys walked by, assessing and quickly rejecting what was on offer. I'm sure there were other girls not being asked to dance, but it didn't feel that way. I only remember the humiliation of standing there alone. I had come to the dance with a friend with big bouncy curls and big bouncy breasts. She danced every dance. After the dance, a group of boys who were hot on her trail followed us out the door. They wanted us, rather *her*, to hang out behind the gym with them to smoke and who knows what. By that time I had somehow found the gumption to resist.

"We can't," I said firmly. "We have to go."

The boys started pressuring my friend. She shrugged. "If she won't stay, I can't stay. We came together." So they turned to lobby me. One of them finally said, "Look, if you stay, I'll kiss you." His tone and the look on his face was not of revulsion; it was the look of a martyr! Maybe I hadn't had the self-respect or wherewithal to leave the gym during the cattle call, but I did have enough to tell my friend I was leaving with or without her and I did. The boy who had so magnanimously offered to kiss me said to my friend, "You don't need her, my brother will take you home." They walked to the back of the gym, and I called my mother to come get me.

When I got in the car she asked if I'd had a good time. I said yes but my body language must have said otherwise. The next day, my parents announced that they had decided I was too young to go to dances. "I'm not too young," I said, but that was as vehement as I got. I was relieved. So relieved.

Because I no longer had to endure dances, and because I'd found a best friend (she also had big bouncy breasts but she was fiercely loyal), I existed below the radar. Popularity didn't matter. Or so I told myself.

Something changed the summer before high school. I don't know what it was but I was no longer booby prize material. At Hollywood High I was rushed by a few of the social clubs and accepted by two—one of which was the one I wanted to get into: Gamma Rho.

It's hard to exaggerate the outsized part these junior sororities played in the social scene at Hollywood High. Eve Babitz, in her book *Eve's Hollywood*, wrote that in that era, she so feared being excluded from the social clubs at Hollywood High that she avoided the whole scene by going to a school out of her district and a long bus ride away. "In Hollywood High School you were at the mercy of your cunty peers who whispered and squealed and giggled and screamed about who was being rushed by what sorority. Even today I am nearly heartbroken not to be invited to something, so you can imagine how the prospect of sororities looked to me at the age of fourteen when I had no control over my sanity."

Gamma Rho was one of three in the top tier, an unspoken designation that I suppose was based on their selectivity. Gammas were known for being wholesome, preppie, and prudish. Our club jacket was a blue blazer. The other clubs had boys' baseball jackets. The other two in the top tier were the Deltas, beautiful, glamorous, smokers, drinkers; and the Lambdas, just as wholesome as Gammas but maybe less prudish, more athletic. Eve Babitz, who subsequently transferred to Hollywood High after all, wrote at some length in *Rolling Stone* about the beautiful girls of Hollywood High, claiming that they were not only beautiful but sophisticated. They were so sophisticated, in fact, that they were "running off to Rome with older men—directors, producers, actors." All I can say is maybe that applied to a Delta or two (Melody did run off with a big movie star but it was years later), but no one I knew either in or out of Gammas was running off to Rome with anybody. Officially anyway, the Gammas had a lock on their chastity until their wedding nights.

My dad and I finished our drinks and returned to the search. He continued his lecture. He said the clubs were based on the Greek system in colleges and universities. Fraternities and sororities, in addition to being intellectually benighted and morally corrupt, were guilty of racism and anti-Semitism. "And they're closed off from other influences. By the way," he said, "just out of curiosity, does the club know that you had a Jewish grandmother?"

I shrugged. "They wouldn't care."

"You're sure? According to Jewish law, you're one hundred percent Jewish because you inherit your Jewishness from your mother."

I laughed. "Daddy, you're making too much out of this whole thing. Kids don't care about these things. The club is just for having fun. For eating lunch together. Having parties. And doing volunteer work. The Gammas help blind kids."

"Don't worry," he said, "we're not going to forbid you to join." He said they simply wanted me to understand the ramifications of the decision. I would be sacrificing values he knew I had, and he wanted me to consider my decision carefully. I said I would but I didn't. Not for a second.

"If you decide to join, you might end up regretting it one day." He was right but for reasons I don't believe even he predicted.

Years later, I thought about this: My brother attended Hollywood High four years before I did. He was in a club at a time when social clubs were no less discriminating. My father never gave him the lecture about joining. I've never known what to make of that.

We never did find the Cessna. Was there a Cessna?

chapter twenty-eight
THE METAPHORICAL MICROSCOPE

May 1998

I was sitting on a park bench in the small civic center complex of a suburban town outside of L.A. waiting for Leslie's mother. She would not have wanted me to tell you what suburban town. She barely wanted to tell me which one. Three decades after the murders she was still trying to protect her privacy. When I was first introduced to her at the prison (she was visiting Leslie, I was visiting Pat), she was courteous but cool. This reserve, Leslie explained later, was the result of the brutal way she and her family were treated by the media during the first trial. Despite this, she eventually agreed to meet with me, much to Leslie's surprise.

The air was moist, the sky a pale gray. The marine layer hangs heavy this time of year, making the late spring close and dreary. But a counterpoint to the gloom was the display of jacarandas. In May, the blossoms of these magnificent trees adorn the L.A. basin with lavender, making so many areas—from the bleakest blocks of South Central to the featureless civic center plaza where I was sitting—look like paradise.

I'd arrived more than a half-hour early. Mrs. Van Houten inspired this kind of punctuality; at least she inspired it in me. When I'd observed her interacting with people in the visiting room, she'd been an erect, well-coifed woman with white hair and sharp blue eyes. She had an air of brisk competence and the sort of authoritative presence teachers once possessed before the 1960s upheaval blurred the dividing line between teachers and students. In her tailored dress and sensible pumps, she'd stood out among the relatives visiting inmates. Most mothers of inmates are too beleaguered—they are often taking care of their grandchildren full-time—to manage anything other than sweats when they visit.

That morning when I was dressing to meet her, I put more thought into my attire than I would ordinarily. Mrs. V. inspired in me, in addition to punctuality, the wish to be perceived as a girl with good breeding. It was the Sabbath. Mrs. V. was a church-goer. I could hear my own mother's 1950s admonishment about wearing my Sunday best. I pulled a dress from my closet. Punctuality. Proper attire. The wish to please. My projection? My regression? Or clues as to what kind of mother she was to Leslie growing up?

In preparation for the meeting I'd reread all of Leslie's psychiatric reports for the preceding three decades. All had attempted, as one prison psychologist put it in 1980, to "bridge the seemingly enormous gap between the high school prom princess and the barefoot participator in murder." Such attempts inevitably focus on the mother. When it comes to mothers of murderers we want consistency, logic, cause and effect. We want their stories to offer clues to the behavior of their progeny. Clues are there, perhaps, but consistency and logic are scarce.

When Leslie got to prison, clinicians examined her relationship with her parents with a fine-grained lens. Year after year of psychological testing unearthed few causal factors. The most damning observation about her parents was made in 1991, though it had a distinctly 1950s ring to it. After administering the house-tree-person projective test, clinical psychologist Dr. J. J. Ponath concluded: "The placement of the tree is characteristic of a person who has grown up under the influence of a dominant mother and an emotionally unavailable father."

Depending on which of Leslie's psychiatric reports you believe and from what year, Mrs. Van Houten was emotionally remote from Leslie, favoring her sons, or an overindulgent mother, spoiling her daughter and preventing her from learning how to defer gratification. Or, if you prefer, she was so strict, so demanding of deferred gratification, of sacrifice and discipline, that it had caused Leslie to rebel in such a disastrous way.

Most evaluators expressed bewilderment that a girl with such bright beginnings had become a murderer. But one, Joel Hochman, stated that he was not surprised. In a 1971 report, he divined homicidal rage from an early age. That rage, he implied, derived from her too-comfortable early years. He described her as a child with poor impulse control and given to temper tantrums, "a spoiled little princess who was unable to suffer frustration and delay gratification." He was not at all puzzled, he wrote, that this rage was directed at Mrs. LaBianca. "Let me make it clear, Mrs. LaBianca was an object, a blank screen upon which Leslie projected her feelings, much as a patient projects his feelings on an analyst whom he doesn't know. These feelings were, in fact, feelings she had toward her mother, her father, toward the establishment."

In 1981, psychologist Ruth Loveys took a different tack. In a letter to the parole board, she described the relationship between Leslie and her mother as having many positive aspects but identified what she saw as significant emotional distance between them, which, in her opinion, led to Leslie's early feelings of emptiness and inadequacy. Earlier reports had suggested that Leslie could be self-critical as well as believing that she was undeserving. Loveys attributed these tendencies to a mother who "inadvertently instilled in her highly imaginative daughter a very heavy sense of social conscience for less fortunate people along with the subtle message that it was wrong to put oneself first. There was a well-intentioned but inordinately burdensome emphasis placed on such values as sensitivity to others rather than to oneself, on being ladylike at all times, not making waves and later having a role in life that was healing to others. The underlying philosophy of the home was that self-effacement and suffering are the greater goods."

In one of her appearances before the parole board Leslie said, "In thinking back, I think sometimes maybe I almost had too much going for me and I just started to put myself down." Loveys interpreted that to mean that the successful life that seemed imminent for her—she was smart, she was pretty, she was charming—was in fact frightening to her because it would mean the loss of her mother's love and sympathy. Because her mother's love and sympathy was always directed toward deprived persons, Leslie systematically embarked on a plan to strip herself of all her attributes that would lead to success.

Loveys later expounded on this theory in an undated article on primal therapy in the *Denver Primal Journal*: "I was absolutely certain of one thing, Leslie had acted out so as to make of her life one long sacrifice and had tragically fulfilled her mother's early teaching that suffering is noble and purifying," thus making her a prime candidate for Manson. This made me angry. I did clinical work long enough to know there is no such thing as the kind of certainty she expressed. It's simply one more example of fitting the patient into the mold of a therapist's theory of human behavior.

If the situation weren't so tragic, much of this speculation would be laughable. The mother was too strict or she was too indulgent, her standards were too high or she had none at all. Leslie couldn't defer gratification or her mother insisted that she always defer it. As I read the reports, I couldn't help thinking about the decades of blame the mothers of autistic and schizophrenic kids have had to endure. From the refrigerator mother theories to the theory of double-bind communication, mothers were in the perpetual hot seat. The truth is, however, that in all but the most egregious cases of emotional or physical brutality (such as Manson's childhood), the "science" of causality is far from scientific. Place most families under a metaphorical microscope and pathology will reign.

Joel Hochman's observation that Mrs. LaBianca was a surrogate for Leslie's mother, however, did make me think of my brother's crime. He and my parents had argued heatedly and often about money. They would make it available to him but only with very short strings attached, strings he believed infantilized him. When he dropped out of school, they refused to continue supporting him. When his girlfriend discovered she was pregnant and wanted an abortion, he refused to talk to our parents about it. He told her they were too frugal to help. (I believe this was a ridiculous misreading of my parents' frugality.) He later said he was forced to do something drastic.

It therefore seems within the realm of possibility that when he was stealing money from that older couple, he was acting out against my parents; there was more than a little anger involved. When he was arrested at the Mexican border he said, "Call my father, he's a big shot at the IRS." A shrink wouldn't have needed to administer a Rorschach test to figure that out. So my problem is not that psychiatric evaluations are without value, my objection is the certainty with which the conclusions are asserted.

At the park, when I saw Mrs. Van Houten get out of her Toyota Camry, I smiled. She was wearing slacks, a blue denim jacket, and a turquoise Mickey Mouse T-shirt. When we shook hands, she looked at my dress and apologized for her informal attire. "I'm taking my granddaughter to the zoo when we're done."

I had made her uncomfortable, not the other way around. What else was I wrong about?

We sat opposite each other at a picnic table. There was a young couple with a toddler having a picnic on the lawn. The baby, her legs bowed, her diapers droopy, was clearly new to the business of ambulation. "That baby is adorable," she said. Was she thinking about Leslie, who'd also been an adorable baby? I have seen photos. The parents hovered anxiously, and when the baby teetered they both rushed to catch her. "I love the way young fathers are so involved with their kids these days," Mrs. V. said. Was she referring to Mr. Van Houten's lack of involvement when Leslie was a baby? I was no better than the shrinks. Everything she said to me, even about other families, seemed freighted with meaning.

We discussed many things: the marine layer, the jacarandas, the end-of-an-era death of Frank Sinatra. From there, we somehow slipped into talk of her childhood in Cedar Falls, Iowa. She reminisced about long summer days, walking in the woods, building mud dams on the Cedar River, and unearthing relics from the Mesquaki and Sauk Indians, the first inhabitants of Black Hawk County. As I listened to her describe the hushed solitude of the woods, the chance to daydream, the feeling of endless space and time, I was struck by the similarity between her observations—her dreamy love of nature, of solitude, even of Native American culture—and those of her daughter. In prison Leslie is exposed to only a sliver of the natural world, but she makes the most of it, describing to me the robins who perch outside the window of her cell, the redolence of the rosemary bushes on the prison grounds, the clarity of the sky on those rare smog-free days, and the lessons she's learned from Native American inmates at Frontera who regularly invite her to their sweat lodge rituals.

After graduating from high school, Mrs. Van Houten attended Iowa State Teachers College in Cedar Falls, now called the University of Northern Iowa. She got a job teaching in a small school in a tiny town—Dumont, Iowa. As was the custom for such teachers in rural America in the 1940s, she lived with a local family but she often ate dinner at the Home Café, which is where she met Paul Van Houten in 1942. He had just come home from five years in the Army. Events went quickly after that. They got married and then he was sent overseas to fight in World War II. He was stationed in Italy and after that Africa. During the war, Mrs. Van Houten taught at a teacher's college.

When the war was over, the Van Houtens were part of a massive influx of Midwesterners into California. Many of the immigrants were GIs who had tasted the fruits of the state—the weather, the beaches, the jobs, the wide open spaces, and, literally, the fruit from the miles of orange groves—on their way to the Pacific theater or when they were stationed in California. This continuous wave created the vast metropolis that is now L.A.

Mr. Van Houten established a well-paying career as a car auctioneer, and with the help of the GI Bill they bought a house for $10,500 in Mayflower Village—the first subdivision in Monrovia. To outsiders, the town is indistinguishable from scores of other suburban tracts in the San Gabriel Valley, but the town, which calls itself "The All-American City," takes pride in its stalwart character and commitment to tradition. Two of its former residents have achieved national attention: writer Upton Sinclair, who lived there in the 1930s, and three decades later, Leslie Van Houten. Sinclair is mentioned in the city's 1986 Centennial Review; Leslie Van Houten is not.

Monrovia in the 1950s was "relaxed and nifty," according to the recollections of longtime resident Mary Lou in a nostalgic piece in the *Monrovia News Post* the year of the centennial. "The second big war had ceased a few years before, Eisenhower was President, and the economy was on the way up."

"Van had survived the war. Life was wonderful," Mrs. V. told me. "We were living an Ozzie and Harriet existence."

In 1947, the couple had a son, Paul; Leslie was born in 1949. The house was only one thousand square feet, but it grew along with the family. They remodeled the kitchen, built another bedroom, and then added a swimming pool. Mrs. V. remembers planting raspberry bushes in the front yard.

The Van Houtens were an enterprising couple. They helped to establish a Presbyterian church in their community, part of the religious revival that swept over the United States after the war, and to build a new school. Once the school was established, they started the PTA. Their community engagement was in full throttle.

After the Korean War, the couple started to hear through their church about what Mrs. Van Houten described as "the mess" the 8th Army had left in Korea. She said it was Mr. Van Houten's idea to adopt one or two of the mixed-race kids abandoned by American soldiers. When Leslie was seven years old, they adopted two who were among the first wave of Korean children coming to the United States.

When Mrs. V. talked about her two adopted kids, I mentioned that I'd read in the court transcript that one of the psychological experts claimed that even as a little girl, Leslie had exhibited an explosive nature, testifying that she'd had tantrums and one time hit her adopted sister with a shoe.

"Of course there was competition between them," she said, shaking her head and clearly exasperated. "Of course there was sibling rivalry, but whoever said Leslie had tantrums was lying. The problem wasn't tantrums, the problem was that Leslie didn't want to fight back. Her sister would sometimes hit her and she'd just keep taking it. Finally, I told her she had to stand up for herself. She looked at me with tears in her eyes and said, 'Mom, I can't.'

"I have no idea where they get that stuff. Leslie was simply delightful. She was the sweetest, cutest kid—a kid who required no discipline. It was her way to try and understand. It was her way to try and avoid conflict, to try and work things out."

In 1963, the year that John Kennedy was killed, Leslie's parents filed for divorce. While Mrs. Van Houten was attending PTA meetings, her husband found another woman, a woman who was younger, richer, and unencumbered by children. I only know this, however, because Leslie told me. Her mother said simply, "Van departed." I started to ask more but she looked away, which I took as a signal that the topic was not up for discussion. It was clear that thirty years later the wound had not completely healed. At first I was struck by the fact that the ancient divorce seemed as emotionally charged for her as her daughter's involvement in the murders, and then I realized that, in her mind, the two were intimately connected. It seemed clear that she blamed the divorce for Leslie's eventual attachment to Manson.

After her husband left, Mrs. Van Houten went back to school, taking classes in special education so she could resume her teaching career. Though she was devastated by the divorce, she loved her new career. She was eventually hired to be part of a groundbreaking program funded by War on Poverty monies. The kids who were brought in from all over the city were high-risk, underachieving, and from the poorest families.

"It was a team approach and we used innovative techniques," she said, her eyes bright with enthusiasm. "And you know what? It worked. We made a difference." She explained that the education department did pre-tests and post-tests that demonstrated how much the kids improved as a result of the program. "It was a thrilling time of my life. I woke up every day excited about going to work."

She loved her new career though she did worry about not being home for her kids after school. But in those first years after the divorce, Leslie seemed to be the same smart, energetic little girl she'd always been. And then she wasn't.

chapter twenty-nine
DECODING MANSON

Summer–Fall of 1998

*I*t was a particularly dreary day at the prison. There was a cloud cover and the sky looked close to a downpour, so everyone crowded into the visiting room instead of going outside. The atmosphere was always close in there; on this day it was even closer and stuffier. I was always struck by how good-natured and polite everyone was, even when we were all bunched together with no privacy for conversations.

I got there late and Pat was clearly irritated. She always seemed this way when I first greeted her, but then again, I was quite often late. On the days that I flew directly from Northern California, there were many variables beyond my control—traffic to the airport during rush hour, flight delays, car rental hang-ups—all of which I explained or attempted to explain, but I'm not sure she ever bought my lack of culpability. Or maybe my tardiness wasn't the issue at all. Maybe she was just moody.

I asked her if she wanted "the usual." The usual was French vanilla coffee from the vending machine. She nodded. Pat had introduced me to this brew. Despite its ersatz ingredients, I liked the creamy sweetness. At the machine, we worked as a team: I put the dollars in the slot—prisoners are not allowed to handle money—

and she retrieved the coffee. When she handed me my cup, it was too hot to drink. It always was and it always cooled in reverse proportion to Pat's warming up to me. By the time the coffee was perfect drinking temperature, her attitude had softened. She smiled more readily, she even laughed. By then she would be asking me questions about my life instead of lecturing me on the bad state of the prison, the Department of Corrections, the country, the world. At the point in our visit when my coffee was decidedly cool, she was making me feel welcome rather than treating me like someone imposing on her time.

On my previous visit, Pat had just started talking about the process of freeing herself from Manson when the guard announced the end of visiting. Today, I asked her about it again. At first, she simply repeated what she'd said before: "It took a long time." When I asked for more—What changed for you? What were the influences?—her replies consisted of shrugs, one-word answers, and short declarative sentences. But then, slowly, question by question, she started elaborating. She told me that the first tentative steps away from Manson occurred because of her relationship with Jean Oliver Carver, an inmate who shared the makeshift death row with Pat, Susan, and Leslie.

Carver, who had killed a woman evangelical minister in the course of a robbery, had seen much of the world's dark side, generally, and a lot of the dark side of men, specifically. When Pat had first arrived she often talked dreamily about Manson, elaborating on the way he made her feel good about herself, the way he was endowed with special powers, the way he knew secret things about her and other people. Carver would say, "Honey, those are all old tricks. He sounds just like dozens of men I've known—hustlers, pimps, convicts."

"That was the beginning of my deprogramming," Pat said.

With Carver's help, Pat started to question her passivity when she'd been with Manson. Fear of his diatribes kept her head down. But it wasn't only fear that made her obedient. The entire time she was with Manson, in spite of his sexual relationships with other women, she harbored the fantasy that one day she would have children with him and they would be a family. "He knew how to pay just enough attention to me to keep that fantasy alive." If he sensed that she was unhappy he'd make love to her or compliment her or make her feel special in some other way. But he also constantly assured her that no one else would ever love her or understand her the way he did. If she ever left him, he'd warn, she'd be dooming herself to a life without love.

At one point when she was talking to me, her mood shifted abruptly. Her mouth morphed from its vinegary pucker to a wider smile; her severe eyes softened, seemed bluer, more liquid, and she seemed far away. I asked what she was thinking about. "All of this talk about family makes me think about Anne Tyler. She's my favorite writer. All of the families in her novels have problems, but reading her books fills me with longing. That's when I most regret that I'll never have a family."

We were both quiet, sipping our very cold coffee.

*L*et's assume, for the sake of argument, that mirror neurons in the human brain exist and play an important role. There are researchers who theorize that there are people whose mirror neurons are absent or whose mirror neurons malfunction. Autism, some researchers believe, may involve broken mirror neurons. A study published in the January 6, 2006, issue of *Nature, Neuroscience* by Mirella Dapretto, a neuroscientist at U.C.L.A., found that while many people with autism can identify an emotional expression, like sadness on another person's face, or imitate sad looks with their own faces, they do not feel the emotion associated with the expression. They do not know what it feels like to be sad, angry, disgusted, or surprised from observing other people.Though many studies like Dapretto's have been replicated, there is no agreement that the cause is a disruption in the mirror neuron system. One proponent of this theory is Simon Baron-Cohen, a Cambridge University psychologist who received considerable flack for it when his 2011 book *The Science of Evil: On Empathy and the Origins of Cruelty* was published. He is the parent of an autistic child and is not suggesting that people with autism are more prone to violence. In fact, in a chapter titled "When Zero Degrees (of Empathy) are Positive," he makes a distinction between the lack of empathy in autism and the lack of empathy in psychopaths.

The book is somewhat limited for my purposes because his major focus isn't on violence committed by ordinary people but on violence perpetrated by people who are borderline, narcissistic, or psychopathic. What was helpful to me, however, was his use of the term "empathy erosion." Erosion implies a process, not an either/or condition or an on/off switch. A decade or so ago the idea of "snapping" was in vogue and people have suggested to Pat and Leslie that they "snapped" and that's what caused them to be violent. But their descriptions of what happened to them with Manson reflect a process that occurred over a period of time.

If, when they first met him, Manson had presented them with a plan to randomly murder people in their homes, they would not have been attracted to either him or his philosophy. Instead, there was a gradual, steady erosion of their core being. (What could be more core than one's empathy circuit?) In framing empathy erosion, Baron-Cohen uses the analogy of a dimmer switch. If we'd been able to hook up Pat and Leslie with electrodes after they'd been with Manson for a while, and if the science had been there, would we have discovered damage to the empathy circuit? Of course we don't know, but there are some tantalizing clues as to the complex interplay of biological and social factors.

By examining the environment created by Manson, it's possible to speculate about what variables might have eroded their empathy. (I'm not proposing that they were totally passive—at this point I'm not willing to abandon the concept of free will. They may have been manipulated by a cunning psychopath, but they did choose to be with him.)

One of the techniques for mobilizing ordinary people to commit mass murder is to identify potential victims as subhuman. None of this is new. The Nazis called the Jews vermin, the Hutus in Rwanda called the Tutsis cockroaches, the Guatemalan military called the Mayans demons during the systematic torture and murder of Mayan Indians in a thirty-four-year civil war. But now there is scientific evidence of how that works in the brain. Numerous studies demonstrate that the empathy circuit can be fired up or tamped down, depending on how people are labeled.

In his 2008 book, *Mirroring People: The New Science of How We Connect with Others,* Dr. Marco Iacoboni, a U.C.L.A. neurologist and neuroscientist and a leading authority on mirror neurons, describes an experiment he performed during the 2004 presidential election. He hooked up people to functional MRIs and he and his colleagues showed Democrats and Republicans photographs of candidates. (The functional magnetic resonance imaging [fMRI] is sister to MRIs. The former measures blood flow; the latter takes images of anatomy.) Whenever they showed a Democrat an image of a Democratic candidate, that individual's mirror neurons fired strongly, indicating empathy for his or her fellow party member. No surprise there.

When they showed that same individual an image of someone in the opposite party, however, it triggered a sequence of activity that did surprise the Iacoboni team. At first, the individual's mirror neurons fired, indicating natural human empathy, but then it seemed that his or her conscious mind kicked in, suppressed the mirror neurons, and reduced empathy. The implication of this sequence is significant. According to Iacoboni, it means that our natural impulse is to create an immediate emotional connection with people. It's only after we label someone as belonging to a different group that we consciously force away that emotional connection.

In another example, subjects who were hooked up to fMRIs were shown photos of people in pain who were sick with AIDS. There was a marked difference in the reaction to that pain. If the subjects were told that the patients had contracted AIDS from a blood transfusion, there was intense firing of the mirror neurons.

If the subjects were told that the patients had contracted AIDS from needle sharing, that is, by being drug addicts, there was significant less empathy for their pain. In a rather complicated study, social psychologist Tania Singer at the Institute of Neurology at University College London tested subjects' willingness to administer shocks to people they perceived as cheaters in a card game. (As in Milgram's study, the shocks were fake.) The empathy circuits in the brains of the subjects were less reactive to the pain of people they saw as "unfair."

Tania Singer conducted another study on couples that also caught my attention. In an attempt to understand the interaction between empathy and pain, she tested nineteen couples who were romantically involved. The woman from each pair was monitored with an fMRI. The researchers gave her a brief electric shock and recorded her neural activity. Then they administered the same shock to her partner. When her partner received the shock, the same critical brain regions involved in processing the physical sensation of pain were activated in each case. Feelings of empathy for the partner's pain triggered regions of the brain responsible for processing pain in the same way it did when the shock was administered to the subject directly.

When I read this study, I couldn't help thinking about Mr. and Mrs. LaBianca. As you recall, Leslie reported that when Mrs. LaBianca heard her husband's cries in the next room, she started to sob. From Tania Singer's study it seems possible that she wasn't only reacting to hearing his cries emotionally, her brain was also registering his physical pain as though it were her own. In that way, Mrs. LaBianca was murdered twice. First when her husband was murdered, and then when she was.

During the past few years, every time I came across an article about empathy and brain cells, I'd write to the researcher asking if he or she could explain what might have been going on neurologically with Pat and Leslie at the time of the murders. The universal response has been that brain research is still too new to answer such questions definitively, but aforementioned neuroscientist Christian Keysers was willing to speculate. In an e-mail, he referred to experiments, such as Tania Singer's, that demonstrate a marked decrease in empathy for people perceived as unfair, and pointed out that Nazi propaganda was centered on making Jews seem unfair. Hitler used this switch of empathy cunningly by portraying Jews as a threat to cooperative Nazi society.

Keysers explained that our success as humans has been dependent on our capacity to work cooperatively. In that kind of system, defectors have to be punished. To that end, evolution has equipped us with mechanisms that make us cut off empathy to individuals who jeopardize cooperation. He wrote that he suspected that this "switch" that turns off feeling is more powerful than, say, anesthesia, because it's at the heart of our evolutionary history. He suspects Manson, after selecting women who were particularly susceptible, exerted this kind of control—the switch from empathy for each other to punishment for 'the other' like the La Biancas who he portrayed as threatening their system of cooperation. "I know there is quite a step from mild electroshocks after a trust game to crushing skulls, but I suspect it is a similar mechanism."

In fact, Manson cleverly utilized "them" and "us" labeling. He hammered away constantly at people who were educated, middle or upper class, or in any way privileged in the way he wasn't. (He did seem to make an exception for people in the music industry who he wanted to help him with his music career.) To his followers, all traces of influence of their families, who were, for the most part, educated and comfortably middle class, were to be expunged. He would say to Leslie, "I still see your parents in you."

It's still difficult to understand how, in the women's eyes, Manson's labeling was enough to render the people in those two houses undeserving of life, deserving only of brutal murder, but there was another way that Manson's categorizing worked to dehumanize "them." The women felt a genuine sadness for the way Charlie had been treated by society—first as a child and then as a teenager and then as an adult in prison. Their own anger against their parents merged with the sadness for Charlie, and both grew into a hate for everything they considered established society.

chapter thirty-one
"LESLIE IS MY DAUGHTER"

May 1998

*M*rs. Van Houten and I met again at the same suburban park. It was a Saturday and there were many more people, but we managed to find an empty bench. This time we were both dressed in casual clothes and the jacaranda were still in bloom, giving the park a lavender cast. We didn't have much time—when she'd arrived Mrs. V. told me she had plans to babysit for her granddaughter, whom she had to pick up in a half-hour.

I wanted to ask her about the final phone call that Leslie made to her from Haight-Ashbury, but I didn't want to pounce abruptly with a question about what had to be a painful memory. I should have raised a neutral topic, such as the jacaranda or the weather, but for some reason, in blurting mode, what popped out of my mouth was the Unabomber. I mentioned that Ted Kaczynski had just been sentenced to eight life terms.

"I heard about that," she said. "Talk about a family's anguish. That poor mother. That poor brother." We talked about how unfair it was that after the brother went to the FBI and they were able to crack the case, the only thing he asked in return was that the federal prosecutor would not go for the death penalty, and then the prosecutor went for the death penalty anyway. That decision was reversed when he was diagnosed as a paranoid schizophrenic. The U.S. government doesn't like to kill people who are crazy.

When we finally got back to her family, I told her that Leslie had described running away to Haight-Ashbury, twice. I waited to see if she would talk about the abortion since that seemed to be such a critical issue for Leslie. What she did talk about was the "good-bye forever" phone call Leslie made when she arrived in the Haight-Ashbury for the second time.

"We hung up on each other. I was angry."

She didn't hear from Leslie for weeks after that phone call, and then some kids in the neighborhood told her that she was living with a group in Chatsworth, northwest of L.A. No one mentioned Charles Manson, but that's who they were talking about. When they described the group's nomadic existence, Mrs. Van Houten was convinced Leslie could never survive that kind of life. "It sounded like total chaos."

Leslie's brother Paul, who was by this time home from his Kerouac adventure, drove up to Chatsworth to try to find her. The longer she was away, the more convinced Mrs. Van Houten was that she was dead. (I remembered how horrible it was for my mother when she was convinced that my brother was dead and, for a minute, I thought of mentioning it and then reminded myself that I was there to talk about her family, not mine.)

And then in June 1969, two months before the murders, Mrs. Van Houten received a call from the Reseda police, who said they had Leslie. "I can't remember what she'd been arrested for . . . it was something minor, like shoplifting." The police asked if she would come and get her.

"When I picked her up, she was filthy and her clothes were ragged. We got in the car and I looked at her and said, 'Leslie, you smell bad.'"

Mrs. Van Houten shifted her weight on the bench and took a deep breath. "Leslie looked at me." There was a flicker of pain in her eyes. "She said, 'Mom, I smell like Leslie.'

"I can't tell you how many times I dissected that exchange over the years. I can still see Leslie's face when I said it. She was still such a child and I was rejecting that child."

The atmosphere had been chilly between them. They said very little to each other either on the drive home from Reseda or in the days following. "I was still cross with her and she didn't have much to say to me." Leslie did talk to her adopted younger sister Betsy, whom she told that her life on the ranch with Manson was wonderful. She also said something that alarmed her mother when Betsy relayed it. She said the dogs at the ranch talked to her. But Mrs. Van Houten held back her questions. She thought it was best to allow time for both of them to calm down before she tried to sort it out. She wanted Leslie to have a chance to bathe, sleep, and eat nutritious meals. As it turned out, there would be no time for more questions. A few days later, when she came home from work, Leslie was gone. Two months later, the Tate-LaBianca murders were headlines.

"When news of the murders and the suspects—a hippie and his band of gypsies—hit the newspaper, I told friends that I was worried that Leslie was involved. My friends said, 'Oh Jane, you know how many runaways there are? Thousands of parents are thinking the same thing.'"

But one of her neighbors who worked at the *L.A. Times* found out that Leslie had been arrested and booked at Sybil Brand, the women's jail in downtown L.A.

Mrs. Van Houten said the only thing that saved her sanity was her job and the support she got from her co-workers, the other members of the teaching team. "They provided me with a protective shell. Sometimes it was all too much for me and I'd excuse myself and go into the cloak room and cry, but their compassion and solidarity got me through it."

She told me about a day at the peak of the media frenzy when the teaching team was meeting with an outside consultant. When he was introduced to Mrs. Van Houten, he said, laughing, "No relation to Leslie Van Houten, I presume." There was a collective gasp and no one knew what to say.

"Yes, as a matter of fact," she said, breaking the silence, "Leslie is my daughter."

When Mrs. Van Houten was recalling this incident to me, her voice faltered as she said "my daughter" and she stopped talking to compose herself. "After I said that there was silence again. As I recall we all just sat there. No one could think of anything to say. What was there to say?"

At that moment, I couldn't think of anything to say, either. Her portrayal of the scene was so vivid, I felt as though I'd been in that meeting with her. I felt the flush of her embarrassment. Platitudes popped into my mind, some version of "that must have been so hard for you." I noticed that a tiny jacaranda blossom had landed in her hair. I pinched it off with my fingers and showed it to her, surprising both of us with the intimacy of the gesture. She smiled but she also blushed and stood to go.

"Maybe we can have lunch someday," she said, and was off.

chapter thirty-two
ICH BIN EIN JUDE

1956–present

On my family's road trip through Europe in 1956, we had stopped in Pisa to see the Leaning Tower. We arrived during lunch so both the Tower and the baptistery beside it were closed until 2:00 p.m. My father and brother set off to find a place to buy film; my mother and I took a nap in our VW bus. When we reconvened, my father told us that in the shop where they'd found film, he had struck up a conversation with a German woman. She was traveling alone and had just come from Rome. Since we had also just come from Rome, the two of them compared enthusiastic observations of that city's landmarks—the Pantheon, Trevi Fountain, the Sistine Chapel. They talked for a few more minutes and then my father said he had to leave to meet his wife and daughter. The baptistery was the woman's next stop, too, and she asked if she might meet us there and spend the afternoon with our family. My father said he would talk to his wife about it and let the woman know after we had all taken the tour of the baptistery.

My father was recounting the story to my mother when a stout woman in a brown tweed skirt suit and a tan pill box hat walked through the enormous carved wooden doors. I remember watching my mother as she watched the approaching figure while listening to my father's account of his encounter. When he said he thought the woman was lonely, my mother's expression went from neutral to sympathetic, but as the woman got closer, I saw her face change. Her eyes narrowed. Her mouth grew rigid. She was about to answer my father when the guide said, "*Attenzione*" and embarked on his narrative. The guide explained that the marble cupola was famous for its resonance. The acoustics were so perfect, he said, that it was believed that the Renaissance architects had designed it to mimic a pipe organ. He proceeded to demonstrate by singing "Figaro, Figaro, Figaro," which echoed and echoed and echoed.

When we had heard the last *"Figaro,"* my mother asked if she could try. "Come no?" he said, clearly pleased by the prospect of audience participation. My mother cleared her throat and intoned, *"Ich bin ein Jude"* (I am a Jew!), which echoed and echoed and echoed.

The stout woman's eyes popped open, the color drained out of her face, she turned and hurried out the door.

Did she walk out because my mother was a Jew? Or did she walk out because the declaration was hostile? I'll never know. I do know, however, what was on my mother's mind. When my parents argued about it later she said that at first she thought of course we should include her, a woman alone without a family, but her thoughts quickly flipped. This was a prosperous, middle-aged woman who had gotten through the war unscathed. "She's healthy and has enough money to travel," she said with tears in her eyes. "What was she doing when my relatives were being made into lampshades?"

My mother's behavior not only embarrassed me, it shocked me. It shocked my brother, too. We knew she had intense feelings against Hitler's Germany, but she was acting out hostility to one lone and lonely German woman. We couldn't believe that this was the same woman who had raised us to fight against prejudice of any kind and to care about people who suffered—from illness, from poverty, from loneliness. She was always inviting people for dinner who lived alone or bringing meals to shut-ins. In fact, sometimes I wish she hadn't sensitized me so much to other people's suffering. Apparently she didn't consider Germans worthy of the empathy she felt for everyone else on the planet.

My father, an Irish Catholic, was more cerebral about his sympathies. He believed in doing the right thing for people less fortunate, but he didn't necessarily feel their pain. What he did feel was a particular affection and respect for Jews. His Catholicism had fallen away when he fell in love with my mother. (Growing up, he had a calling to be a Jesuit priest.) Because of his respect for Jews culturally and intellectually, he, more than my mother, would in years to come be concerned that his grandchildren were too removed from their Jewish heritage. He gave them books like *A History of the Jewish People* and *The Jewish Book of Why.*

I mention this only to point out that his refusal to share my mother's prejudice against Germans didn't have anything to do with not caring about Jews. But he was disturbed by her behavior, so disturbed that early in the morning after the incident, while my mother was still sleeping in our hotel, he rousted me and my brother from our slumber and asked us to dress. We followed him a few blocks to a nearby park. It was barely light as we walked. My father was quiet and I started to worry that he was going to announce that he and my mother were getting a divorce. Instead, he said, "It's dangerous to hate the Germans because it assumes that what happened under the Nazis couldn't happen anywhere else." It could, he said, and if the world wasn't careful, it would.

My father, of course, was right and he instilled in me a determination to be as unlike my mother as I could be, at least when it came to Germans. But less than a decade after that day in Pisa, I was in Germany with my new husband and a visit to Dachau triggered in me a hatred for Germans that was so pure, it was as though I was channeling my mother. I hated the language, I hated the food, I hated the Autobahn. I had not inherited my father's lesson of universal truths; I had internalized my mother's belief in German anti-Semitism and racism. Genetic? Cultural? Who cared? It was immutable.

It was unsettling, but I was also aware that disliking Germans was not altogether unpleasant. For one thing, it made me feel closer to Jews, a closeness I welcomed as a young adult, unlike the detachment I felt in high school. As we all know, when you're a member of a group, animosity toward another group, "the other," can be a powerful bonding agent.

Then, gradually, it changed again. I learned of Germany's determination to make amends, to prosecute the culprits, and, unlike the Austrians, to teach younger people about what happened. I learned that Germany, more than any other European country, welcomed poor immigrants and, even more important, I got to know some Germans. And of course, atrocities, both large and small, fueled by hatred of "the other," continued to occur. Again and again and again. In the killing fields of Cambodia, in the jungle at My Lai, in Rwanda, in Bosnia, in Darfur.

And it happened on two successive nights in Los Angeles in the summer of 1969. A small group of people who had committed no other crime than being human were savagely murdered by a group of young people who felt not an ounce of empathy toward their suffering. How many times did I have to learn that my father was right? It wasn't a German cluster of culture and genes, it was a human cluster.

I thought of what a survivor of the Holocaust told Robert Jay Lifton, a psychiatrist who has studied the social and psychological causes of violence.

VICTIM OF AUSCHWITZ: When they did what they did
   were they men or were they demons?

ROBERT JAY LIFTON: Well, of course they were men; that's why I went to study them.

VICTIM: Ah but it is demonic that they were not demonic.

ROBERT JAY LIFTON: They were very ordinary men who became demonic, doing demonic things. They weren't inherently evil. Human beings aren't inherently evil. Rather we have the capacity for good or for evil and we become what we are through our own personal decisions.

chapter thirty-three
BAD APPLES OR BAD BARREL?

May 2004

The country was in an uproar. Photographs of prisoner abuses at Abu Ghraib, a prison in Iraq, had surfaced. When I first looked at those images, the horror made me ill, but it was the images of Lynndie England that held my attention: Lynndie England, a petite tomboy, giving a jaunty thumbs-up and pointing at the genitals of a young Iraqi who is naked except for a hood over his head; Lynndie England holding a leash that encircles the neck of a naked Iraqi man lying on his side on a cell block floor, his face contorted in pain and humiliation; Lynndie England, laughing, arms around her boyfriend while bloodied, naked Iraqis writhe in pain in front of them.

I know it was the juxtaposition of her femaleness and youth—that smirk—that was partly responsible for my wave of nausea. I should know better, but I simply expect more compassion from women. Looking at those photographs, I didn't care who bore more responsibility: the higher-ups who either ordered her to do what she did or were responsible because they created the toxic system in which it could occur, or Lynndie England herself. The woman was barbaric. She was evil. All of the adjectives that Bugliosi and Steve Kay had used for Leslie and Pat came to mind.

Even now, as I write this and look at the photos, I can barely contain my rage.

When social psychologist Philip Zimbardo saw those images, he was also appalled but not surprised. He said he understood what happened inside the walls of that prison. Three decades earlier, he'd conducted research demonstrating that brutal institutions produce brutal behavior even among mentally healthy individuals with no previous sign of psychopathology.

In 1971, seeking to expand Stanley Milgram's work on obedience, Zimbardo set up a mock prison and recruited Stanford University undergraduates to staff it and to act in the role of prisoners. The Stanford Prison Experiment became so brutal that the project, designed to last fourteen days, was called off after only six. The students assigned to be guards were so abusive that the students assigned to be prisoners began to show signs of extreme stress and anxiety to such a degree that five of them had to be released from the study even earlier. Zimbardo himself was not immune to the negative conditions. In his role as prison warden, he overlooked the abusive behavior of the prison guards until a graduate student, Christina Maslach, his girlfriend and future wife, was so horrified at what she observed that she pled with him to abort the project. And he did.

The experiment revealed the extent to which ordinary, normal, young men would succumb to or be seduced by the social forces inherent in that behavioral context. "The line between good and evil, once thought to be impermeable, proved instead to be quite permeable," he later wrote in *The Lucifer Effect: Understanding How Good People Turn Evil* (Random House, 2007). And it happened in a very short time.

When Lynndie England's family and friends saw the images of her brutalizing prisoners, they said this was not the Lynndie they knew and Zimbardo agreed. He became an expert witness for the defense in her court-martial. The military hierarchy, in-

cluding Donald Rumsfeld and Dick Cheney, maintained that she
and her brutalizing cohorts had something twisted inside of them
that had caused them to act aberrantly. It wasn't the fault of the
military. England and her buddies were "bad apples." Zimbardo
countered that the apples weren't bad, the barrel was.

What made him so sure? The students who participated in the
Stanford Prison Experiment who behaved so brutally toward their
charges had been normal, ordinary kids when he'd accepted them
for the project. He maintained that the same dynamic was operating in Abu Ghraib: brutal systems produce brutal people. In his
book, he describes the shock of recognition he felt when he saw
the photographs, photographs that made him relive the worst
scenes from the Stanford Prison Experiment. He claimed that the
bags placed over prisoners' heads, the forced nakedness, the sexually humiliating "games" were comparable to the abuses imposed
by his clean-cut college students on their student prisoners. When
placed in a situation that granted them absolute power, only a few
were able to resist abusing that power. He confessed that he was
not among the ones who resisted.

What does any of this have to do with Pat and Leslie? Though
they weren't inmates in a physical prison, they were in a psychological one, and many of the same variables that existed at Abu
Ghraib and at the Stanford Prison Experiment prevailed under
Manson's lethal rule. In all three situations, the reduction of the
cues of social accountability produced deindividuation, the stripping away of one's core identity.

There has been no shortage of challenges to the conclusions of
the Stanford Prison Experiment. One is that the participants were
not, as Zimbardo claimed, "average, healthy guys." Though none
of the participants were overt, diagnosable sadists before the
study, an ad seeking volunteers for "a psychological study of
prison life" would likely attract a subset of "normal." The other
principal criticism has to do with expectations. Years later, a cou-

ple of the men who'd been assigned the role of guards said they behaved tyrannically because they thought that's the way Zimbardo wanted them to behave.

Neither of these criticisms invalidate the usefulness of Zimbardo's research for my purposes. The young people who were attracted to Manson did not represent a cross section of normal people; they, too, while not being overt sadists before meeting Manson, were a subset of presumably normal people who were vulnerable to manipulation. That's precisely why Manson picked them. And Pat and Leslie didn't come up with murder on their own. As with Zimbardo's guards, the ones who now say they were acting out Zimbardo's expectations, the women were acting out what Manson ordered them to do.

The point, or at least one of them, is that certain leaders in certain situations produce brutal, at times extremely brutal, behavior. If the guards at Abu Ghraib were mistreating the prisoners because they thought it was expected of them, it rather proves the point that situations and leadership matter.

The research may be flawed, but I believe Zimbardo's inquiry into the conditions that promote barbaric behavior is invaluable in understanding the way techniques are able to erode or destroy the very souls of human beings.

chapter thirty-four
A PSYCHEDELIC CITY-STATE

1998, 1968

It had been more than an hour since I slipped my request to visit Leslie through the slot in the waiting room, but there was still no sign of her. I started to worry that they had forgotten about me. It had happened before—more than once.

"Do you think there's a problem?" I said, leaning into the microphone so the guard on the other side of the bulletproof glass could hear me.

"No," she said.

"It's been over an hour."

She shrugged. "It happens." She looked down at the stack of forms she was shuffling. She was not going to provide me with the gift of eye contact.

I sat back down.

A man sitting in an adjacent row looked at his watch and let out an exasperated sigh. He'd been waiting when I arrived so his impatience was well deserved. "She said the same thing to me," he said, motioning in the direction of "it happens" Hannah.

He was a slender man who looked to be in his fifties with a sun-weathered face and faded blond hair. He looked nautical or a good imitation of nautical in a pale yellow Ralph Lauren polo shirt and Vans. He also had the ever-so-slightly shell-shocked expression of a straight-arrow guy who hadn't yet adjusted to the necessity of having to deal with the Department of Corrections. He told me his daughter had recently been convicted on a drug charge. He had a string of complaints against the judicial system, starting with the district attorney who prosecuted her for what he considered a minor offense right up to and including the snotty guard behind the glass. He raked his fingers through his thinning hair and said, "To think I voted for Pete Wilson."

This was not the first discussion of its kind I'd had with people in the waiting room. If there are no atheists in foxholes, there are no law-and-order Republicans, or at least not many, in prison visiting rooms. I'd wager that prisons have been responsible for converting more people to progressive politics than any other single institution or organization. The first time many Americans come into contact with a totalitarian regime is when someone they care about goes to prison. You don't have many more rights than a prisoner when you're visiting one, except that you get to go home when the visit is over.

And then I saw Leslie, handcuffed, entering the visiting area with her minder. It was always a shock to see her escorted in handcuffs, standard operating procedure.

After we settled outside with drinks, chips, and cigarettes, I asked her to tell me more about her experiences in Haight-Ashbury in the 1960s. She said the first time she went there she was too young and not at all prepared for the trials and tribulations of emancipation. The second time she was eighteen and ready to make the break with her mother permanent. "I was older and I wasn't as frightened," she said, lighting her filtered Camel. "It was exciting and I wanted an adventure."

I told her that I, too, had lived in the Haight in the 1960s and it *was* exciting. That era, defined by its swirl of garish tie-dyed colors and stoned lingo is so effortlessly caricatured that it's easy to forget the pervasive joy and optimism that prevailed in the early days. There was a feeling that something important was happening—rules were being broken, advances were being made—and you could sense it by walking down the street. There was an innovative spirit everywhere: in the music, the art, the sciences, in the academy. Much has been written about the rage of the 1960s—David Horowitz and Peter Collier, former radicals and born-again right-wingers, titled their book about the '60s *The Destructive Generation*—but the overall momentum was propelled by idealism.

The vibrant twenty-five-square-block area at the eastern edge of Golden Gate Park—journalist Warren Hinkle called it "a psychedelic city-state"—was characterized by two- and three-story Victorians built in the 1890s. Over the years the once-upscale district had depreciated, and by the 1960s housing was a bargain. A group of kids could rent a five-bedroom Victorian with stain-glassed windows, wainscoting—gas lamps, though wired, were still in place—and a sun-drenched backyard for a few hundred dollars a month. These circumstances were perfect for communal living, and communality was the order of the day.

When Leslie and I compared notes on our time living there, we agreed that there was something about the place that felt uniquely welcoming—in fact, no neighborhood, before or since, made me feel as safe, nurtured, or entertained. In the *S.F. Examiner*, Michael Fallon described the Haight as "part old Calcutta, part circus."

At the time, I was in graduate school and in a new marriage to a medical student, and we had some adjusting to do. Occasionally, as a symptom of that adjustment, I would angrily bang out of our apartment at 2:00 or 3:00 a.m. and walk two blocks to the House of Donuts on Stanyan Street. I wish I'd taken photos: even at those hours it was an all-night costume party with people wearing topcoats and ponchos, granny dresses, serapes, and a variety of robes—from bathrobes to monk's robes.

What started as a party, drawing kids from all over the country, took a more sinister turn as social upheaval roiled the country. The rage over the war in Vietnam was ignited daily by televised images of mothers and children fleeing from napalm and carpet bombs; by 1968, the body count of American servicemen killed had reached an average of fourteen hundred a month. Martin Luther King Jr. was assassinated, in April 1968, in Memphis; the following June, the month Leslie arrived, Bobby Kennedy was assassinated in Los Angeles.

Social scientist Helen Perry, one of the early observers of the Haight in the 1960s, likened the scene to the delta of a river where all the uprooted sediment of America was washing ashore. The uprooted sediment she was talking about were disaffected kids like Leslie fleeing their parents. Michael Fallon is credited with coining "hippie," a word, so the story goes, that he created out of "hipster." Norman Mailer, in his 1957 essay "The White Negro," defined hipster as someone who, because of World War II, the brutality of concentration camps, and the diabolical invention of the H-bomb, had divorced himself from society, "to exist without roots," Mailer wrote, "to set out on that uncharted journey into the rebellious imperatives of the self."

Kids in the Haight like Leslie may not have been reading Mailer, but they were definitely acting out their own imperatives. The most sheltered generation in history now rejected the very institutions that had sheltered them. The conformity of the 1950s gave way to an infatuation with change. Alter your clothes, grow your hair, change your name, unleash your sexual inhibitions. Try everything, experiment constantly, accept nothing as given.

The context for the so-called Manson Family was a subculture committed to communal effort and social change. In 1967, Dr. Dave Smith opened the Haight-Ashbury Free Clinic for medical problems, and the Diggers, a group founded by Peter Coyote in 1966, established crash pads for the kids pouring into the district.

Charles Manson, 1969. *Everett Collection Historical/Alamy Stock Photo.*

The house at Barker Ranch. *William Girard/Alamy Stock Photo.*

Leslie Van Houten leaving the courthouse in 1978 after her third trial.
AP Photo/Nick Ut.

Leslie Van Houten at age 53, pleading her case to the parole board in 2002.
Reuters/Alamy Stock Photo.

Patricia Krenwinkel, March 3, 1970, as she entered the Los Angeles Superior Court for arraignment on murder charges. *Zuma Press, Inc./Press/Alamy Stock Photo.*

Patricia Krenwinkel, 63, appearing before the parole board in January 2011.
AP Photo/Reed Saxon.

During the August 1970 trial, and for years afterward, Leslie Van Houten, Susan Atkins, and Patricia Krenwinkel buttressed each other with Manson's pathological ideology.
Everett Collection Historical/Alamy Stock Photo.

Squeaky Fromme (left) and Catherine "Gypsy" Share are shown outside the courtroom during the January 1970 trial of Manson, Watson, and the three women.
AP Photo/David F. Smith File.

Susan Atkins at age 54. Eight years later, in 2009, she died in prison of brain cancer. *Photo courtesy California Department of Corrections and Rehabilitation.*

Charles "Tex" Watson at age 61. *Photo courtesy California Department of Corrections and Rehabilitation.*

Los Angeles Deputy District Attorney Stephen Kaye, shown here in 1996, worked closely with prosecutor Vincent Bugliosi in the 1970 trial. *AP Photo/ Michael Caulfield.*

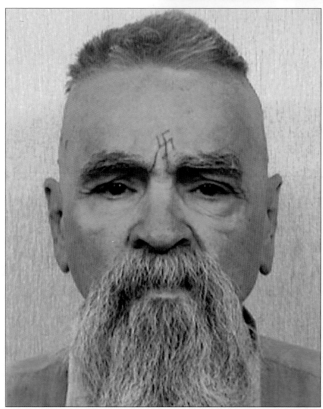

Charles Manson at age 80 in 2014. *Photo courtesy California Department of Corrections and Rehabilitation.*

The Diggers also distributed free clothing from a storefront and served free food in the Panhandle every day to more than two hundred people. One of the units of social change in this era was the group, and there were groups of every stripe on every corner: consciousness raising groups, encounter groups, Gestalt groups, sensitivity training groups, Synanon square games, community organizing groups, and group therapy.

At the time, I was in graduate school at San Francisco State and married to a medical student at the University of California, San Francisco. Political activity was fervent on both campuses, but the proximity of the medical school to the Haight—the buildings on Parnassus Hill loom over the district—created an uncomfortable coexistence of counter-culture and institutional practices. It's hard to overstate the upheaval and the contradictions.

A few examples: to the astonishment of the chancellor, the once-staid Dean of Students, after a weekend at Big Sur, reorganized his office, doing away with the hierarchical structure so that the secretaries had as much say as the dean; medical students started challenging big pharma, though it wasn't yet called that, vilifying lazy doctors who relied on drug company hucksters for prescribing information; my husband and I, along with six other couples, were part of an encounter group organized by a faculty psychiatrist who facilitated marathon weekend sessions. These encounters challenged what had once been solid boundaries. The word "inappropriate" had vanished, and if someone had "boundary issues," another term not yet in vogue, it was because he or she felt pressure to cross them, not maintain them.

Not only did the medical students and their wives and girlfriends bare their souls in these groups, the faculty advisor who led the group did as well. These intense sessions routinely produced confessions of infidelity, accusations of infidelity, expressions of aggression, and lots of crying. Early Monday morning, the same guys (in this group, the med students were all guys) who had peeled off their crisp white coats on Friday night to expose their soft underbellies put the coats back on and, with very little sleep, showed up for rounds where humiliation by arrogant superiors, in effect since the time of Hippocrates, continued to be the order of the day.

The friction between hide-bound tradition and the counterculture was the environment Manson discovered when he arrived on the scene. Shedding the past was one of the themes, and potent agents for doing so were drugs: marijuana, mushrooms, and LSD. Taking acid, Ken Kesey called it the "acid test," was a way of nullifying the values you had internalized and thumbing your nose at everything your parents, your schools, your church considered worthwhile.

Timothy Leary, with his tune-in-turn-on-drop-out exhortation to young people everywhere, promoted "the death of the mind" through LSD. Reality, he declared, is an illusion. At the 1967 Human Be-In in Golden Gate Park, dressed in white robes, Leary, sounding very much like Manson would later sound, proclaimed, "The only way out is in," and urged people to start their own religions. "You are a god, live like one," was the refrain. Proselytizers like Leary, drunk on drugs, spirituality, and their own grandiosity, either didn't know or didn't care how this death-of-the-mind message got translated to kids who had barely formed minds to begin with or how literally some might take the invitation to act like a god.

Four months after the Be-In and two months before the summer of love, thirty-year-old Manson moved out of federal prison and into Haight-Ashbury. He'd been in and out of prison for the previous seventeen years for a variety of crimes, including grand theft auto, pimping, mail fraud. The Haight was a predator's paradise. "Pretty little girls running around every place with no panties or bras and asking for love," he said in *Manson Speaks*, a book written with Nuel Emmons, a former prison mate. "It was a convict's dream after being locked up for seven years."

By then the hazards lurking in an open, accepting community of young people intent on shaking off parental shackles were beginning to be apparent. To the everlasting regret of many, Ken Kesey had already invited the Hells Angels to the party. "We're in the same business, you break people's bones, I break people's heads," he was quoted as saying during the summer of love. By that time, many of the flowers cited in Scott McKenzie's "San Francisco" ("For those who come to San Francisco, be sure to wear some flowers in your hair") were pinned to the dirty matted hair of bikers and hard drug users.

When Leslie and her friend arrived in the Haight, they stayed with a young couple and their baby in a railroad flat near the panhandle. One night, Leslie went to a party at a house on the corner of Stanyan and Carl, across from Golden Gate Park. There she met Gypsy, aka Catherine Share, and Bobby Beausoleil. Bobby, a guy with hazel eyes and a heart-shaped face, was cute and cocky, a bad boy like the other Bobby, but with a harder edge. He had worked as a child actor in Hollywood, a sometime musician, and had played several parts in offbeat films—one of them being *Mondo Hollywood*, a film with a segment featuring Jay Sebring's hair salon, another of many synchronistic tendrils connecting the victims to their eventual slayers but having no causal relationship. Gypsy was a musician, making her living playing music in films. She had hooked up with Bobby on a film set in Topanga Canyon, and he, a couple months later, introduced her to Charles Manson.

(If this were a movie, it would be at this point that a split screen would appear showing parallel narratives. On one screen we'd see Leslie's fateful meeting with Gypsy and Bobby; on the other, we'd see Charles Manson driving up and down the coast with Pat and Mary Brunner, collecting new recruits. Leslie didn't know until years later that Gypsy was doing exactly the same thing— collecting girls for Manson.)

At the party in San Francisco, Leslie got stoned with Bobby.
They flirted, they danced, and later had sex. She assumed she was
going to be his girlfriend but he already had one: Gypsy. No problem, explained Bobby. He was adept at parceling out his favors to
more than one woman at a time.

Gypsy and Bobby, who were living in a bread truck with RANDY'S
TRAVELING CIRCUS painted on the side, invited Leslie to hit the road
with them. She agreed and they headed south along the coast. "It
was our version of the Merry Pranksters," she recalled. "We'd
drive along the coast tripping out and picking up people as we
went. Gypsy kept telling all of us about this wonderful commune
near Los Angeles where people were present in the moment,
where they lived for the day, not the past or the future."

At one point when Leslie was describing her experiences in the
Haight, we noticed a young woman standing nearby trying to get
her attention above the din in the visiting room. She was young,
maybe early thirties, and though she had a broad smile, there was
something timid and almost fearful about her.

"Leslie, I'm so sorry to interrupt but I wanted you to meet my
husband." A slim young man who looked even more timid than
his wife stepped forward, and Leslie extended her hand to shake
his. She introduced me to the couple, we exchanged comments
about the weather—it was hot and humid—and Leslie and the
woman talked about an inmate they both liked who had recently
been released. And then the couple moved along.

Once again, I was struck by Leslie's warmth. She gave this
small interaction her all. It was easy to see why so many people at
the prison sought her out and why she had so many long-term
friends on the outside.

"Where were we?" she asked. I reminded her that we'd been
talking about Catherine Share. "Oh, yeah." She told me that she
didn't know until years later that Gypsy was scouting girls, pretty
girls or girls who had cars or cash or their parents' credit cards.

"Gypsy called me in prison in the early nineties to apologize for recruiting me. That was the word she used. 'Recruit.' She said that was her assignment from Manson. I was stunned. I had no idea that it was that well planned."

I told Leslie that Catherine and I had been in the same high school sorority at Hollywood High.

"Was she pushy then?" she asked.

"No," I replied. "Actually I thought of her as quiet, reserved."

"She's one of the pushiest people I've ever known."

The commune Gypsy was talking to Leslie about, the commune near Los Angeles where she said people lived for the moment, not the past or the future, was at Spahn Ranch, the destination for Randy's Traveling Circus truck.

1954–1960

I lived fourteen years before I heard the verb "to Jew." The first time I heard it was from one of the older girls in my social club when she was talking about her father's purchase of a car, as in "He Jewed the guy down on the price." I was familiar with the concept: my father's mother and sister used to take my mother along on shopping trips because they were convinced her Jewishness would enable them to get better deals. My mother joked about it—it was one of many anecdotes in her repertoire of marrying into an Irish Catholic family. So when I first heard this girl use the expression, I felt I had permission to not be offended. I wasn't yet sophisticated enough to know the rules of the road. Later I would understand that it was one thing for my mother to talk about her family's provincial attitudes and quite another for someone outside the tribe to do so.

The longer I was in the Gammas, the more aware I was of ethnic and racial slurs. One of the other older girls (it was always the older girls), for example, had a penchant for doing riffs in a fake Yiddish accent: "Oy vey," usually followed by a crack about Jewish frugality or big noses. Slurs against Asians were not uncommon, either, and African Americans were not left out of this, though the latter didn't come up much because there were only two or three in the entire school and they were only there to attend special classes for the deaf.

When I started noticing these remarks, I thought my father had been prescient that day at the airport. How did he know that's what the club was like? Did he have inside information? I realized later that the club members weren't any more anti-Semitic or racist than other kids in the school or, for that matter, society at large in the 1950s. This was the language they heard at home.

There was, however, a particularly gut-churning incident for me, primarily because it involved one of the girls I really liked, a popular, effervescent senior, who, early on, had taken me under her wing. A bunch of us were riding in her car to a basketball game at University High School. Her method for deciding who would be assigned to the backseat, who in the front, was to employ the "eenie, meenie, miney, mo, catch a n—ger by the toe."

When I was very young, my mother had used this children's counting rhyme as an opportunity to teach me about the maltreatment of African Americans. She didn't just say don't ever use the n-word, she talked about the history of slavery and how, to that day, there was no equality for Negroes. (Decades later I Googled the rhyme and discovered that it might not have had anything to do with slavery.) She said the word was hurtful and that she couldn't think of another word in the English language that was as horrible and I was never, ever, under any circumstances, to use it and if I ever heard anyone else use that word, I had to speak up and tell them it was wrong. As a little girl, I took this responsibility seriously. If any other kids used that word, and it was usually in the context of eenie, meenie, I would deliver my version of my mother's lecture.

But now the stakes were too high. This girl liked me and her status in the club enhanced my status, or at least that's what I believed. There wasn't any part of me that was even tempted to correct her. When she recited "eenie meenie," my mother told me to choose "the very best one," and when this girl's finger landed on me, she laughed, squeezed my hand, and said, "Good, now you can sit in front with me." It's hard now to remember which was more acute: my excitement over her public anointment of me, my disappointment in her for using the n-word, or my distress at my cowardice for not correcting her.

Not using the n-word was a rule, but the overarching imperative was that you speak up when you hear bigotry. Throughout my childhood, my mother had been vigilant about this. One situation that stands out happened when I was in the fifth or sixth grade. She was one of the leaders of my Campfire Girl troop—a circumstance I was not thrilled about from the outset. This was the era of Ozzie and Harriet, and my mother was no waspy Harriet.

The kids in my class were all, as far as I knew, churchgoing Christians whose parents had Eisenhower bumper stickers on their wood-paneled station wagons. My parents were atheists who voted for Adlai Stevenson. None of the other mothers worked. They made lunches for their kids and were home to serve them milk and cookies after school. I made my own lunches and was a latchkey kid.

The worst for me, though, was my parents' art. Hanging in our dining room was a print of Paul Gauguin's *Two Tahitian Women* that featured bare-breasted women. Every friend who came to the house was shocked by that picture, so when my mother offered to hold the annual Campfire Girl party at our house, I begged her either to withdraw the offer or to take the picture down. She said she would not take the picture down but she would withdraw her offer out of deference to my prudish sensibilities. That was a solution to the immediate problem, but worse than my embarrassment about the bare breasts was my fear that my parents' taste in art suggested that they were perverted freaks.

The annual event that year was to be a mother-daughter sing-a-long. The theme: Italian crooners. My mother, who was in charge of entertainment, passed out the lyrics to Dean Martin's *That's Amore* and *When You're Smiling* along with a couple of Perry Como and Frank Sinatra songs. Because of her involvement I was nervous about the event, but I relaxed as soon as it got under way. Everyone seemed to be having a good time—the mothers and the daughters.

At the end of the evening, after most of the guests had left, there was a group of mother-daughter teams in the living room cleaning up. One mother held up a record jacket with a photo of Dean Martin and said, laughing, "Look at him, he's as dark as a wetback." Holding my breath and praying that my mother hadn't heard her, I inched my way toward the kitchen.

No such luck. She whipped her head around to face the woman. "I'm sure you didn't mean to say that," my mother said.

"Didn't mean what?"

"The word you used for Mexicans."

The woman made a brushing-away gesture. "Don't be silly. I was kidding. Anyway," she said, looking around, "there aren't any Mexicans in this room, are there?"

"That really isn't the point," my mother said. "At least it's not the only point." And then she turned to the few remaining girls and said, "Part of being a Campfire Girl is being a good citizen. I know Mrs. G. didn't mean to hurt anyone's feelings, but you need to know that it's not right to talk about people that way."

It was very quiet for what seemed like forever. I know time stood still for me. In those few seconds or minutes, I decided I would have to drop out of school. Move to a different district. Maybe, even, to a different city. I couldn't imagine facing any of these kids or their mothers again.

Finally, the woman whose house it was started jabbering nervously about how late it was and why didn't everyone leave the rest of the cleanup to her? She and her daughter would finish in the morning. As I recall, everyone promptly left.

To this day, I don't know what I think about what my mother did. Was it appropriate to turn a kids' sing-a-long into a teaching moment at the expense of that mother and that mother's child, to say nothing of the humiliation suffered by my mother's daughter? Many years later, I asked my mother why she didn't speak to the woman privately. She didn't miss a beat. "Because it was my responsibility as an adult to let the other girls know it wasn't acceptable. If people say or do something despicable, you're just as bad if you don't publicly challenge them."

So, in high school, from the moment I declined to challenge the use of the "n" word, I realized my membership in the club was problematic. It's hard to say, however, how soon that realization overshadowed my happiness at being accepted. Perhaps it seems trivial to discuss my problems with a high school sorority in the context of the circumstances that worked together to cause two young women to become murderers, but I'm interested in looking at parallel pressures even if those pressures were small by comparison.

The path to Manson started out as small, innocuous steps. I know that I coped with the disparity between the values with which I was raised, the ones my father underlined for me that day at the Santa Monica Airport, and the modus operandi of the club by creating, if not exactly a false self, then a false*ish* self. For the first two years of high school, when I was around the Gammas, especially the older girls, I kept both my opinions and my Jewish origins to myself.

And it wasn't only my uneasiness over the ethnic and racial slurs that posed a problem. I wasn't crazy about pledging. Pledging is supposed to be uncomfortable, but the older girls in the club took it a step or two beyond discomfort. The group persona of Gamma Rho may have been wholesome, but some of the older girls had a decidedly dark side, some might say sadistic, and their sadism had free rein during Hell Night. I had a large, weeping cold sore on my lip that one older girl rubbed hot peppers into. For years after that, I dreamed about the menacing gleam in her eyes as she did it.

Later that night, they made me strip down to my underwear. I don't remember all that they made me do, other than shouting questions at me, and when I got the answers wrong making me do jumping jacks as penance. I do remember the humiliation of standing alone in some girl's rumpus room with all of the older girls staring at me. I wanted to quit that night but I talked myself out of it—there was a reason they called it Hell Night. I don't remember how I later rationalized the racial slurs, the riffs in the Yiddish accent, or the use of the n-word. What I do remember is the shame of remaining quiet. The worst part was my cowardice and the feeling that I was betraying my family and my family's values.

1977–1978

I'd known Leslie for some time before I discovered that she was released from prison in 1977 and lived a quiet, unobserved life for six months on Micheltorena Hill in the Silver Lake District just a few blocks from where I grew up.

Here's how it happened: In 1976 the California Court of Appeals threw out her conviction, ruling that a mistrial should have been declared during the first trial because her attorney, Ronald Hughes, had disappeared during the trial—apparently having drowned on a camping trip. The new attorney, Maxwell Keith, had to take over mid-trial, requiring him to familiarize himself with over eighteen thousand pages of transcript in a very short time. The appellate court ruled that this burden put him at a decided disadvantage.

The new trial, this time separate from that of her co-defendants, was set for Leslie in 1977. She was transferred from Frontera to Sybil Brand, the downtown women's jail.

Stephen Kay was the prosecutor, and he tried Leslie on "conspiracy to murder" charges. The conspiracy involved the accusation that she was in on the planning of the murders at the Tate house on the first night though there was no evidence that she even knew about them. Those charges allowed Steve to expose jury members to the grisly details of those five murders and to show them enlarged color photos of those victims along with the photos of the LaBiancas.

Leslie's lawyer, Maxwell Keith, who had represented her during the death penalty phase of the first trial, went for a diminished capacity defense based on her drug use and Manson's brainwashing. The diminished capacity defense is no longer permissible, but according to California state law at the time, a first-degree murder conviction required that the state of mind of the accused be capable of pre-meditation, deliberation, and harboring malice. Keith argued that Leslie had not been capable of any of those things at the time of the murders.

Steve's summation to the jury not only included a rehashing of the horror at the Tate house, but also an admonition to the jury that something other than justice was involved: "When you go in that jury room, society will be watching you."

After twenty-five days of deliberation, the trial ended in a hung jury—seven voted for conviction on first-degree murder and five voted for manslaughter. (If she had been convicted of manslaughter she would have been eligible for immediate release for time served.) This gave Leslie hope that there could be a plea bargain. Usually, with a widely split decision, a defendant would be able to plea bargain to second-degree murder. According to Leslie's mother, Steve was particularly upset that so many jurors had held out for manslaughter and was in no mood to plea bargain. This was the first time in California history that a hung jury in a first-degree murder case led to another trial. I wasn't following the case then, but given how high its profile, I believe that most likely even a deputy DA not as obsessed as Steve would have insisted on another trial.

The third trial was scheduled for March 1978 and the court granted Leslie the right to be released on bail. For the next six months, she lived quietly in an apartment on Micheltorena Hill, driving herself to court every day.

Steve adopted a new strategy. He changed the charge to "felony murder committed in the act of robbery," a crime for which state of mind was not legally relevant. The felony robbery consisted of the food, clothing, coins, and wallet that had been taken from the LaBianca house. This was a reversal of the strategy Bugliosi had pursued in the first trial. In *Helter Skelter*, Bugliosi stated that there had been no evidence of robbery and the LaBiancas' son testified in that trial that nothing was missing except for a few coins and some clothes. The wallet had been taken by Manson when he went into the LaBianca house and tied them up. This was a tactic in his inspired plan to start a race war. Because he wanted the police to think a black person had stolen it, he had the group drive to a gas station in a black neighborhood and leave the wallet in the bathroom. Only problem: he selected a neighborhood that wasn't predominantly African American. No race war. Not even a racial skirmish.

Bugliosi had rejected this approach in the first trial because a robbery motive made the crime seem too pedestrian, but Steve had to settle for a mediocre motive. The judge in the third trial instructed the jury to disregard Leslie's state of mind at the time of the crime. In spite of that, Maxwell Keith argued to the jury that she could not have understood the nature of the crime because of the cumulative effects of LSD and the intensity of Manson's power over her. His goal was to win a verdict of voluntary manslaughter—unlawful killing without malice aforethought.

The jury voted unanimously to convict her on two counts of first-degree felony murder. But it was not all bad news, or so it seemed at the time: Leslie would be forevermore separated legally from Manson, Pat, and Susan; when Superior Court Judge Gordon Ringer sentenced her to seven years to life in prison, the new sentence automatically carried with it the possibility of parole after seven years, which she had already served. Her mother and other allies believed that the judge had been encouraging about the possibility that Leslie could become a beneficiary of that provision.

There was another reason for optimism: Leslie was no longer what's called a "death penalty overturn." Though the death penalty had been reinstated, the crime for which she was convicted was not subject to the death penalty. While this put her in an improved position technically, it is a point routinely missed by parole panels. They assume she's a death penalty reversal so they approach her with a "you're lucky to be alive" attitude. "No," she will say patiently, "I'm not a death penalty reversal," and she explains why. The educational process is continual because the panels change constantly. (The board is composed of twelve full-time commissioners who are appointed by the governor to staggered three-year terms.)

It's bewildering that the court felt okay about allowing Leslie—who is, to this day, according to the DA and the parole board, a dangerous murderer—to live among us for six months only eight years after the murders and only three years after she had freed herself from Manson's hold on her. I think of her driving to court every day and then I think about what it must have been like for her to go back to prison.

She told me that it wasn't as terrible as it sounds because so many people really did believe it was just a matter of time, a short time, before she was paroled.

chapter thirty-seven
MULE CREEK PRISON

1998

*I*t was early. The sun hadn't fully come up, and tule fog softly blanketed the cars trickling into the parking lot of the Mule Creek Prison. I was looking for Tex Watson's wife. (Tex no longer uses that nickname—he goes by his given name Charles—but I use it in this book for the sake of clarity.) When we'd arranged to meet, I'd forgotten to ask what make car she'd be driving. Also, I hadn't counted on such low visibility. For a minute I worried that I wouldn't find her. And then I saw a young woman emerge out of the mist and walk toward me.

Because she was a born-again Christian, because I'd heard an interview with her in which "praise the Lord" larded almost every sentence, marking pauses in her speech the way some people use "uh"—and because of the heaven-like swirls of fog, there was something otherworldly about my first glimpse of her. But then she waved and we were earth-bound again. She was pretty with dark hair, and she looked very young. She had a sober quality that tempered her youth. There were three children walking behind her.

I knew she and Tex had children, but I hadn't expected her to bring them. Perhaps I should have. It was, after all, Sunday, visiting day, and, if they hadn't come, they would have missed family time with their dad that week. Early on in this project, I had decided that I wouldn't contact Charles "Tex" Watson, Manson's henchman. Initially my reluctance was due to the desire to limit the scope of my inquiries, but as time went by and my feelings for Leslie and Pat intensified, I think I had another agenda, though I didn't realize it at the time. I wanted him as backup to Susan Atkins for the role of scapegoat, in the event that she failed to continue serving that purpose. (And in fact, Susan eventually did fail in that role. As I observed her getting increasingly debilitated from cancer during my visits to the prison, it was difficult to continue conjuring her as a receptacle for the rage, fear, and sadness about the murders that I hadn't shaken.) As it turned out, though, Tex wasn't such a good substitute.

Two things changed my mind about meeting him: I read *Will You Die for Me?* A book he wrote with a chaplain nine years after the murders. I was surprised to find it very readable and, even more surprising, I trusted the voice. It seemed to be an honest rendering of what had attracted Tex to Charles Manson and a straightforward account of the murders. I wouldn't say it was overflowing with psychological insight, but, on the other hand, it was not filled with the-devil-made-me-do-it rhetoric. It was an as-told-to book, so the quality of writing isn't Watson's, but I assumed it represented his experience and perspective.

The other thing that piqued my interest: I had heard that Tex had a friendship with Susan Struthers LaBerge, Mrs. LaBianca's daughter. How in the hell did that happen? I certainly know relatives of victims who believe in forgiveness but not to the point of friendship. I wanted to learn more about it.

I wrote to Tex at Mule Creek Prison asking if I could visit. He responded by suggesting that I contact his wife, Kristin, who would make the arrangements. Kristin and I talked on the phone and planned to rendezvous at the prison the following month. (As with Pat and Leslie, I couldn't formally interview him—no paper, no pencil, no recorder. I would have to visit as a friend.)

I didn't know much about Tex, other than imagining him as a one-man killing machine on those two nights of terror. In the photos from his time with Manson, he looked a little deranged, springing from the same gene pool as *Mad* magazine's Alfred E. Neuman. He did not look like the babe magnet he was purported to be. In his before-Manson photos, he looked like the strapping young man he'd been in Texas and later in California—a man to whom many women were apparently attracted.

In high school he'd been popular with his teachers and peers, excelled academically, lettered in sports, and he was a member of Future Farmers of America. After the murders, his mother had famously said, "I sent a nice boy to California and he came back a killer." He was not with the Manson group when they were arrested. He fled home to Texas and was later extradited.

The day I drove to Ione, the town where Mule Creek is located, the tule fog was hugging the road, making the drive a little treacherous. Actually, one stretch always felt treacherous, even when there wasn't a trace of fog. Whenever I drove past Rancho Seco, the decommissioned nuclear reactor, I noticed that I held my breath the way I did as a little girl going through tunnels. After the movie *The China Syndrome* was released in March 1979, I was sent to the area by an editor to interview people about how they felt living close to a nuclear reactor. Residents seemed equally divided between those who thought it was dangerous and those who thought it perfectly safe and blamed one of the stars, Jane Fonda, for fanning the flames of foolish paranoia.

As it turned out, the paranoia was not so foolish. Twelve days after the movie was released, there was a partial meltdown at Three Mile Island, a nuclear reactor in Pennsylvania with the same design as Rancho Seco. Radioactive gases and iodine were released into the environment. Later, it was disclosed that there had been a series of accidents at Rancho Seco that had gone unreported in the press, and citizens voted to close the plant in 1989. The cooling towers were now empty, but abandoned air raid sirens scattered throughout the area were reminders of past danger.

Even knowing that the cooling towers were empty and the plant decommissioned, as usual, I held my breath. The twin towers, as they appeared through the fog, seemed particularly ominous that morning, but I was on my way to meet a man who had murdered seven people and it was hard to separate my uneasiness about lingering radiation from the horror I always felt whenever I thought about the murders, the murderers and the victims.

Tex's children sat very quietly in the visiting room. It was difficult to tell if they were shy or extremely well behaved. The oldest boy stands out in my memory—a kid with neatly combed dark hair, fair skin, and freckles. I think he was probably twelve or thirteen. He was wearing slacks, a white dress shirt, and a blazer. His mom, Kristin, was wearing a navy shirt-waist dress. Sunday best. No jeans and sweatpants for this handsome family. (There are now a total of four children.)

The children are compliments of the conjugal visit program started under the administration of Governor Ronald Reagan in 1971. When the program was proposed initially, there was much opposition from the guards, who claimed that it would increase drug smuggling, violence, and child molestation. There was, however, abundant research demonstrating that conjugal visiting strengthened families and encouraged rehabilitation. Doris Tate, Sharon's mother, cared not a whit about this research. Before she died in 1992, she was one of the most insistent voices demanding that the legislators end the program, which they eventually did in 2000 for inmates serving life terms. (As I indicate in an earlier chapter, family visits were eventually reinstated for lifers, but only for those whose crimes did not involve violence.)

Tex, his family, and I sat at a table in the visiting room. As their dad and I talked, the kids sat looking sober, which I interpreted as boredom. I wished I'd brought something for them to do. I wondered why their mom hadn't thought of that. On second thought, other than a coloring book, not exactly a pre-teen boy's métier, I'm not sure what would have been on the approved list. So Dad and I talked while Kristen and the kids observed.

I asked Tex how he happened to become friends with Mrs. LaBianca's daughter, Susan Struthers LaBerge. I knew from Steve Kay that Frank Struthers, Susan's younger brother, had struggled mightily, both as a kid and as a young adult. I'm not sure precisely what "struggled" referred to but could imagine the kind of suffering a boy who found his parents dead would endure. At one point, Steve used the term "lost." Somewhere along the way he seemed to have found some footing by allying himself with Debra Tate, the youngest of the three Tate sisters. He now shows up at parole hearings along with the ever-growing crowd of parole deniers, arguing against release for any and all of the people involved in the murders. His testimony seems to get ever more bitter as the years go by.

His sister, Suzan, was a teenager when their parents were killed, and her life was in no less turmoil after the murders than her little brother's, but as part of her quest to make sense of what happened, she started writing to Tex under a different name. After corresponding for months, she asked if she could meet him. He agreed and at that meeting she told him who she was. At first he didn't believe her, but eventually he did and after he recovered from the shock, they slowly built a friendship. They were both born-again Christians, and that helped intensify their bond. In a subsequent interview on a Christian network, Suzan explained how getting to know Tex and forgiving him released her from her grief. Her explanation: "He's new in Christ. I'm new in Christ." She also became friends with Kristin.

At the time of my visit, the two women and their children lived in the same neighborhood not far from the prison. Eventually, Susan came to believe that Tex should be out of prison and started attending his parole hearings to promote his release. Sharon's mother, Doris Tate, was outraged. After one parole hearing, she accosted Susan in the prison parking lot, demanding that she reconsider her support for Watson, a verifiable serial killer.

Charles "Tex" Watson grew up in Copeville, Texas, thirty-five miles north of Dallas. After a promising tenure in high school, he attended North State University in Denton, Texas, but he didn't graduate. According to his first memoir, he was lured to California by the drugs, sex, and rock 'n' roll of the 1960s. He found all three in abundance when he arrived.

After he'd been in California for a few months and living in Malibu, he picked up a hitchhiker on Sunset Boulevard who was also heading to the beach. The hitchhiker was Dennis Wilson, the drummer for The Beach Boys, who explained he was without transportation because he had wrecked both his Rolls Royce and his Ferrari. Tex had grown up listening to the band—his brother was a fan—so when Wilson invited him to come into his house in Pacific Palisades, Tex accepted enthusiastically. This is where he first met Charles Manson, who was sitting on the floor in the living room surrounded by five or six girls and strumming his guitar. Watson said that when his eyes met Manson's, he felt "a sort of gentleness, an embracing kind of acceptance and love."

Though, initially, Wilson was also taken with Manson's message of love and acceptance, he subsequently tired of the hangers-on and kicked them out. Tex left with them.

Tex, like Pat and Leslie, was besotted with Charles Manson, the embodiment of all things mystical. At one point, he telephoned his parents in Texas and told his mother that he had met the Jesus she had preached about his whole life. "Charlie was

Jesus. He was my messiah, my savior, my soul," Tex wrote in *Will You Die for Me?*

The book's title came from an incident after the Tate-LaBianca murders when Manson pressed the point of a long knife against Tex's chest and asked, "Would you die for me? Would you let me kill you?"

Tex wrote that his reply was instantaneous and automatic. "Sure, Charlie, you can kill me."

In the book he explains that he was so filled with the love of God that nothing was too great to ask. "I was filled with Charlie. He was God to me. He could ask anything, even my life . . . And it wouldn't be any great thing, giving him my life, because I knew everything but my physical, animal body was already dead anyway. My ego was dead; anything that asserted I, me, or mine was dead. My personality had died, now I was only Charlie, and Charlie was all of me that mattered."

When he told Charlie that he could kill him he knew that the person he had been before was "totally dead." He felt no remorse for the murders, no revulsion at the brutality of the killings. He felt nothing at all.

In the prison visiting room, Tex and I talked about his history, his life at Mule Creek, and his religion, which figured prominently in his life. It was through his church connections that Tex and Kristin had started corresponding. She lived in New Jersey, and at the time, he was incarcerated at California Men's Colony in San Louis Obispo. He persuaded her to move to San Louis Obispo, and they got married when she was twenty-two and he was thirty-three.

Tex was "born again" in 1975, six years after the murders, and ordained as a Methodist minister in 1981. At the time of our meeting, he was assisting a minister from the community who came weekly to hold services for the prisoners. Our conversation was easy and friendly until I referred to "the murders." He shot me a "look," the kind I used to get from my mother when I mentioned a family secret in front of outsiders.

Clearly he hadn't told his kids. He must have told them he was convicted of something—he was, after all, in prison—but I didn't know what. Given that, I wondered why he had wanted his kids to be present for the interview. What did he think we would talk about? Later, I thought about the conversation he would eventually have to have with them. How and at what age do you tell your kids you murdered seven people?

Aside from that bit of discomfort, the visit was pleasant. I hadn't expected to like him but I did. I'd anticipated that his religiosity would dominate, but it didn't.

At one point, Kristin and the kids walked over to the vending machines to buy chips and sodas. In the short time they were out of earshot, I told him that I was getting to know Pat and Leslie.

"Those poor girls," he said, a pained look coming over his face. "They just got caught up in it." He looked genuinely aggrieved.

"What do you mean?" I asked.

"I mean they just got caught up in the moment. They didn't kill on those nights."

At first I thought I'd misheard him. What did he mean they didn't kill? Leslie stabbed Mrs. LaBianca nineteen times.

"I don't understand," I said.

And then I remembered Pat telling me that she stabbed Abigail Folger first and then got Tex to come and finish killing her. So I assume what Tex meant was that they didn't administer the *coup de grâce*—he did. Of course, in the eyes of the law, that made no difference. They were as guilty as he was. (Though, when I was driving home that night, I thought that if the women hadn't been so sturdily under Manson's influence at the time of the trial, a

good lawyer might have been able to use this testimony as a miti-
gating factor. Then again, if they hadn't been under Manson's influence none of it would have happened in the first place.)

I was surprised. It seemed like a generous thing to say because
the implication was that he was responsible for doing it all, if not
legally or morally, then physically. I couldn't think of any benefit
he would gain from portraying them as more innocent than he. At
that point, anyway, his account of the murders didn't seem strate-
gic.

Since then, Tex has changed his story a bit. Tex now says that
Pat is the one who killed Abigail Folger. According to an April 6,
2016, article in the *Daily Mail*, he has written to Wikipedia asking
that the entry on him be corrected to reflect that Pat was the primary killer of Abigail Folger, although he admits he "assisted."
Patricia has never denied her involvement in Folger's murder. It
does seem to contradict what he told me about the primary responsibility for the murders.

I'm not sure why he took so much of the blame when we talked
or why he later changed his mind. At the time, he clearly expressed sympathy for both Pat and Leslie. I don't attribute any
sinister motives to his change of heart. Perhaps it was on the advice of a lawyer. It's possible that a fact like this could make a difference at a parole hearing. Or, maybe now that his kids are older
and might read these accounts, he wants to minimize his culpability in any way he can.

On the drive home from Mule Creek, I wondered again about
the presence of his kids. Had it served a purpose other than (or in
addition to) the fact that it was visiting day? I suspected that the
tableau of the perfect Sunday best family was contrived to counter-
balance the criticism they were getting for producing a family in
the first place. If I'm right, they needn't have bothered. While I
understand why this sort of thing makes taxpayers angry (there is

a possibility that the kids were on Medi-Cal), and especially tax-payers who have in any way been victimized by violent crime, it's simply not in me to be upset about creating a new family in which the kids are wanted, loved, and treated well.

According to information in the transcript of his last parole hearing, the couple has since divorced and Kristin has remarried, but Tex told the panel that the two have an amicable relationship and continue to co-parent the kids.

In 1980, Tex founded Abounding Love Ministries and it now has a website, *AboundingLove.org*. (Someone else must manage it for him. He wouldn't be able to do that from prison.) The website tells his story, quotes Scripture, and talks a lot about love and forgiveness. I may not have a problem with Tex fathering children while in prison, but the website doesn't sit well with me. He's capitalizing on the interest people have in Manson and it seems dishonest, especially because he states on the site that he "no longer allows his crime to identify who he is."

It's hard to reconcile that with the fact that talk of the murders is threaded throughout the site and the title of his latest memoir is *Manson's Right-Hand Man Speaks Out!* And in bold letters on newer editions of his previous memoir, *Will You Die For Me?* is *Once Ready to Die for Manson Now Living a New Life for Christ.* From what I can tell, he isn't receiving money and I assume it would be illegal for him to do so. There's no obvious way to donate, though there is an address should someone want to contact him.

Ostensibly, the purpose of the website is to spread the word about Jesus Christ and to reach out in the spirit of love and forgiveness, but it seems to me that he, like Catherine Share, also uses the murders as a platform for public recognition. And why not? They both have a story to tell. I'm not suggesting they be prevented from doing so, but I do think it's significant that neither Pat nor Leslie has done anything this self-serving.

chapter thirty-eight
EVERY FACET OF HER MOTHERING

1998

Leslie's next parole hearing took place a week after I last saw Mrs. Van Houten. At the hearing, Deputy District Attorney Stephen Kay could barely contain his excitement: he'd found something new he could use against Leslie. In her most recent psychiatric report there was a reference to how thin she'd become. "She has a history of anorexia," Kay told the panel. "Everyone knows anorexia is anger turned inward. What if she gets out and that anger is turned outward again? We can't take that chance."

Also, he had unearthed Mr. LaBianca's first wife. Though they were divorced long before Mr. LaBianca and the second Mrs. LaBianca were murdered, Kay had arranged for her to speak on behalf of the couple. She appeared before the board to say that Mr. LaBianca was a very nice man and to argue against Leslie's release.

The board, once again, refused to grant Leslie a parole date, but this time the panel did ask that she return in one year instead of two. This seemed to be an acknowledgment that they were running out of reasons to keep her incarcerated. Even so, members of the board serve at the pleasure of the governor, and no governor of any political stripe is going to win votes by releasing one of the Manson group no matter how justified it may be under the law, under the policies that guide release or under a reasonable interpretation of justice.

When I called Mrs. Van Houten later that week to confirm our next meeting, I asked how she was feeling—she had complained of a cold the last time we talked on the phone.

"I'm not going to discuss that on the telephone," she said. I was puzzled, actually not puzzled, stunned by her tone. She was so snappish, you'd think I'd asked her something as personal as "female" troubles.

We met a few days later for lunch at an outdoor Mexican restaurant. The Los Angeles County Health Department had recently started assigning letter grades to restaurants, reflecting how compliant they were with health department rules. There was a "B" prominently displayed in the window. We talked about how to interpret the grade. According to recent news reports, restaurant owners had been paying inspectors under the table for high letter grades.

"Does that mean their standards are only above average or that they didn't pay enough?" she said, laughing. "Do I dare order a *chile relleno*?"

After we ordered I asked about her snappishness on the phone.

"I had made up my mind that if you were going to be blunt enough to ask me about Leslie's parole hearing on the phone, I would be blunt enough to tell you I didn't want to talk about it on the phone." When I explained that I was merely asking if she'd recovered from her cold, she blushed and apologized. I believed, however, that I'd gotten a glimpse of her formidable nature. After all, would it be so terrible to ask her about a parole hearing on the phone? It was clear that she had firmly etched in her mind the dopey television reporter who sticks a microphone in the victim's face and chirps, "How do you feel about your whole family dying in this car wreck?" I knew she had many scars. I remembered Leslie talking about how brutal the media had been to her family during the trial.

Once we'd straightened that out, I did ask her about the parole hearing. "The whole thing is so unfair. Leslie is thin but so is her dad. It's in the family. Steve Kay will find anything to hold against her. *Anything.*"

I asked Mrs. Van Houten how she and Leslie had repaired their relationship after her incarceration. She described it as a long, arduous journey.

When Leslie was first arrested she gave an alias—Lucy Sankston—and after her actual identity was revealed she did everything she could to renounce her family. Mrs. Van Houten was not so easily renounced but finding a way to connect was not easy. Leslie was so weirdly out of touch with reality, Mrs. V felt as though she was visiting a mental patient. As a way to reorient her to her past she decided the first task would be to reintroduce her to the Van Houten family. She brought boxes of family photos and asked Leslie to help her put them in albums. And while they did this together, it was natural to talk about the images—who was in them and what they were doing. "I'd say, 'Leslie, do you remember what we were doing there? Where were we? Wasn't that a picnic?'" And this stimulated extended conversations about each family member and memories Leslie had about her childhood.

Mrs. Van Houten brought needlepoint, something they had done together when Leslie was younger. Later, when they were able to have overnight family visits, she brought literature for them to read together. They read Eudora Welty. They read Faulkner. "I tried to build on what we had and could have together that was less threatening."

Very slowly she began to see changes.

Leslie had told me in an earlier conversation that she never would have survived prison without her mother. "She made a decision to reclaim me as a daughter. I remember at one point I said to her, 'Why don't you forget about me? It would be so much easier for you and perfectly understandable.' My mother said, 'I'm not made of that kind of stuff.'"

In spite of those assurances to Leslie, Mrs. Van Houten told me that in the beginning she wasn't actually sure of what kind of stuff she was made. She struggled mightily with the knowledge of what Leslie had done. I asked her if she had ever discussed the murders with Leslie. She shook her head.

"I learned a long time ago not to ask a question I couldn't bear to hear the answer to," she said. "I had to try and commit myself to reclaiming Leslie as my daughter . . . to do that I had to develop tunnel vision. I had to block out the images of the murders and focus on what it would take to bring Leslie back to the land of the living."

Before my first meeting with her mother, I had asked Leslie if she had any advice for me. She was quiet for a while. "Don't ask her why it happened," she said, referring to the murders, "she doesn't know." Not knowing, however, did not shield her from the where-did-I-go-wrong question familiar to all mothers whose children's lives take a tragic turn. Over the years, she'd examined every facet of her mothering, no matter how minute, held it up to the light, turned it over and over again. Every question asked, every answer given. Every limit imposed or not imposed. Every lesson taught or not taught.

When Leslie was a little girl, she believed in elves. Would a good mother have discouraged that belief? Did that fantasy set her up for Manson's craziness? What about the family's religious practices? What about their religious teachings? "I wanted the kids to know about the Jewish religion so when we had dinner at Passover we set a place at the table for Elijah. Did that set her up to be predisposed to magical thinking? Was I too restrictive?

Maybe I should have let her have a Barbie doll." (When Barbie dolls came out in 1959, Leslie was ten and her mother thought the dolls were too sexualized for a young girl.) Leslie wanted to attend modeling school. Her mother said no. "It seemed like such a shallow career. But . . . maybe I should have let her. Was I too critical generally?"

Mother and daughter have come a long way since their nasty parting on the phone when Leslie called from the Haight. Mrs. Van Houten expressed great admiration for how hard Leslie's worked, not only on herself—her therapy, her education—but also on projects that benefit other people. She said the many hours they were able to spend together on overnight family visits in the trailer cemented their closeness. They talked, they cooked, they read together. "In addition to our Southern period when we read Faulkner and Welty, we had our Russian period when we read Tolstoy and Dostoyevsky."

In the very early days of family visits, Mrs. Van Houten was so determined to do everything she could to reintegrate Leslie into the family, she agreed to include Mr. Van Houten in an overnight visit. For a brief time, they were a family again—cooking, talking, playing cards and board games. She told me the visit had gone well and served its purpose, but she didn't elaborate. I found the thought of the three of them living under the same roof for the first time since he abandoned the family touching and, given how much acrimony there had been, a testament to how much they both loved their daughter.

One day in the visiting room, I was talking to Pat when Mrs. Van Houten walked over to say hello to me. She was courteous but seemed cool to Pat. The next time I saw her I asked her about it. "I have wanted to distance myself. Even more, I've wanted Leslie to keep her distance." This had a familiar ring to it. Though Mrs. Van Houten said her purpose in keeping Susan and Pat at a distance was so that other people would believe that Leslie wasn't like them, I wondered if it was a version of the way I had wanted to keep Susan and Tex at a distance.

August 1998

Mrs. Van Houten and I met at a Starbucks close to her home. We talked about movies—I had just seen *Shakespeare in Love* so I mentioned Gwyneth Paltrow and we talked about language, Shakespeare, beauty. We talked about the recent U.S. Embassy bombings in which hundreds of people were killed in simultaneous truck bomb explosions at the U.S. Embassies in Kenya and Tanzania. We talked about religious zealotry, suicide bombers, mind control.

We sparked each other. We'd go from one topic to another, each of us interested in what the other had to say. These are also the kinds of conversations I have with Leslie. There is much similarity between them. They both read a lot, they are both alert to the hopeful signs in the world as well as to the tragic state of so much of the planet. They are both lively and, each in her own way, participating fully in life. Somehow we got on to the topic of Hugh C. Thompson, a hero of both of ours. He was a U.S. Army helicopter pilot who, in 1968 during the Vietnam war, had, along with his crew, risked his life to stop the My Lai massacre in which a group of U.S. Army soldiers deliberately murdered hundreds of Vietnamese civilians—women, old people, babies. In March 1998, thirty years after the fact, he and his gunner were awarded the Soldier's Medal.

I asked her whether she thought the kind of character displayed by Hugh Thompson is inborn. She said she didn't know whether it was inborn, but she didn't believe you could teach it. I realized that we had veered into Leslie territory. One of the questions I had pondered more than once: What did Hugh Thompson have that Leslie didn't? And why would I compare them? In my mind, the commonality in the two situations—the massacre at My Lai versus the slaughter of the LaBiancas—is the issue of following orders. I believe that the Leslie I know now is someone whose character and humanity would force her to override an order to hurt someone no matter what the situation.

Over the course of hours and days, Mrs. Van Houten and I talked of many things existential and spiritual. She was a woman approaching eighty who was still in search of answers; in fact, she was still in search of questions. She said that over the years her religious beliefs had changed. "I'm completely turned off to the idea of retribution now. To me, God is love. I'm rereading *The Sound and the Fury*, and when Benji's mother says, 'What did I do that God would present me with this?' I want to scream, 'It was a horrible coincidence! God didn't do it to you!'"

And then in a very soft voice she added, "The truth is that I am also guilty of asking 'why?' There's still so much I don't know. So much I don't understand."

Because I knew how much pain she'd suffered and the dignified way she'd coped, and because I knew how hard she'd struggled to lead a life of consequence in spite of everything, and because I knew how seriously she took questions, when she looked at me with those clear blue eyes and said, "God is a puzzle to me now," it broke my heart.

chapter thirty-nine

A LETHAL CONVERGENCE

*A*s hard as I tried, I could not find a single clue—a smoking gun—to explain why these women had been willing to sacrifice their humanity to Charles Manson. I'm not saying there was nothing in any of the backgrounds of these people, the members of the so-called Manson Family, that contributed to their vulnerability—Leslie's absent father, the teasing Pat suffered as a kid and her father's rejection of her sister, Catherine Share losing her mother and emotionally abandoned by her father, Susan Atkins's grim childhood—but I don't think the explanation is to be found with their families. You have to give the psychologists and psychiatrists credit for trying, but, unlike Manson's history, there just isn't enough there. As I've said, take any ordinary family and apply close enough scrutiny and you will find enough pathology to fill volumes.

My family was such a family. There were few answers to the questions my parents asked over and over. Like Leslie, my brother was a bright, attractive kid, who, again like Leslie, started fooling around with drugs as a teenager. There was no divorce but there are clues that his birth might not have been entirely welcomed by my father, who, as a young man, had planned to be a Jesuit priest. That changed when he met my mother, but they waited ten years before having children. By his own admission, he wasn't ready to be a father even then.

After my brother was arrested, my father scrupulously reviewed what kind of parent he'd been. An incident haunted him: he was buying my six-year-old brother an ice cream cone and, because my father liked chocolate and assumed all kids liked chocolate, he ordered them both chocolate ice cream cones. When he handed my brother his cone, the little boy looked at it and said, "I don't like chocolate. I wanted strawberry." My father grabbed the cone, walked to the trash can, dumped it, and walked out of the store. I'm not proposing that my brother robbed an elderly couple because of that incident, but it did say a lot about my father's thin skin. Why would the feelings of an adult man be hurt because his kid wanted strawberry?

Unlike Pat and Leslie, post-crime, my brother's situation was, to use a shop-worn expression, a perfect storm of positive forces converging. Neither of his victims died and his years in prison were as good as it gets. He was in an elite program, a minimum-security prison on the grounds of the maximum-security prison. The inmates fought fires every day and had group therapy every evening. He was only in prison for three years and probably would have gotten out sooner except the parole board was convinced that he had money stashed away. They couldn't believe that he had burned through his share of $100,000 in just a few months.

After he was paroled, he got his undergraduate degree, then his PhD, and eventually became a tenured professor at a university. In other words, he became the person my parents had wanted him to become in the first place.

I'm not suggesting that his situation was strictly parallel to Leslie's. He didn't kill anyone. And that is not a small difference. But for me, the hardest part of my brother's crime was his apparent indifference to the terror the couple must have felt as they were being tied up. Like Leslie, he was young, but he wasn't a teenager. He was a young adult. Like Leslie, he'd been raised with good values by educated parents who agonized about the best course of action when he ran into trouble. And as was the case with Leslie, by the time he planned to enter that house to rob that old couple, it was too late. At that point, my parents had no influence on him.

So, no single factor for the kids attracted to Manson but most certainly contributing ones. Divorce is painful and disrupting for kids; drugs are destructive; social upheaval was the order of the day. All of those elements converged in a lethal and tragic way. In their case, it was a perfect storm of unfortunate circumstances that led those women to Manson. But after concluding that, and after getting to know Leslie and Pat, I remained perplexed. At the risk of tedium I will repeat: these two women not only caused horrible suffering, very intimate suffering, they felt nothing, *nothing* about it. Natural human empathy for their victims did not surface for five years. How could that be? Even after years of knowing them, I didn't feel any closer to understanding that.

chapter forty
"YOU COULDN'T FIND A NICER GROUP OF PEOPLE"

1969

*W*hile I had trouble with Bugliosi's original characterization of the women as soulless monsters, I did have to acknowledge that killing someone so intimately and feeling nothing came pretty close to a definition of soulless. Certainly it was an example of a total lack of empathy. When I first got to know Pat and Leslie, I assumed that while they were with Manson and later, still under his influence, the empathy dial wasn't turned down; it was turned off. But as I listened to them describe their lives with him, it was clear that the situation had been more complicated.

They had compassion and concern for each other and they had intense sympathy for Manson. When he talked about his childhood, they wept for the little boy who was abandoned and abused. When he talked about his life in institutions, they got angry and blamed society. Manson was an expert at selecting young people who were longing for an intense group connection, and he was skilled at reinforcing the bond that kept them together. It's no accident that it was called the Family. In fact, it may be that the empathy they felt for each other, particularly for Charlie, made them so dangerous.

Emile Bruneau, a cognitive neuroscientist at MIT, has spent

years studying intractable conflicts around the world including Israelis and Palestinians in Israel and the West Bank, Mexican immigrants and Americans along the Arizona border, and Democrats and Republicans. As part of his research, he's analyzed programs designed to improve relations between antagonistic groups. Increasing empathy is a central goal of every conflict resolution program he has examined, but he now believes that increasing empathy might be exactly the opposite of what's needed to reduce conflict.

According to Bruneau, there is a widespread assumption that the type of people who engage in political violence are sociopaths, but he contends that is not the reality. When I interviewed him in early 2015, he said that suicide bombers tend to be characterized by very high levels of empathy. "Increasing empathy might be great at improving pro-social behavior among individuals, but a program that succeeds in boosting an individual's empathy for his or her own group might actually increase hostility toward the enemy."

His theory is that the mind generates an "empathy gap" when considering an enemy. It mutes the empathy signal, and that muting prevents us from putting ourselves in the perceived enemy's shoes. He said we don't know what mechanism controls this, but he believes that it has nothing to do with how empathic a person is by nature. "Even the most deeply empathetic people can mute their empathy signals under the right circumstances."

Bruneau points out that empathy is flexible and that flexibility is a feature of being human. "Milgram and Zimbardo have demonstrated that context can be far more powerful than our own values and personality traits in determining how we treat other people."

I told Bruneau that his theory helped me understand the gap in empathy displayed by Pat and Leslie but, it was still puzzling to me that it took them so long to reconnect with the values with which they were raised. He said it was also puzzling to him.

When I think of the importance of context and the way a group influences the perception of its members, I think about Leslie's unswerving loyalty to the Family after she was arrested. There is very little in this saga that's amusing, but there is one thing that always makes me smile. At a time when the country was reeling from fright and the Manson Family had infiltrated the nation's collective psyche, Leslie provided the pull quote of the year, if not the century when she told her interrogator, Sergeant Michael McGann, without a hint of irony, "You couldn't find a nicer group of people."

chapter forty-one
PAT'S ANGER

Fall of 1998

Once again, I was late, and once again Pat was chilly, but today there seemed to be an extra iciness. I didn't want to ask her directly what was wrong—with Pat that didn't usually work—so I steered the conversation to something I'd been wanting to ask her. I told her I'd noticed in a parole report that one of her jobs at the prison was training women to fight fires (as a lifer, she wasn't allowed to travel to fight fires herself), and I know she'd received commendations for this work.

"What happened to that job?" I asked.

"I quit," she said.

"You didn't like the work?"

"I loved the work and I miss it, but the prison cut way back on the amount of training the women received and after that, I just couldn't do it anymore. In good conscience, I couldn't send those women out to front lines of dangerous wild fires without adequate training no matter how much I loved the job."

She said quitting the job was another manifestation of lessons learned from her relationship with Manson. "When I was with him, I did what I was told. I obeyed. I won't do that anymore."

She said she was passionate about the plight of abused women;

she placed the relationship she and the other women had with Manson in that category. She said one of the things she felt guilty about was the role she played with the women. As surrogate mother, she may have made it more comfortable for some of them to stay, women who might otherwise have moved on and gotten out of there before their lives were so messed up.

She had opinions about everything and considered it a badge of honor that she challenged what she heard and what she read. (She was a fan of *The X-Files*, whose motto is "trust no one.") She accepted nothing as true, she said, before investigating it on her own, reading about it, and turning it over in her own mind. She read whatever she could get her hands on in the prison—*Newsweek* cover to cover every week and, when she borrowed it from Leslie, the *New Yorker*. She also loved the *Nation*, which she saw from time to time. She spent her share of time in the prison law library and was particularly fond of Supreme Court opinions written by Justice William O. Douglas.

An hour into our time together that day, I said that she seemed upset. Had something happened? At first she denied it and then she acknowledged that she'd had a bad week and yes, she was upset, really upset with the psychiatrist who did the evaluation for her last parole hearing. In their session together she'd mentioned an incident that had happened with another inmate, and he used that incident against her in his report.

An inmate who was on washing dishes detail started horsing around and accidentally sprayed Pat with a hose. According to Pat, the woman was horror-stricken when she realized she'd gotten Pat wet, but Pat's reaction was to laugh it off and walk away. She mentioned it to the shrink only because she wanted him to know that she was now able to shrug off incidents that once would have angered her. But in his report he wrote that it was evidence of Pat's insensitivity. He believed the inmate was terrified because she had sprayed "the most notorious woman murderer in the country." In his opinion, Pat's laughter at the time was a continuation of the insensitivity to others she showed when she murdered Abigail Folger and the LaBiancas.

Pat said his interpretation demonstrated a complete lack of understanding of the prison culture: "The woman, who, by the way, is covered with tattoos and is a member of a gang, wasn't afraid because I'm the most notorious woman murderer in the country, she was afraid because gang members seek violent retribution for something as minor as being sprayed with a hose. I can't tell you how ridiculous it is for him to say that a woman here is more fearful of me than she is of the Crips and the Bloods."

Pat's explanation sounded credible to me, certainly more credible than the psychiatrist's. (It's hard for me to get past his use of the word "insensitive" in the context of murder.) But later when I was at McDonald's writing up my notes, I realized that I had been momentarily bothered by her anger. Not because it signaled that she was dangerous. I didn't believe that Pat was dangerous. But maybe I do believe that she's forfeited her right to express anger at anyone . . . ever. It didn't take long for me to talk myself down from this position. No one can live without expressing anger, especially someone who's been in prison for as long as she has. Even if you believe that she deserves to be there, the prison/parole system is unimaginably irrational, frustrating, unfair.

I tried to imagine myself in her situation. I spend an hour—given current budgetary constraints, probably less than an hour—with a psychiatrist who doesn't know me, and based on one incident that I tell him about, he arms the district attorney with ammunition that damages my record of twenty-seven years of hard work and good behavior. How could anyone not be enraged?

Wanting the record to be fair may have nothing to do with parole. I'm pretty sure Pat knows the chances are slim that she will ever get out of prison, but it's understandable that she would want some recognition for working so hard. Or if not recognition, at least not misrepresentation. What's called for is a measure of justice, honesty, fairness.

At the same parole hearing, Stephen Kay, who claims to have made a "study" of her but who hasn't actually talked to her since 1970, told the panel that Pat only sees people as objects: "She has as much regard for you and me as she would a piece of Kleenex she'd blow her nose into."

I'm sure there are convicted killers about whom what he said is true, but I know it isn't true of Pat. Unlike Kay, I have spent time with her. But who is going to object to the injustice of saying something undeserved and negative about someone convicted of murder? Kay's continued depiction of her as dangerous was not only dishonest, it was unwarranted and unnecessary. If the chance that Pat will be paroled is very slim, why not give her credit for what she has accomplished? The only purpose his remarks serve is to whip up the old rage.

I know Pat's psychological makeup is complicated and contains vast unexplained areas of emotion—I discuss those later—but she is not without compassion. When I tell her about a friend who is dying of cancer, I know her sympathy is real. When I tell her about the work my daughter is doing at a massive refugee camp on the Somali border with Kenya, I know both her interest and her compassion are genuine. When she points out women in the visiting room, women in wheelchairs or with oxygen canisters who have terminal diseases and whose appeals for compassionate release have been turned down, I do not doubt her concern.

One day, she asked me if I'd ever been to the Vietnam Memorial in Washington, D.C. I said I had. She asked me if it's as beautiful as it reads in the photographs. I said it is. We talked about the initial controversy surrounding the design, and we both agreed that, contrary to the critics, it's a perfect tribute. She told me she had friends in high school who were killed in Vietnam and her pain about them is still acute. Tears rimmed her eyes when she talked about them. "I know I'll never get out of here but if I did, the very first thing I'd do would be to go to the Vietnam Memorial."

Stephen Kay would no doubt challenge my belief in her authentic compassion, but that's because his thinking is binary. You are either not a murderer or you are a murderer, and if you are, you deserve to have verbal abuse heaped on you eternally. It is a black-and-white world, and perhaps this outlook is precisely what we need in prosecutors. But perhaps that's not what we need at parole hearings.

chapter forty-two
SCAPEGOATS—THE NEED TO BLAME

*A*t some point I stopped talking about Pat and Leslie to my friends. I stopped because no matter who these friends were, no matter how progressive politically or committed to social justice, no matter whether they were men or women, no matter how generally sympathetic to people caught up in the criminal justice system, most were unable to locate that sympathy for Leslie or Pat. Their names, almost as much as Charles Manson's, still conjure both the terror and the anger that gripped the country at the time.

As I got to know the women better, the harsh opinions toward them made me feel increasingly protective. It wasn't as though I'd forgotten the murders; it was that I knew the women to be more than the murders they'd committed. I knew and trusted their remorse and their concern for their victims. I knew and trusted their concern about society's problems in general and their empathy for people, especially women and children, who have a hard time of it. I knew and trusted their renunciation of all that was Manson and the beliefs they held when they were under his sway.

But avoiding the topic among my friends didn't avoid the problem. Outside of my social circle, I continued to be surprised by the vehemence of the hostility toward them. A few years ago I was in a writing workshop where, as in most such groups, the woman who led the group routinely insisted that we create a tolerant, nurturing atmosphere for each other so that our creativity could flourish. One day I wrote a paragraph about Leslie, describing the nature of her interactions with fellow inmates and the families of her fellow inmates. I tried to capture her sunny disposition and how it seemed infectious; I described the way people brightened when she talked to them. While I was reading the piece to the group, Lorna frowned. When I stopped reading, she shook her head and said, "I don't understand."

That bad? I thought. The prose seemed straightforward.

"I'm sorry," I said, "but I don't understand. Could you be more specific about what you don't understand?"

"I don't understand why," she said, shrugging her shoulders to illustrate her confusion, "with all of the worthy causes in the world and all of the worthy people in the world you would select this woman to write about."

First I was surprised and then I was angry, but in between the surprise and the anger was amusement. "It's my turn to be perplexed," I said with what I intended as a sarcastic smile on my face. "Lorna, I'm wondering about that creating a safe, nurturing environment thing?"

"I guess there's a limit to my tolerance," she said, ignoring my smile and looking at me with a most un-amused look on her face.

Of course the right answer, or at least one of them, was: I wasn't writing about Leslie to advocate, I was writing about her to understand—to understand her, to understand human nature. She only needed to be worthy of exploration, not advocacy. But that was all beside the point. Lorna was not interested in any portrayal of Leslie as a multi-dimensional person; she was only interested in judgment. Eventually, I did advocate for Leslie's release, so Lorna had apparently seen the writing on the wall.

The next day she called to apologize. "I'm sorry but I couldn't help myself. I guess my feelings are still pretty intense about those murders. Those feelings override everything else."

The more I thought about it, though, the more her reaction gave me pause. She had echoed the sentiments expressed by many of my friends. I recoiled at her attempt at censorship, but it also increased my awareness of the prejudice I was up against in writing about the women. And I couldn't help wondering about myself. If one of the other participants in the group brought in a sympathetic portrayal of someone like Pauline Nyiramasuhuko, the social worker now serving a life term for being responsible for the murder and rape of hundreds of Tutsi women, could I stomach any attempt to depict her as anything but despicable? I doubted it. Unlike Leslie, she denied her participation, but what if she, too, was assuming responsibility and expressing genuine remorse? Would I feel the way Lorna did? I think so because every time I think of Pauline Nyiramasuhuko, when I think of the way she engineered some of the most depraved actions on the face of the earth (forcing a boy to rape his own mother, for example), I feel such intense hatred it scares me.

A few years ago, the film director John Waters, who's been friends with Leslie for many decades, wrote *Role Models* (2010), a book about people who have inspired him. It is an eclectic collection—ten profiles that include, among others, Johnny Mathis, Tennessee Williams, and Leslie Van Houten. In his chapter on Leslie, he praised her hard work, her tenacity, her patience, and her willingness to assume responsibility for her part in the murders. He also wrote that he respected that she resisted the temptation to adopt religious fanaticism, a route that would provide her instant forgiveness. "She has managed to live through bad times without despair and inspire others to do the same."

When Waters appeared on HBO's *Real Time* to promote the book, Bill Maher asked him about Leslie. Waters, while acknowledging how horrendous the murders were, talked about how much he respects and is inspired by her, adding that she had paid her dues and that it was time for her to be released. And then Maher asked a version of what Lorna had asked me in the writing group. I can't remember the exact words and I can't find the clip on the Internet, but his point: this woman is not worthy of your attention.

For a long time I dismissed these attitudes as parochial and small-minded, but the question I had asked myself about the Rwandan social worker continued to bother me. It became increasingly clear that I was not immune to these feelings, and it wasn't limited to the Rwandan social worker. Karla Faye Tucker, a young woman who was convicted in 1984 for the brutal murder of two people, was another one. I knew very little about the circumstances of the murders until George W. Bush, then governor of Texas, refused to commute her death sentence to life imprisonment. When the state eventually killed her in 1998, she was the first woman to be executed in the United States since 1984, and the first in Texas since 1863.

When I read about Bush's coldhearted refusal to consider mercy, I was angry, but then I'd been angry at Bush since he'd unseated Ann Richards, a woman I greatly admired, for the governorship of Texas. When I read a detailed account of the grisly murders, my rage transferred from George W. to Karla Faye herself. She'd found Jesus in prison and after that, people from all over the world rallied to the cause of saving her life. Supporters included the United Nations Commissioner on Summary and Arbitrary Executions; the World Council of Churches; Pope John Paul II; Italian Prime Minister Romano Prodi; the Speaker of the U.S. House of Representatives Newt Gingrich; conservative pundit Tucker Carlson; televangelist Pat Robertson; and even Ron Carlson, the brother of Karla Faye's murder victim Deborah Thornton. When the pleas reached fever pitch, I read *Crossed Over,* an account of the friendship between Karla Faye and novelist Beverly Lowry. After reading *Crossed Over*, my anger then targeted Beverly Lowry as well. I didn't understand. (When you could pick anyone to defend, why pick her? Sound familiar?)

She pled for Karla Faye's life on the basis that she was under the influence of drugs at the time of the murders, she would not have committed the murders otherwise, and that she was now a reformed person.

But Lowry's pleas left me cold. No matter how sympathetic her portrayal of Karla Faye, I simply could not get around the brutal, graphic details of what she had done. Yes, she'd had a difficult childhood and yes, she had a spiritual awakening and yes, she expressed profound remorse. No doubt, she had an appealing, fresh-faced girlishness about her, but look at the crime: There was a motorcycle that Karla Faye's boyfriend Danny Garrett wanted and that the victim, Jerry Dean, owned. There were drugs, there was partying, and one thing led to another. Karla's boyfriend bludgeoned Dean with a hammer. The blows caused his head to become unhinged from his neck and his breathing passages to fill with fluid. He began making a "gurgling" sound that Karla Faye didn't like, so she grabbed a pickax and smashed it into him.

The blows stopped the noise but didn't completely kill him, so Karla's boyfriend, who'd taken time out from murdering to load motorcycle parts into his truck, re-entered the room, dealt the final blow, and then went back to his task. Meanwhile, Karla Faye noticed a woman hiding under bed covers. Deborah Thornton was there because she'd had the great misfortune of meeting the first victim, Jerry Dean, at a party earlier that afternoon. Karla Faye went after her with the pickax, eventually embedding it in Deborah's heart. She told friends and later testified in court that she experienced intense multiple orgasms with each blow of the pickax. (Could there be a more perfect example of the blood lust killing that Chris Browning referred to in his book about Battalion 101?)

Upon reading the description of Karla Faye's murders, I couldn't help thinking about Bugliosi's characterizations of Pat and Leslie in 1970 as human monsters. But I also felt that their total lack of feelings, empathy or otherwise, put them in a more elevated category, mutation-wise, than the state of a woman bragging about multiple orgasms as she plunged a pickax into Deborah Thornton's heart. Part of this weird mechanism I'm trying to understand is that I could always find a way that Pat and Leslie, as bad as they'd been, were not as bad as whoever I was thinking about when these issues came up. *Your murderer is much worse than mine.*

I noted with dismay that I derived a measure of satisfaction from the anger I felt toward Karla Faye. It seemed very much like the anger I'd heard others express toward Pat and Leslie or that I'd seen on Lorna's face in that writers' workshop. I didn't understand what function these intense negative feelings served. I only knew that they seemed important, almost necessary. Necessary for what?

There was no way for me to absorb the savagery of the Tate-LaBianca murders without blaming someone. I needed someone other than Leslie and Pat to be the repository of these feelings. It helped me live with the material and it protected my feelings for the two women. At any given time it was necessary for me to have one or more persons whom I blamed, disliked, distrusted.

Manson holds permanent first place but, irrationally, he's inadequate to the task. The world continues to be fascinated by him, but he holds no interest for me. He knew intuitively how to manipulate young people—I suppose you could say he had a gift—but he also learned some tricks of the trade in prison. If it hadn't been for certain external factors converging, what I've described unoriginally as a perfect storm, he wouldn't have been as effective. Psychopaths are a dime a dozen. Kids who grow up being loved and who are socialized with humane values and end up committing senseless murders are much less common.

In the beginning of this journey, I didn't understand my need

for scapegoats. I thought my lack of interest in Susan was primarily due to her identification as born-again. I saw the conversion as
lazy, a shortcut for taking responsibility. I think that's what John
Waters meant when he said he admired Leslie for resisting the
temptation to adopt "religious fanaticism," a route that would
provide her instant forgiveness.

When Leslie's mother told me she always urged her to keep her
distance from Susan Atkins and Pat Krenwinkel, I think she was
using a similar mechanism to cope. (She had needed more than
one.) She believed that Leslie was made of different stuff than
they were, and she wanted the world to think so, too. But before
she died, she told me she was rethinking this attitude as she was
rethinking many things. She realized that her commitment to
these categories hadn't helped; it certainly hadn't helped get
Leslie out of prison. "Recently I happened to talk to Susan Atkins
and her husband and I quite enjoyed it. She seemed pleasant and
he's so bright."

As I've indicated, when the photos from Abu Ghraib prison
surfaced, I was acutely aware of the similarity between me and
those people I had accused of being narrow-minded. Despite the
consensus of many experts that it was the system that was evil,
not the individuals at the bottom who were acting out the pathology of the system, I had a problem with letting those people at the
bottom off the hook—in particular, Lynndie England. She's the
one laughing and smiling while those men were so palpably suffering. The government may have treated her as a scapegoat,
Philip Zimbardo certainly thought so, but to me her participation
was unforgivable. England was convicted on September 26,
2005, of one count of conspiracy, four counts of maltreating de-
tainees, and one count of committing an indecent act. Along with
a dishonorable discharge she received a three-year prison sentence. She was paroled on March 1, 2007, after serving 521 days.

It hasn't escaped my attention that every example I've mentioned is a woman, and apparently I'm not alone in this focus. According to researchers Georgie Ann Weatherby, Jamie Blanche, and Rebecca Jones, the public has a particular fascination with cases that involve women, and certainly the media coverage is more sensational when the murderers are women. "When the media (and thus the public) learns of a violent female crime they automatically enter a frenzied state," they write in "The Value of Life: Female Killers & the Feminine Mystique" (*Journal of Criminology and Criminal Justice Research & Education* Volume 2, Issue 1, 2008). They maintain that this frenzied state leads to distortions. "In order to deal with such a rare occurrence, society's rules automatically shut down, which causes people to bring forth biased and stereotypical notions about these women."

I'm convinced that the unforgiving anger expressed toward Pat and Leslie is more intense because they are women. But maybe I'm talking about my own unforgiving anger when it comes to women other than Pat and Leslie.

There are many reasons, I suppose, that the image of a woman murdering in situations other than self-defense is more threatening to me than the image of a murdering man. For one thing, women grow up with the awareness that men can hurt us; we're practically socialized to believe this. From the local news to mainstream TV series, we're bombarded with images of men hurting women. We can't help but be desensitized to it. On some primitive level, perhaps women believe that men's sexual drive renders them incapable of self-control and capable of atrocious brutality. Much of this is myth, and some of it is perpetuated by men themselves. For the most part, I think this expectation operates on a subconscious level.

There is something particularly chilling about a woman without empathy—much more frightening than a man without empathy. The anger I feel about the women I've listed above is qualitatively different from any anger I've ever felt toward male murderers. It feels as though it comes from a different part of my brain. The most obvious basis is our original relationship with our mothers.

The part I have the most trouble understanding is how oddly committed I am to my negative feelings about poor Lynndie England. It seems connected to my humanity and not in a good way.

For me, one of the problems with Lynndie is that, because of the photos, her laughter in the face of all of those suffering men is frozen in time. It's a problem for me but apparently not for Lynndie. She feels no remorse. In 2013, she told NBC news she does not regret her actions. "They [Iraqis] got the better end of the deal. They weren't innocent. They're trying to kill us, and you want me to apologize to them? It's like saying sorry to the enemy."

As I've said, when I think of Mrs. LaBianca I feel a heartbreaking sadness. She not only suffered on her own behalf, she heard her husband being killed in the other room. Does it help that Leslie didn't experience any pleasure from the killing? What she describes is a state of numbness, of unfeeling. If that's true, and I believe her (though there are those who don't), does it make the act more palatable? It doesn't in any way absolve her of responsibility, she's the first to say that, but in terms of her humanity, does it make a difference to me that she was an automaton rather than a sadist?

But how can I forget one very important distinction? Lynndie didn't kill anyone. She may have inflicted horrible psychological, emotional, and spiritual damage, but she did not murder anyone. That makes it all the more puzzling that I cannot find it in my heart to feel forgiveness for her while I feel true compassion for Leslie.

chapter forty-three

"SHE DID APPEAL TO MY HUMANITY BUT I HAD NONE TO GIVE HER"

*O*ne day I told Pat about a recurring dream I had as a child that involved appealing to Hitler's humanity—begging him not to kill me because I was just a little girl. Before I even had a chance to get the whole question out, Pat said, "If you're asking me about Abigail Folger, she did appeal to my humanity but I had none to give her."

As usual, Pat's response was straightforward and blunt and, as usual, I was startled by it. Her brand of honesty always feels like a door being slammed. I think the question of what happened to her humanity that night is still, to some extent, untapped. I'm not sure Pat can truly let herself feel the depth of this. Not because she doesn't want to, but because she doesn't have the psychological tools to do so. The born-again Christians don't need those tools. Religion provides them with automatic redemption.

And that leads me to the issue of remorse. I have no doubt that Pat feels remorseful about the murders; I also believe her remorse is complicated.

In a 1988 psychiatric report, she told a psychiatrist that while she knew it was wrong to kill Abigail Folger, it was also true that Folger, who was known to use drugs, "could have made more out of her life." One day I asked her about this statement, expecting her to claim it was distorted, taken out of context, not what she meant at all. But she repeated it. It's part of a rap she does about drugs and bad behavior and you reap what you sow. In essence, if those people at the Tate house had been leading more honorable lives, none of this would have happened to them. She seems not to recognize that she is in no position to be making any kind of moral judgment about the life of the woman she murdered.

I pushed her a bit on her logic: "But Mr. and Mrs. LaBianca didn't take drugs and they were murdered anyway." Instead of reflecting on this, she immediately pointed out that a neighbor of the LaBiancas, but someone they didn't know, did take drugs. In fact, Manson knew him through partying, and he may have selected that neighborhood simply because he was familiar with it.

That day when I was driving back to L.A. from Frontera, I thought about an interview I'd once heard with Robert Jay Lifton, the psychiatrist who has done considerable research on Nazi doctors. He said most of the doctors were candid about the war crimes they committed, but they expressed very little true remorse. He concluded that what they'd done was so horrendous they couldn't come close to truly looking at their guilt. (Lifton said, from that point of view, the experience of interviewing them, while psychologically valuable, was not morally satisfying.)

The conversation with Pat, when she mentioned Abigail Folger's drug use, was a reminder of how difficult it is to peel away layers of guilt and remorse. I was also aware of being deeply disappointed though it took me awhile to understand why. I wanted to see her in the best possible light because I know how hard she's worked on her rehabilitation, and I also know that she's never given any acknowledgment for that when she goes in front of the parole board. The thought that I would write anything that could contribute to the brutal and unfair way she's treated in those sessions is hard to accept.

I think I understand her position on Abigail Folger's drug use, but it doesn't sell well. She has accepted responsibility for her behavior and, in her mind, if she's going to judge herself for her past behavior, she's going to judge everyone. I'm not sure she's capable of the kind of nuanced thinking that would let either herself or her victims off the hook for anything. Her perspective is black and white—just as black and white as the district attorney's. That doesn't mean that I believe there's any reason for her to remain in prison. I don't. She's not a danger to anyone. If we kept people locked up forever because of their psychological shortcomings, no one would ever be released. And I do believe she has found her humanity. She just can't explain it very well.

In my early conversations with her, some of her softest feelings emerged when we talked about Leslie. One day we somehow got onto the topic of legacies. She said Leslie was the only person in the world to whom she would leave whatever possessions she owned. (This conversation took place many years ago.) I've never been able to visit them together, but they talk respectfully of each other and they know each other better than they know anyone else in prison. I believe they have a different circle of friends, both inside and outside the prison.

As far as I know, they have never talked to each other about what happened that night at the LaBiancas'. At first that surprised me, but the more I thought about it, the more it made sense. What, after all, could they say to each other that wouldn't be horrible?

chapter forty-four
THE HOLE-IN-THE-WALL GANG

March 1997

*M*y daughter was home for spring break from college when I decided we should travel to Death Valley to take a look at Barker Ranch, the Manson desert outpost where he was arrested a month after the Tate-LaBianca murders. The ranch held so much significance that it had been designated a national monument. We rented a four-wheel-drive Ford Explorer and took off for the desert.

We slept the first night at the Furnace Creek Lodge. Actually, she slept. I didn't. At 2:00 a.m. I was lying in my bed, my heart pounding. What was my problem? I'd carefully planned the trip. I had maps, many maps, including the forest service topographical map, and I had stocked up on food, water, extra sweaters, and even a blanket. We were only going to the Barker Ranch for the day, but I knew that many people who rent cars to explore unfamiliar deserts end up dead—it's not called Death Valley for nothing—and usually those people had set out unprepared.

Since 1970 when I read Diane Kennedy Pike's account of having to drink her own urine after she and her husband, James Pike, a former Episcopalian bishop, got stranded in the Judean Desert,

I've had a keen interest in being prepared in such circumstances. (The couple set off for a journey in their Avis rental car with only two bottles of Coca-Cola to drink. The car got stuck in a rut. When Bishop Pike was unable to walk with her to get help, she continued without him. He died. She didn't but before she didn't die, she drank her urine.)

But, as I say, we were well prepared and we had four-wheel-drive to deal with the ruts. My panic had little to do with the desert. It had to do with Barker Ranch, which had become a shrine to Manson, attracting all sorts of bikers, survivalists, Satanists, and who-knows-what-ists. Or so I had heard. And Manson still had a couple of crazy women followers from the old days who occasionally threatened people they perceived as his enemies. I knew people occasionally camped there, but otherwise I didn't know what to expect. Why was I going? What could I learn from the place?

But my panic also had to do with my daughter, the very same daughter who had been a newborn infant when I first read *Helter Skelter*. All of the fear I felt then came roaring back—a primitive, almost reptilian fear combined with intense protective instincts.

All I could think of were the ways I had been a bad parent when my kids were young: slapping my son once in the face, leaving a red mark; subjecting my daughter to Mommy and Me swim classes; on a couple of occasions being late picking them up from summer camp. These failings may seem totally unrelated to driving out to Barker Ranch with my college-age daughter, but in those hours before dawn there was hardly anything too trivial in the parenting department for me to dredge up, and by first light I had decided to call off the excursion. It was way too risky.

When my daughter woke up, I announced my decision. Responding in a calm and clinical voice, the kind of voice you use with someone you're trying to coax down from a ledge or a bad acid trip, she said that perhaps my lack of sleep had made me a bit overwrought. She said she wasn't frightened and she didn't think I should be.

So we embarked on our journey, following the homemade wooden signs to Golar Wash, the area where the Ranch was located. It was slow going; the sandy road was arduous, with deep potholes and giant boulders, but we were doing it. We had gone about ten miles when we came to a fork in the road. No signs, hand-painted or otherwise. We studied the maps. We studied the directions. Neither provided a clue.

We got out of the car and I looked up at the rugged Panamint Mountains. In my concerned state, they were casting deep, sinister shadows as the sun seemed to be sinking toward them at an alarming rate. We had just about decided to turn back when a pickup rambled up behind us.

A couple, Joe and Maggie, stopped and got out of their truck. She was a big-boned, freckled thirtyish blonde wearing short cut-off jeans and Frye boots. He was a burly forty-something man with pumped-up muscles and his shiny black hair in a modified mullet. He was short and very sweet and, best of all, because he was a Manson buff and lived in the area, he'd been to Barker Ranch before. He knew which fork to take and invited us to follow. Not only that, his pickup, a fire-engine red, four-by-four, Dodge Ram included an off-road winch on its front bumper, which came in handy when our car did indeed get stuck in a particularly deep rut. We caravanned the ten miles, and whatever fears I'd had the night before were completely erased. I was pretty sure neither of us was going to have to drink our pee that day.

Barker Ranch sits high on a hill at the end of a canyon, with lookouts perfectly situated to spot any strangers coming up the canyon. Those of us of a certain age have all seen many hideouts for hole-in-the-wall gangs like this in Western movies—where scouts were assigned to watch for the U.S. Marshal. Golar Wash is a desert oasis and one of the prettiest I've ever seen. The homestead is surrounded by rocks and boulders and fed by crystalline streams that nourish cottonwood trees. I had not expected it to be beautiful.

I remember feeling this kind of surprise, on a much broader scale, when I visited Rwanda post-genocide. The verdant beauty of the country was disorienting. It seemed utterly impossible that people had been hacked to death with machetes in such lush surroundings.

The Tate-LaBianca murders hadn't taken place at Barker Ranch, but the evil was hatched here. This was where Manson socialized or, rather, de-socialized, his acolytes, stripping them not only of their consciences, but also of their ability to think rationally, and this is where he trained them to be murderers. This is where they, in turn, nurtured him and surrendered their very humanity to him.

The main house was a wood and stone structure and looked to be sturdily built. It was clear that, in the decades since the murders, it had been home to campers passing through and to squatters who stayed awhile. It was generally tidy—the concrete floor swept clean, the tiny assortment of dishes and pots on the shelves appeared to have been washed—and there was a note on the kitchen table asking people to keep it that way. Someone had put a bedspread, pillow, and pillowcase on the single bed.

As the four of us walked around, Joe started taking photos of Maggie in various poses to suggest she lived here—stoking a pretend fire in the stone fireplace; sitting at the kitchen table pretending to read an issue of *Life* magazine with Manson on the cover she'd found on the shelf: December 19, 1969, "The Love and Terror Cult." At one point, she stood at the stove holding a wooden spoon and pretending to stir soup. Maggie in no way resembled Pat, but the little drama she was acting out brought to life domestic scenes Pat had described to me.

We moved on to the bathroom, where a non-functioning toilet had apparently been used anyway, but someone had removed the sink and vanity. The vanity had been Manson's hiding place when the ranch was raided by Inyo County officers two months after the murders. The raid was not connected to the murders but the result of auto thefts, primarily of dune buggies, and of arson fires, which seemed to be motivated by vandalism in and around Death Valley. At the time of the raid, most of the group of seven had been sitting at the kitchen table, but Manson was not among them. When a sheriff's deputy went into the bathroom he noticed long brown hair peeking out of the bathroom vanity. He opened the cupboard door to behold Charles Manson, dressed in fringed buckskin, hiding in the very cramped space.

Outside, there was a stone and concrete structure—either a very small pool or a very large bathtub—that looked to be spring fed when there was enough water to feed it, and nearby, a corroded porcelain bathtub. I wondered if this was the bathtub Leslie had described when she told me one of her jobs was to read the Bible to Manson as he bathed.

After their photo session, Joe and Maggie went to their truck to eat lunch. My daughter and I retrieved our sandwiches from our car and sat down in a couple of wooden folding chairs on the veranda where we had a panoramic view of the little valley. Amidst the sagebrush, there was a scattering of tiny yellow flowers, desert gold, I think, and the leaves on the cottonwoods were a dusky ochre. I again thought about the juxtaposition of the beauty and the grotesque history of the place. But the longer we sat there, the more my focus shifted from the beauty to the isolation, the desolation. And then I knew why I'd come: for the first time I understood the extent of the group's primitive, regressive existence. This was a world unto itself, suspended from temporal, familial, societal considerations. The little oasis was buffered by the rugged primeval and empty terrain of Death Valley, so empty and so rugged it looked like a moonscape and served as a virtual moat. The sky, washed out by the sun, felt higher and more infinitely infinite.

I thought of the *Be Here Now* credo of the '60s. Such a total emphasis on the present is a fine goal if you're practicing mindfulness, but Manson used it to strip away all other influences but his. As both Pat and Leslie report, he banned clocks and he openly chastised (and worse) manifestations of the life led by the young people before they hitched their wagons to his star.

This was exactly what Zimbardo meant when he described what can occur when people are trapped in what he calls "an expanded present moment." "When we stop relying on our sense of past commitments and our sense of future liabilities," he writes in *The Lucifer Effect*, "we open ourselves to situational temptations to engage in Lord of the Flies excesses." He explains that under normal circumstances, when you experience an abusive person, you are able to resist by relying on a temporal perspective that stretches beyond what he calls "present-oriented hedonism." When your behavior is guided by the past, it is informed by your personal values and standards. When your behavior takes the future into account, you automatically engage in what he calls a "cost-benefit analysis," which evaluates your actions in terms of future consequences. Situations where both past and future considerations are obliterated can result in what he calls deindividuation. This, he writes, was responsible for the abuse in Abu Ghraib and in his own faux prison experiments at Stanford. And this, I believe, is what happened under Manson's rule where the goal was to erase all traces of the people his subjects had been.

As we sat eating our lunch, except for the periodic rustling of a squirrel or the plaintive whimper of a quail, there was total silence. The hushed emptiness seemed to blot up everything into itself, even the passage of time.

chapter forty-five
HEAVEN'S GATE

March 1997

That night, on our way to our room after having dinner at the Lodge, we looked up, in wonder, at the sky. Away from the wash of city lights, the stars were dazzling, and though we were exhausted, we didn't want to pass up the chance to take in the be-jeweled sky. We got chairs from the room and brought them down to the lawn. As we tried to identify the constellations we knew, the ones everyone knows, we noticed what looked like a UFO low in the northern sky. I thought it must be a satellite, though I'd seen satellites before and they moved faster; this seemed to be drifting slowly, if it was moving at all. Also, the shape—a bright glowing head trailed by the fanned-out tail—was very un-satel-lite-like. And then we both remembered: on the drive to Death Valley we'd heard on the radio that the comet Hale-Bopp was the closest it would ever be to the earth. And there it was. So many words are thrown around at a time like that and we used them all: magical, astonishing, miraculous, historic, surreal.

The sight of that comet that night in Death Valley struck me as synchronistic, another "sign" connected to the murders. For the life of me now, I can't remember what I thought it was a sign of, other than that perhaps I was a little too immersed in my quest.

Two days later, however, we learned that while our eyes were trained on the comet, a group in Rancho Santa Fe near San Diego had been focused on it for their own eccentric reasons. The members of Heaven's Gate were preparing to be rescued by a spaceship they believed to be traveling behind the comet, a spaceship that would take them to a higher plane of existence. In order to board the spacecraft, they would need to leave their bodies, which they did by eating phenobarbital mixed with applesauce and washing it down with vodka. To ensure asphyxiation, they secured plastic bags over their heads. Each person carried exactly $5.75 in his or her pocket, passports, and all wore Nike "Windrunner" athletic shoes and armband patches reading "Heaven's Gate Away Team." "Our planet earth is about to be recycled," Marshall Applewhite, their leader, explained in a video. "Your only chance to survive or evacuate is to leave with us."

In the days that followed, much was learned about Applewhite and his group. Like Manson, he required his followers to give up their families, their friends, and to renounce all worldly possessions. They were told they must battle spiritually with dark forces known as Luciferians, a label applied to anyone and everyone outside the group. The passports and cash were related to a short story written by Mark Twain in 1907 having to do with travel on the tail of a comet.

What they did was not strictly analogous to what the Manson group did. They didn't kill anyone but themselves. What was similar was the way in which the two men—Manson and Applewhite—were able to get smart, presumably sane people to abandon their values and reject what was familiar and rational. Instead of being delivered to safety in a spacecraft, Manson's tribe would be transported in dune buggies and be saved from the apocalypse, a race war, by retreating to a bottomless pit in Death Valley. When arrested, the group had been actively looking for this pit and were stealing dune buggies because Manson claimed they were

the ideal vehicles for entry into the city housed within the bottomless pit.

It's hard to say which of the exit/entry plans (exiting one reality, entering another) hatched by the two men displayed more lunacy. There is something about the brand specificity of Nike
"Windrunner" athletic shoes that seems, if not comical, then jarring. The imagery involved in Manson's exit/entry plan had a
more artistic touch. He allegedly purchased a "golden" rope that
would be attached to the dune buggies for the purpose of lower-
ing the vehicles into the city in the bottomless pit.

chapter forty-six
A DIFFERENT PAT

1997–2016

In contrast to my visits with her, Pat's letters were consistently filled with warmth and optimism. While she made references to politics, she didn't dwell obsessively and the comments were usually positive. In 2008, she wrote that she was thrilled that Obama was elected and, though our country was in dire straits at the time, she hoped that his election would lift the nation's spirits. She felt blessed to have witnessed his election. "JFK and now Obama."

I always looked forward to her notes during the holidays. No one in my life sends me greetings that are as sweet, non-generic, and sincere. She vividly conjured the aromas, the treats, and the good cheer of the season and good times with family and friends. She always asked about my family. In the years that my daughter worked in Africa with Doctors Without Borders, she never failed to ask me about her, expressing admiration for her work and what the organization accomplishes.

Reading these letters is always bittersweet for me, though. I'm touched by her generosity of spirit, but I can't help feeling sad for her. I remember what she said many years ago about Anne Tyler— that reading her novels always makes her feel the saddest about never having a family. (What she had with Manson was really the only family experience she had as an adult.)

In 2002, she wrote that she had started obedience-training puppies, the ones who would eventually be trained to be service dogs for the disabled. This is an intense program; the inmates spend twenty-four hours a day with the dog during the training period. She wrote glowingly of the puppy she was working with at the time, a golden retriever named Joshua who she described as a sweetheart.

This was a contrast to her attitude later when I got a puppy. At one of our visits I asked her for training tips—by that time she'd been at it for a few years. She offered some basic advice but gone was the enthusiasm she'd expressed in her letters. I don't know what to make of this difference. None of her bitterness or anger came out in her letters. I'm glad that I had this experience to counter the discomfort I felt after our visits, but I'm as puzzled by the contrast today as I was when I first met her.

chapter forty-seven
THE TERROR OF BEING EXCLUDED

*I*n *The Lucifer Effect*, Philip Zimbardo, citing decades of research, details all of the ways that ordinary, average individuals— whether they be soldiers in Guatemala, doctors in Nazi Germany, Hutus in Rwanda—can be stripped of their values, their morality, their souls. After elaborating on the variables that contribute to this process—isolation, drug use, denying people identities—he declares that the most important variable, far and away more important than the others, is the fear of being excluded from the in-group. Manipulating this fear, he asserts, is the most effective way people are transformed from ordinary human beings into human beings capable of evil. We tend to associate the desire for acceptance by the in-group with high school, but according to Zimbardo, this need does not stop at adolescence but continues through adulthood. He cites people's willingness to suffer painful and or humiliating initiation rites in return for acceptance in fra- ternities, cults, social clubs, or the military.

When the desire to be included is coupled with the terror of being excluded, Zimbardo writes that it can cripple initiative, negate personal autonomy, and lead people to do virtually any- thing to avoid rejection. "Authorities can command total obedience not through punishment or rewards but by means of the double-edged weapon: the lure of acceptance coupled with the threat of rejection."

I believe that Manson was a genius at wielding this double-edged weapon.

chapter forty-eight
HATRED MORE POWERFUL
THAN A MOTHER'S LOVE

December 2015

When I first heard about Tashfeen Malik, the young wife and mother who, along with her husband, slaughtered fourteen of his co-workers at the San Bernardino Health Department in December 2015, I wondered about similarities between her story and what I know about Leslie and Pat.

I've discussed in another chapter why I, like most people, are more unsettled when women kill; it is in part, I believe, because we associate that gender with nurturing. Malik was not only a woman, she was, according to early reports, the nursing mother of a six-month-old baby. If killing fourteen people in cold blood is inconsistent with how we view motherhood, abandoning your nursing child while doing so challenges an unfathomable quantity of what we hold dear.

In recent years, with the rise of terrorism, social science researchers have paid increasing attention to young people who are drawn to this kind of violence. Though the research on jihadists is still in its infancy, there is much that sheds light on the dynamics of what was once called the Manson Family.

I've seen only a few photos of Malik; they were all headshots and seemed to reflect only a hint of the woman's true nature. Unlike the first image I saw where she was cloaked in black and her face expressionless, in this one, she's wearing a white hijab and her eyes seem softer. I think I can detect the faintest of smiles, though her expression is mysterious enough it could be something besides a smile. What was I looking for in her face? I was trying to see past my assumption of her rage and heartlessness and the complete disdain for her victims; I was trying to detect some trace of her humanity. It was a painful exercise.

Because what she did was so horrible, it's difficult to imagine this woman as anything but monstrous. That's why words of that nature seem to fit. In the original Tate-LaBianca trial, when Vincent Bugliosi argued in favor of the death penalty for the women and Manson, he had said, "These defendants are not human beings, ladies and gentlemen. . . . These defendants are human monsters, human mutations."

Bugliosi was using those words for effect with the jury, and when I first read *Helter Skelter*, I agreed with his characterization. Those labels are a response to our fear and provide a sense of comfort because they put distance between us and murderers. Those people aren't us. But the labels lead to a dead end when it comes to understanding behavior, and I don't believe we can afford the luxury of dead ends.

What are the similarities between Tashfeen Malik in 2015 and Pat and Leslie in 1969? For one thing, the murders in both cases were not abstract. The suffering they inflicted was palpable. From their own descriptions, we know how physically close Pat and Leslie were to their victims; Malik had to have seen the terror in the eyes in some of those fourteen people who died and the twenty-one who were injured; she had to have seen the blood spatter, the agony. As she aimed her AR-15 assault rifle, witnesses said that unlike her husband who hesitated, she did not.

Pat and Leslie did not know their victims; Malik apparently did not know her victims well but she knew about them. She knew they were welcoming and generous to her family. (There was one exception: one of her husband's co-workers had expressed anti-Muslim feelings, but it's not believed that he was the one who inspired the massacre.) Among the people she killed were people who had given the couple a baby shower and had purchased gifts they'd requested when they registered at Target. She knew her victims were parents and husbands and wives, daughters and sons, brothers and sisters. Given all of that, how was she able to so completely detach herself from their humanity?

Was there something in her history to explain her cruel detachment? If so, it wasn't economic deprivation. As was true of Pat and Leslie and so many of the young people enticed by ISIS, Malik did not come from hardship. She was born into a middle-class family in Pakistan. Her father was a landowner, an engineer, and at some point he moved his family to Saudi Arabia where she attended university, eventually completing a graduate course in a school of pharmacy.

We know that Pat and Leslie, at least in part, were vulnerable to Manson because of their youth and their struggle with identity, but Malik was twenty-seven years old and in a settled life. Her husband made a good living and they owned a condominium. She was a mother. She had in-laws who provided babysitting.

Given the barbaric acts ISIS displays on TV and the Internet, it's reasonable to assume that some kind of pathology is what drives people from comfortable lives in the West into the arms of ISIS. Social science researchers, however, take issue with that assumption; the attraction, they say, is far more complicated. "These young people are not psychopaths," Scott Atran, an anthropologist wrote in the September 4, 2016, issue of the *Guardian,* "but rather everyday young people in social transition, on the margins

of society, or amidst a crisis of identity." He explained that recruits for ISIS from Western countries are in transitional stages in
their lives—between jobs, schools, relationships, countries—and
are looking for new families.

Given their desire to be part of the caliphate, you'd think they'd
be spurred on by traditional religious fervor, but not so. By and
large, most of them are "born again." They are self-seekers who
have found their way to jihad in myriad ways, ways that include a
need for what Atran calls "a sense of power, destiny . . . a giving
over to the ineffable and unknown."

The most surprising aspect of the initial attraction to ISIS is
that for most of these young people, idealism is what prompts the
appeal. They want to be a part of something that enlarges their
lives and makes them more meaningful. And that was certainly
true of Pat and Leslie who say that initially, Charles Manson
stood for peace and love, a beacon of hope in a society torn apart
by disagreements over the war in Vietnam. Even more important,
he offered a family to these girls who were adrift from their own.
This is also true of the young people attracted to ISIS.

Who was Malik's inspiration? His name was Abu Bakr al-
Baghdadi, the ISIS leader to whom she posted her allegiance on
Facebook the day she prepared to slaughter her husband's co-
workers. Al-Baghdadi was, in many ways, Charles Manson writ
large. According to David Ignatious in a June 24, 2015, issue of
The Washington Post, al-Baghdadi was a master opportunist with
gang leader charisma. Like Manson, he was schooled in American prisons. He spent time as a prisoner at Camp Bucca, a U.S.-
run detention facility. Manson claimed the mantle of Jesus Christ;
al-Baghdadi claimed to be a descendant of the prophet Muham-
mad. Like Manson, he was an unexceptional child. He never excelled at religious scholarship but was talented at the recitation of
Quranic verse. In spite of his other limitations, al-Baghdadi was a
genius at exploiting the anarchy in the Middle East, leveraging

his biography, and taking advantage of the far reach of the Internet. Manson, who encouraged the belief that he was the embodiment of Jesus Christ, leveraged his knowledge of scientology, the Bible, and Dale Carnegie to the same effect.

Time magazine called al-Baghdadi "the brooding muezzin of death" because of the way he turned an early affinity for Quranic recitation into a grandiose claim to be the caliph. (Muezzin is a man who calls Muslims to prayer from the tower of a mosque.) Rumors of his death have been reported sporadically since 2014 when the cleric made a public appearance announcing the creation of Isis' so-called caliphate from the Iraqi city of Mosul. In June 2017 Russia claimed to have killed him in an air strike in Syria. As of this writing, the United States has not confirmed his death.

Dead or alive, his ability to attract new followers or keep his existing ones has not diminished; he lives on in perpetuity through videos. Al-Baghdadi, like Manson, is able to inspire such intense support that his fighters seemingly will go anywhere and do anything for the cause, either destroying themselves or others in the process.

One of the researchers who's been studying young jihadists is Dr. Bill Swann, a psychology professor at the University of Texas. In late 2016, I sent him some background on Manson and the former Manson Family, and asked him to compare the techniques employed by Manson and what is being discovered about ISIS leaders today. In a subsequent phone interview he said there were many parallels. Both targeted people whose social identities were deficient in two crucial ways: they lacked closeness with individuals as well as collective ties to a group. The resulting void left them without a sense of worth or competency. This sort of dislocation is problematic for everyone, but according to Swann, the sense of isolation and insignificance is particularly hard on young people.

What Manson provided four decades ago and what al-Baghdadi (or his avatar in videos) serves up today, in its simplest form, is a sense of an all-encompassing family. It's not surprising that Manson could snare vulnerable youth in his trap, he had 24/7 access to his acolytes, but ISIS manages to do the same through the Internet. It's a testament to the power of carefully honed messages sent to targeted populations, but it also points to the power of screens. I find it astonishing that inspiring young people to change their lives so profoundly can be accomplished through computers, iPads, and cell phones, and even more astonishing that such transformations can be sustained remotely.

Swanson calls the experience that results from these recruitment strategies "identity fusion": an exceptional form of alignment in which members experience a visceral sense of oneness with the group. The power it wields is formidable.

chapter forty-nine
THE SHADE TREES OF HOLLYWOOD HIGH

Spring of 1960

When we walked into our first-period class, our Spanish teacher, Mrs. Jimenez, who usually greeted us standing ramrod straight at the blackboard, was slumped at her desk weeping. No conjugating irregular verbs today. "I've been at Hollywood High for twenty years," she said, removing her glasses and dabbing her cheeks with a handkerchief. "Nothing like this has ever happened." Over the weekend shade trees on the quad had been chopped down. The carnage was the result of yet another battle in the ongoing war between the school administration and the social clubs they were attempting to banish.

The administration's first salvo was aimed at the clubs' dominion over the benches in the inner quad. The benches surrounded hundred-year-old pepper trees whose spreading branches provided the only shade to the central part of the campus. There were no signs—DELTAS ONLY or BETAS ONLY—the control was exerted by tradition. Actually, if signs had been posted it would have been less humiliating for new students.

I remember watching a boy wander over to the Athenian bench with his lunch box and sit down. He was a reedy kid with a crew cut and wearing jeans that were a little too short. I remember how skinny he was because I also remember thinking he had selected the worst bench for his introduction to Greek life at Hollywood High. The Athenians were husky, well-muscled football players, guys who had five-o'clock shadows. This boy didn't even have peach fuzz. Both he and I must have gotten out of our third-period class early because at first we were the only ones around. I watched him from an adjacent bench, the bench that "belonged" to my club, Gamma Rho, wondering what to do. Do I walk over there and warn him? I'd be saving him from embarrassment, but I'd also be enforcing the part of club life I knew was wrong.

Though the exclusion at Hollywood High wasn't racial, if I'd been honest with myself, I would have acknowledged that the invisible signs on campus reminded me of the WHITES ONLY signs I was exposed to on my family trip to the segregated South. As I debated what to do, I watched him take out the contents of his lunch box and pictured his mom packing that lunch, chopping the carrots, washing the apple, spreading tuna salad on whole wheat bread, feeling good about sending her son off to school with a nutritious meal. Could she have imagined that there was a system in place that conferred second-class citizenship on him, a system that prevented him from eating that lunch wherever he wanted to?

"You can't be here," a burly Athenian said, walking up to confront him.

The kid looked around. "Why?"

"This bench belongs to my club."

"Where does it say that?"

"It doesn't."

The boy started to reply, "But, I . . ." The enforcer edged closer. The boy shrugged and put the contents back in his lunch box. He looked around, apparently trying to scout another bench on which to alight. The Athenian read his mind: "You can't sit on any of these benches," he said with a sweep of his hand, "unless you're in a club and"—he gave the boy an appraising look—"I don't think you are."

Again, for a moment, the kid seemed like he was going to say something . . . ask a question? Challenge the rule? Ultimately, though, he said nothing and walked away.

Later in the semester, the principal called an assembly to announce an end to the practice. The benches belonged to all students. Excluding non-club members would no longer be tolerated.

Outrage erupted. Club members said the new rule was un-American, unconstitutional, something Communists would do. Nothing changed. Club members continued to eat their lunches under the shade trees, shooing away everyone else. The administration devised a new tactic: one Monday morning when we arrived on campus there were fat white lines painted around each tree. In homeroom that morning it was announced that everyone would have to stay outside the white lines. The benches on the inside of the white lines would now be off limits to everyone.

The clubs continued to commandeer the space by standing along the white lines that defined their former benches. It was inconvenient to eat lunch standing up, but, hell, this was war. For a while, club members got a thrill out of sabotaging the new rule but soon tired of standing for the whole lunch hour. The anger mounted. And then one weekend, a girl I'll call Melody, a budding starlet who landed a starring role on a popular TV show, got together with a couple of her guy friends, one of whom was a freshman at University of Southern California and a recent graduate of Hollywood High where he'd been in a club. Melody was a Delta. Rumor had it that they got drunk and decided to exact revenge. They drove to the school and chopped down trees.

Even before that, Melody had made news in club circles. She had dropped out of the Lambdas to join the Deltas, something heretofore unheard of. Both were top-tier clubs, but the Deltas were at the pinnacle. They were the beauties. The speculation was that the plastic surgery Melody had to repair an alleged broken nose the summer before newly qualified her for the super elite.

When we arrived on campus the next morning, it looked as though a tornado had swept through. As we stepped over the piles of broken limbs —you could no longer see the white lines—even club members were stunned. It felt shockingly violent, the more shocking because a girl was involved.

Had it really been a drunken whim? Did Melody carry around an ax in her car? Or was it planned?

"I feel as though someone has amputated my limbs," Mrs. Jimenez said to the class, hugging herself. "I loved those trees. They were so beautiful."

I don't remember what happened after that. Was Melody arrested? Suspended? What about the white lines? I do remember that the next year Melody starred in the school musical and both her talent and her confidence made it clear she was headed for fame. Maybe her obvious star quality made people forget the damage. It didn't make me forget. I had tried to pretend, if only to myself, that my club membership had not compromised my values, had not compromised me. The destruction of the trees symbolized ugly entitlement. And though my club wasn't directly involved, Melody represented the club culture and I was a part of that culture. I was on the wrong side of this war, a war my father had implored me to be on the right side of.

chapter fifty
FUSED IDENTITIES

*M*ost of us, at some point in our lives, identify, to varying degrees, with a group: girl scouts, fraternities, labor unions, political parties. How is identity fusion different? According to Bill Swann, a professor at University of Texas, allegiance to the group in most associations, even active ones, does not eclipse the self. Fused identity does. (I recall that early in my relationships with Pat and Leslie, they both, independently, said that they had "no self" when they were with Manson.) "You give the group strength and the group gets strength from you," says Swann.

The concept of identity fusion has provided a different way of looking at the dynamics of the Manson Family. So much of my thinking about the women and much of the research on violent group behavior has emphasized the primacy of the leader and the way the situation, as designed by the leader or institution, manipulates and enforces obedience (as it did at Abu Ghraib). More recent research has focused on the relationship between the members of the group and the influence that has on behavior.

Identity fusion may explain one of the most puzzling aspects of the behavior displayed by Pat and Leslie in the aftermath of the Tate-LaBianca murders—the five years it took for them to have any feelings about killing their victims.

I had assumed that the women continued to be disconnected from the reality of their behavior because Manson was still managing to control them even though they were in prison. If, however, identity fusion is as powerful as Swann suggests, it seems just as likely that it was because the three women, Pat, Leslie, and Susan Atkins, continued to reinforce and gather strength from each other at Frontera.

How does fused identity lead to cold-blooded killing? The necessary ingredient for that conversion, according to Swann, is the perception that the group is threatened and that dramatic action is required to defend it. "This completes or amplifies the process of fusion with the group."

Before this step, however, the leader must get them to sever ties with their existing groups, usually families. Swann calls this, "switching worlds." Manson not only discouraged his followers from maintaining contact with their families, he used those relationships as weapons. "I still see your mother in you," he would yell at Leslie if she challenged his dictates or expressed values he considered bourgeois. ISIS, who targets vulnerable young people through various social media outlets, has a similar approach, pressuring recruits to cut off ties with their families and to renounce their countries of origin.

The following is an appeal by Aqsa Mahmood, a British woman living in Syrian territory controlled by ISIS. "The family you get in exchange for leaving the ones behind are like the pearl in comparison to the shell you threw away into the foam of the sea, which is the Ummah [community of believers]." Mahmood is involved in a campaign to urge Western women to abandon their homes and join her there. "The reason for this is because your love for one another is purely for the sake of Allah."

For ISIS, there is no shortage of enemies. Any infidel will do. The formula is simple: people who don't practice the ISIS fundamentalist brand of Islam are infidels. An infidel is an enemy. All enemies must be destroyed.

Swann describes members of these groups as having a "visceral sense of oneness." When I imagine how the Manson Family defended itself from external threats I picture a sea anemone. When you poke it with a stick, the whole organism shrivels in response.

chapter fifty-one
A DROP OF JEWISH BLOOD

Summer of 1961

It was Sunday, family day at Don Lugo, the then minimum security wing of the California Institution for Men where my brother was incarcerated. There were four of us that day: my brother, his girlfriend, Candace, me and my college boyfriend, Craig. We were sitting at a picnic table in a grassy area dotted with ironwood trees and next to a pasture of grazing Holsteins. (My brother always joked that the men were so hard up for females they referred to the herd as "the girls.")

Although that campus is close to the prison where Pat and Leslie are now housed, the methane haze that persistently hovers over them was not there—at least, not in my memory. Instead, when I picture the sky that day, it's a lovely David Hockney blue with a mottled scattering of clouds. I even remember a babbling brook running through the grounds. If there was no babbling brook, the fact that I remember one is a reflection of how idyllic that day seemed. I also picture us eating fried chicken and potato salad served on a red-and-white-checked gingham tablecloth that Candace brought in an old-fashioned wicker picnic hamper.

Is it possible that life was so different then that the prison allowed outside food? Or is this a complete distortion? Maybe because of what came before and immediately after, that day seemed near perfect. Near perfect, or any kind of perfect is not what one normally associates with prison memories, but there was something joyful about that day. The only exception was how uncharacteristically distant my boyfriend was. I passed it off as a hangover. He'd been out late the night before.

My brother was a changed guy since those first days when we talked through the thick glass in the maximum security unit. He was certainly in better shape than he'd been before his arrest when he was using drugs and leading a life of debauchery. I don't actually know if he'd been leading a life of debauchery. That's how my mother referred to it. But he was, by his own admission, taking drugs—most of them, as far as I know, hallucinogens— and he had that pallor and slightly wasted look that people who take drugs and spend a lot of time debauching indoors have.

In prison he was tan and muscled, not from lifting weights but from hard physical labor. He was fighting fires every day—all of Southern California was ablaze, as is usual every summer. He also radiated emotional well-being. This I attributed to therapy. Every evening the inmates at Don Lugo, no matter how fatigued from a day on the fire line, were required to participate in group therapy. The program was experimental, and the guys were hand selected for their intelligence, their attitude, and their promise. As far as I know, it was very successful.

I later wrote a paper on the unique features of Don Lugo for a criminology class at U.C.; I don't now remember the exact stats on recidivism, but I do know that the data looked very good. Don Lugo no longer exists; such programs were not repeated once California took a hard right and decimated budgets for rehabilitation.

(This destruction was not only Ronald Reagan's handiwork; Jerry Brown, in his first two terms as governor, was a criminal justice hardliner. His father, Pat Brown, was the governor during my brother's incarceration. He wasn't exactly progressive but compared to his son, he was the Charles Dickens of California prison reform.)

The warden at Don Lugo was a humane, good-humored guy with a smart, pretty wife who was equally good humored and humane. They were an energetic couple who lived on the grounds with their young children. With them at the helm, Don Lugo felt like a family.

There was another reason my brother glowed. He was in love. A few months after he was sentenced, Candace, who'd been his junior high school girlfriend, called my parents to say hello. When they told her what had happened to my brother, she wept and then she asked when she could see him. She was an almond-eyed beauty whose loyalty and girlish sweetness was irresistible to him. People laugh when I say this, but prison relationships have all of the ingredients of a perfect romance: intensity, thwarted sexuality, idealization, and singularity of focus. One of the most joyful magazine articles I wrote as a young journalist was "Wedding Day at San Quentin" for *California Living*, the Sunday magazine of the *San Francisco Examiner*.

While in prison, my brother turned into the person he was meant to be. (This is a version of something I've heard Leslie say about her transformation, once she had rid herself of Manson's influence.) I believed, though I never said this to him or to my parents, that getting arrested saved his life. Before that, his behavior was increasingly reckless, and he'd picked up unsavory companions along the way.

We laughed a lot that day. I know because for some reason I brought along a tape recorder. My brother and I reminisced about growing up in Hollywood in the 1950s. Candace joined in with her own version; Craig, who grew up in Ontario, was our audience. He was taken by the mythology of Hollywood High, and once he discovered that was my alma mater, he pressed for information about the celebrities I knew, despite the fact that they were mostly of the B-list variety.

That day, my brother and I compared notes. I had more on my side of the ledger, but in terms of star power, he won the competition. On my list: Linda Evans, Stefani Powers, Tuesday Weld, Yvette Mimieux, various Mouseketeers. On my brother's list: Ricky Nelson and Mike Farrell (of *M.A.S.H.*).

Candace had a list, too, but the people on it were less well-known in mainstream culture. Her mother was a delicate blonde beauty who supported her two children working as a dancer. One day, a well-known bookie and a member of the L.A. Jewish Mafia walked into the club on the Sunset Strip where she was working. He fell in love and the two subsequently got married. (Relationships with exotic gentile dancers was a tradition with his Jewish Mafia compatriots—Mickey Cohen, for example, had well-publicized relationships with Tempest Storm and Candy Barr—both big names in the world of burlesque.) The career wasn't a good fit for Candace's mother. After she married Max, she got out of the business.

While my parents liked Candace, her involvement with my brother had a serious complication. Max was on the list of mobsters my father's IRS team had targeted. He thought he could avoid awkwardness by assigning one of his guys to investigate. It wasn't so easy. At one point, Max pressured Candace to call my father to ask if he would intercede on his behalf. Clearly Max didn't know anything about my father who must have erected some kind of Chinese wall to avoid a conflict of interest. It all had a happy ending: Max had very good lawyers who kept him out of prison. By the time my brother was released from prison and he and Candace got married, my father had retired so both sets of parents were able to attend the wedding. My father and Max actually liked each other and eventually became friends.

As I say, the only thing to mar that day at Don Lugo was Craig's apparent detachment. It wasn't until I listened to the tape that night that I realized that his distance from me, from all of us, wasn't short, it was planetary.

Craig and I had a date to meet for dinner the next night in Los Angeles at *El Cholo*. It was one of my old favorites and he'd never been there. I arrived a little late and he was already seated. Before he noticed me, I stood to the side, watching him for a minute. He was holding up the large menu displaying every combination imaginable, but his eyes looked unfocused. I remember, I will always remember, the pained look on his face. It was memorable but, at that moment, not decipherable—as mysterious as the Mona Lisa . . . except there was no smile. Annoyance? Anger? Guilt? And then I knew: *I'm about to get dumped.*

I'd been half-expecting this outcome since the first time he asked me out. By every measure, he was out of my league—way out. For one thing, he was a striking physical specimen. When we met I was studying somatypes in Psychology 1A. He was a classic mesomorph: athletic, well-developed musculature, rugged, and perfect posture. He hewed so strictly to type that it looked as though he had posed for the sketch of the mesomorph in my textbook. (After I'd seen his body unclothed, the sketch in my textbook was, in my mind, replaced by Rodin's *Thinker.*)

Craig had a lot of other boxes checked. He was ambitious, smart, and disciplined—so disciplined that during Finals Week, while I and everyone else I knew were pulling all-nighters cramming for tests, he was so up-to-date with his classwork, he spent the week reading novels. Even more appealing, unlike the other guys I had dated, he had a self-made quality. His family was blue collar and in no financial position to put three kids through college. Starting in high school, Craig worked as a bricklayer in the summers and was supporting himself.

He had political ambitions and made almost every decision based on what he believed would serve that purpose. He'd been offered a scholarship at an Ivy League school but chose to go to

Cal because he figured that when he ran for governor of California, he would have more contacts in the state. Governor would be a stepping-stone to running for president. I believed in him and his ambition so much, I had no doubt that he would some day be president. He decided to live in the dorms rather than join a fraternity. His plan was to live in a different dorm every semester so he could maximize the number of contacts he could make. Looking back on it now, some of this seems creepy, but at the time John F. Kennedy's presidency gave these Machiavellian plans a certain credibility, at least to me.

I knew who he was before he knew who I was. He was running for some kind of campus-wide office, and I'd seen his campaign poster on the bulletin board in the dining hall. I didn't just see it, one night when I was walking back to my dorm room and there was no one around, I stole the glossy black-and-white headshot and stuck it in my notebook. When I got to my room, I hid it in my underwear drawer. A few days later my roommate discovered it when she was looking for a scarf to borrow. She never stopped talking about it.

One night at a Valentine's dance, a "social" between my dorm and Craig's dorm, I found myself standing alone by the punch bowl watching my roommate do the twist with a guy she'd met the night before at the library. I never met anyone in the library. As I drank my punch watching couples gyrating to Chubby Checker and feeling invisible, I thought I might as well have stayed in junior high. I tossed my plastic glass in the trash bin and started walking toward the elevator to go back to my room. I heard, "Hey, don't leave." I turned around and saw Craig. He was extending his hand out to me. "Come dance with me."

That was in February. By the end of that semester in June, we had spent part of every day with each other in Berkeley, but we'd be apart for the summer. He was living at home with his parents in Ontario working at his job at the local brickyard. I was living with my parents at their beach house in Santa Monica and taking summer classes at Santa Monica City College.

Since his parents lived so close to the prison—Ontario is only a few miles from Chino—I invited him to meet me there on a Sunday so I could introduce him to my brother. They hit it off. He said, "I've met your family. It's time for you to meet mine." He suggested I come for Sunday brunch the following week before going to the prison. We agreed to withhold the information about my brother until his parents had a chance to get to know me.

As soon as I saw the home he grew up in, a snug craftsman bungalow, I knew I would like his family. It had the kind of front porch I had always wanted with an old-fashioned glider and a well-worn overstuffed couch. The stucco exterior was powder blue with white trim and, of course, the lawn was bordered with a white picket fence.

His dad worked in a factory; his mom was a homemaker. They were proud of their kids—all three of whom worked to put themselves through college. That wasn't unusual. What was unusual, in my experience, was that they weren't threatened when their kids talked about issues with which they weren't familiar: art, literature, philosophy. At breakfast, when Craig and his sister got in an extended argument about Nietzsche, they observed it like a tennis match, the scoring of which they didn't quite understand but nonetheless enjoyed.

Both of Craig's siblings were getting married that summer—his sister's wedding was in three weeks; his brother's in six weeks. While passing platters of pancakes and sausages, there was a lot of wedding talk.

The next day Craig called me. "They loved you."

The next week I got an invitation in the mail to his sister's wedding. Two weeks later, I received one to his brother's wedding.

I was excited about the invitations. My mother was, too. She said she wanted to take me shopping at the Broadway Hollywood for dresses. We hadn't shopped together since high school—it always led to conflict—but she insisted. I was mixed about her enthusiasm. Sometimes she was embarrassingly pleased about whatever popularity I managed to garner and would bring it up with people who were neither impressed nor interested. The shopping foray went surprisingly well, except for a little skirmish in the beginning. She said I only needed one dress. I said I needed two; clearly some of the same people would be at both weddings. She said since they were six weeks apart, no one would remember. I told her they would. We agreed that I would pay for one dress out of my savings from waitressing. She would pay for the other.

I loved the dresses we found— cotton sundresses that could be dressed up with strappy high-heeled sandals. We had lunch afterward at the Pig'n Whistle a few blocks up Hollywood Boulevard from the Broadway. Before I hit puberty and started challenging my mother at every turn, this had been our tradition. In those days the restaurant had a special kid's menu—a pig mask—and provided crayons. After lunch we walked farther up Hollywood Boulevard to Grauman's Chinese Theatre and strolled through the forecourt where there are imprints of the hands, feet, and signatures of movie stars. When I was a kid my favorite had been Roy Roger's horse Trigger's hoofprints. Later I was more partial to Betty Grable's legs. And then we went next door for another mother-daughter tradition—sharing a hot fudge sundae at C.C. Brown's. I was happy that day. We both were.

The following week Craig's parents were going to visit a relative in one of the L.A. suburbs, I think it was Monterey Park, and they invited me to meet them at an over-the-top Polynesian-themed restaurant—exotic drinks in coconut shells, water falls, jungle trails. I loved it. At one point, after taking a few sips of Craig's rum drink (he was twenty-one, I was not), I vowed that if I ever had kids, I'd bring them there.

The night before I had talked Craig into allowing me to tell his parents about my brother. I worried that when they finally found out that I'd been visiting him during those weeks Craig was home, they would be distrustful of me forever. But I realized that the jungle setting with the attendant monkey and waterfall sounds would not be conducive to a serious heart-to-heart.

At dinner I told his mom about the dresses my mother and I had bought to wear to the weddings. "Oh, no," she said. "That must have been expensive. Can you return them?"

I was confused. Why would I want to return them?

"I don't think so. We got them on sale."

She put her hand on my arm and told me she would love to make them for me. "I'm finished making the bridesmaids' dresses for my daughter's wedding."

All of them?

She smiled. "There are only five."

"She's a master seamstress," her husband said.

"Oh, no, I'm not. I'm a good seamstress . . . by no means a master."

She asked again about whether I could return the dresses. I shook my head.

"I'm pretty sure I can't."

"That's okay," she said. "Next time." I wasn't sure what next time meant. Neither did Craig or his father.

"Are you trying to marry off our Craig?" his father asked, slapping his son on the back. We all laughed.

When I described Craig's parents to my mother—their house, their kids, their warmth, their generosity—she said, "Salt of the earth?"

I told her I thought that she and my father would like them, though I wasn't sure they'd find a lot to talk about. "They're Democrats. They voted for JFK."

All was not so rosy that day at El Cholo. When I sat down, I saw that Craig's face looked even more pained up close. I took what practitioners of yoga call a cleansing breath, but it had little effect on the fluttering in my chest. I started to talk and I kept talking, emitting a stream of words from my mouth . . . no, not a stream, a fire hose. In some lunatic way I thought that if I kept talking he couldn't break up with me or maybe it would give him time to change his mind. I told him about El Cholo's green tamales. How they were only available that time of year. I told him that I had eaten there regularly with my best friend's family and how we went there after Mass on Sundays. I pointed out celebrities on the wall. "Let's see, I think there's a photo of Bing Crosby, Gary Cooper . . . oh, there's Jack Nicholson." I walked over and pointed to Jack's photo. I said I was sure there was a photo of Frank Sinatra. I said that restaurant had been there so long, there were probably photos from silent pictures. I said I was sure I'd seen a photo of Charlie Chaplin and his daughter.

I was still standing up near the wall when he blurted: "You can't come to my sister's wedding." The fluttering had migrated from my chest to my gut. I sat down at the table.

"You want to bring someone else?" I remembered that he had a high school girlfriend in Ontario. I felt tears forming.

"No," he said. His tone was gruff. He sounded angry. "I don't know how to tell you this. It's my parents—"

"I thought they liked me. You said—"

"They do . . . I mean they did—"

"Oh, you told them about my brother—"

"No. I never got that far."

I had run out of steam. I was utterly confused, but I had no more energy to divert whatever was about to come my way.

"It's because you're Jewish."

This seemed so crazy that it occurred to me that he was just using it as an excuse. He wanted to break up with me for the reason I feared. It was general: I was not in his league and he finally realized it. Or it was specific: he met someone new. And then there was the old girlfriend. I'd seen a photo. She was beautiful . . . a blonde, with a creamy complexion and huge blue eyes. Hitler would have swooned. And then I remembered the hybrid thing, *mischling*. It seemed nauseatingly disloyal, but I couldn't stop myself from asking if his parents knew the degree of my Jewishness.

"Yes, they do, and it makes no difference." He shook his head. "They said terrible things about Jews and how it doesn't matter to them how diluted it is. A drop of Jewish blood is the same as a gallon of Jewish blood except they didn't use the word 'Jewish.' And they certainly don't want grandchildren with tainted blood."

The flutter was now in my head, making me dizzy. I was having trouble imagining the conversation. How could these people, people who apparently used the word "kike" or its first cousin, be the same warm, generous . . . salt of the earth folks with a glider on their front porch?

"How did it even come up?"

"Last night on the drive home my mother asked me about your religion. I hedged a little but finally said I thought you were an atheist. They didn't like that much, but that was nothing compared to what came next.

"'She's a Jew!' My mother said it accusingly, like, 'She's a murderer!' She had such an ugly look on her face. I wanted to throw up."

The waitress came over to take our orders, but Craig told her to come back later. Much later. We were both quiet. Finally, I said, "How could you not have known they hated Jews this much?"

He shrugged. "I guess I didn't want to know. Or I did know but we haven't had conversations about that sort of thing for a long time. When I was in high school we fought about Negroes who they dislike even more than they do Jews. I wanted to ask a Negro girl to a dance and they flipped out. They said that as long as I lived under their roof, I would have to abide by their rules. Maybe we fought so much about Negroes, I forgot about the Jews. Or maybe I was hoping they had changed."

We never ordered. Neither of us felt like eating. He walked me to my car, actually to my mother's car. She'd recently bought a VW Bug.

"I thought your mother hated German cars." I had told Craig about our contentious trip to Europe. Thinking about the trip and the new VW suddenly lightened my mood.

"You see, people can change," I said, kissing his cheek. "My mother loves this car. Maybe your parents will change . . . maybe they'll change before your brother's wedding and I won't have to try and return two dresses. Just one."

chapter fifty-two
A MAKE-BELIEVE DODGE

1968–1969

Spahn Ranch, the group's second outpost, was in the northern part of L.A.'s San Fernando Valley, and though it wasn't as remote as Barker Ranch in Death Valley, according to Pat and Leslie, it, too, felt like a separate reality. It was surrounded by steep, bouldered foothills, and the property had its own creek and waterfalls, which fed a crystal-clear swimming hole. To the kids in Manson's tribe, most of whom grew up watching *Gunsmoke*, the town was the perfect setting for a make-believe world. The ramshackle buildings, once used for cowboy movies and TV shows, may have been falling down and covered with dust, but they were intact enough to serve as a make-believe Dodge. Just as in Dodge, there was a rickety boardwalk that ran along Main Street—the first building was the Rock City Café and the Long Horn Saloon, which had a jukebox. Down the boardwalk farther there was a jailhouse, a funeral parlor, and a carriage house full of old stagecoaches.

The exteriors were make-believe as were the identities of the people inside. Manson orchestrated the shedding of former identities through role-playing and costumes. There was a huge pile of dress-up clothes for that purpose. Every day, a new costume. Every day, a new identity. According to Leslie, there was a different theme every day: one day they all dressed as cowboys, the next as pirates, the following day as gypsies. It was a never-ending Halloween party . . . playtime, but playtime with an agenda.

Zimbardo calls this peeling away of former identities the "Mardi Gras effect." Mardi Gras, he writes, was originally a pagan ceremony and was incorporated by the Romans along with Christianity. In practice, Mardi Gras celebrates the excess of pleasure-seeking, living for the moment. Responsibilities are tossed aside while participants indulge their sensual nature in communal revelries. There's a reason this period of loosened constraints comes right before Lent when there will be a relatively tight lid on pleasure. Mardi Gras, which he calls "deindividuation in group action." involves temporarily giving up limits on personal behavior without concern for consequences.

Manson promoted an ongoing Mardi Gras, leading the way by constantly changing the style of his clothing, his beard, the length of his hair, and even his personality, alternating between slow-paced and soft-spoken to boisterous and wired. His unpredictability kept everyone on edge but also gave them permission to try out new personas; in addition to changing appearances, everyone adopted aliases. Leslie was LuLu, Pat was Katie, Susan was Sadie, Catherine was Gypsy. A new costume, a new name, a new identity—all of it helped to shed inhibitions and old values acquired from parents, church, teachers. Smoking weed and dropping acid also played a part.

The system was patriarchal: Manson was the boss; men like Tex Watson were his top deputies; women were subservient and their roles rigidly structured. The "backstreet" girls, the women Manson deemed less attractive, were assigned to care and maintenance. "Front street" girls were more attractive and used as bait to lure new male recruits into the fold. But that didn't mean they had more standing in the hierarchy. Pat, who functioned as a surrogate mother, managing meals, laundry, and child care, was, according to Leslie, at the very top. "I don't think Pat ever recognized how much status she had among the women. I, for one, worshipped her."

Leslie said that when she found out that Pat had gone to the Tate house that first night, it gave legitimacy to Manson's "Helter Skelter" plan. "It had a huge influence on me," she said. "That doesn't mean that I blame her for my actions, I don't. It's only to describe how influential she was in the group." (For an explanation of Manson's "Helter Skelter" scheme see chapter 13.)

Pat's view is a little different. She knows that she provided support and comfort to the other women and feels guilty about it because she was responsible for some of them sticking around. But she was unaware of Leslie's adulation and didn't realize that her actions the first night inspired Leslie to go the second night. She said her focus was on keeping her head down to avoid Manson's wrath.

Manson intuitively knew how to manipulate their anxiety about their place in the hierarchy, keeping them constantly off-balance. With one hand he conferred status; with the other he took it away. Pat may have been the designated surrogate mother, but when she made mistakes—a shirt crease in the wrong place, the soup too cold, the lemonade too warm, his dinner not warm enough—he would berate her mercilessly, claiming that if she really loved him, she would take care of his needs properly.

The very qualities that earned Leslie the "front street" designation—her coltish beauty, her good breeding, her solid middle-class background—also earned her Manson's scorn. At first it was subtle. He never called her by name, only "whatshername." Eventually, whatshername became "stupid," and then he started savagely criticizing her for questioning his philosophy or any of the increasing number of rules. "There you go again," he'd say. "That question is just another example of your parents . . . you haven't gotten rid of them yet."

This left Leslie longing to be on the inside with the ones who were close to Charlie. According to Leslie, Manson held up a girl named Dianne Lake (nickname Snake) as a role model. When she was a little girl, her parents had joined a commune where she was introduced to group sex and LSD. When she joined Manson at the age of thirteen, it was with her parents' approval. He said she was the ideal: an empty vessel. "She was very young and we were all jealous of her," Leslie said. Eventually, however, even Dianne Lake wasn't submissive enough for him. One day when he was angry at her, he hit her over the head with a chair and kicked her across the room.

In *The Lucifer Effect*, Zimbardo contends that almost any individual is capable, depending on the circumstances, of being transformed from an ordinary person to someone capable of committing horrendous acts. "That knowledge does not excuse evil: rather it democratizes it, sharing its blame among ordinary actors rather than declaring it the province only of deviants and despots—of Them, but not Us."

Zimbardo reviews case after case of these kinds of situations worldwide. In a study of torturers in Brazil, torturers and death squad executioners were not unusual or deviant in any way prior to practicing their new roles, nor were there any persisting pathologies among any of them in the years following their work as torturers and executioners. Their transformation was caused by a combination of factors: intense camaraderie, indoctrination around ideas of national security, and the whipping up of anger that socialists and communists were enemies of their state.

Their actions were entirely explainable as being the consequence of a number of situational and systemic factors, such as the training they were given to play this new role; their group camaraderie.

Since 1971 when Zimbardo conducted the Stanford Prison Experiment, numerous studies have been done that demonstrate to what an alarming degree anonymity diminishes accountability. Perhaps that's not surprising, but what is surprising is how quickly it can happen.

While I believe that Pat and Leslie were subjected to extremely manipulative techniques, it's still astonishing that the socialization of a lifetime was stripped away in a few months and that it took more than five years for their basic humanity to re-emerge.

chapter fifty-three
"A Damn Good Whacking"

1968–1969

*M*anson gradually, if somewhat chaotically, created threats from several quarters. He became expert at inciting anger in the group on his behalf; his supply of enemies wasn't quite as vast as those ISIS has in its inventory, but, while he couldn't go wide, he went deep; he drew from a reservoir of his own anger and transferred it to Tex and the women. The source of the anger included:

- *Manson's dreadful childhood.* His stories of abuse and neglect by parents drew on the women's sympathy for him and stimulated anger at society; eventually that anger generalized and was used to justify murdering the Tate-LaBianca victims who represented middle-class society.
- *Manson's fixation on getting a deal with a record company.* He was a mediocre talent at best, but his hopes were inflated when Dennis Wilson of The Beach Boys and Terry Melcher (Doris Day's son) hung out with him. Melcher ultimately declined to produce a record. To save face, Manson lied and told the members of the group that he had made a deal and Melcher reneged. His humiliation was converted to anger at Dennis Wilson and Terry

Melcher. That anger, which his followers absorbed, consumed him.

- *The convoluted mess that was "Helter Skelter" and the race war.* According to the book *Helter Skelter*, this delusion of Manson's was based on a blend of messages he gleaned from the Beatles' *White Album* and the New Testament and fueled by the racial tensions that existed in the late 1960s. When the *White Album* was released, he gathered the family around and made them listen to it over and over and over. Each song had prophetic significance and provided a musical road map to the future. "Piggies" described the disgusting sense of entitlement enjoyed by the rich and powerful and concluded that the rich and powerful needed a "damn good whacking." "Blackbird" predicted an uprising by the downtrodden blacks—"this was the moment for them to arise"—"Revolution" was a call to arms. "Helter Skelter" was the name for the chaos to come.

Manson was a disciple of Dale Carnegie, and by using his techniques, he got the group to take ownership of the words of the *White Album*. He convinced them that it was not only a call to arms to the entire world, it was specifically directed toward Manson and the Family. He was convinced also that the Beatles would become followers of his. Mixed in there were prophesies from the New Testament—further proof that all of this was divine intervention.

The Family was collecting dune buggies that would provide them with transport to the bottomless pit in the desert; they would hide out in said bottomless pit until called upon by the victorious blacks to govern.

It was never entirely clear when the race war would start, but in the process of selling drugs to accumulate money for the dune buggies, Manson killed a black drug dealer. After that he was convinced and convinced his followers that the Black Panthers were after them. They started amassing weapons along with the dune buggies. Charlie told them that anyone who defected would either be slaughtered in the racial cataclysm or they would be made into slaves serving black masters. Their choice was to be a slave or a ruler.

In Swann's terms, identity fusion coalesced around two beliefs: members of the Family were the most special people on earth; Manson must always be obeyed. And then there were his mumbo jumbo proclamations. He constantly reminded them that all things are the same: love and hate, sanctity and sin, life and death. The Family was meant to rule the earth. After "Helter Skelter," they would reign benevolently and the world would become a far better place, so they had to do whatever was necessary to bring about that era. If it meant killing, so be it. It would not be murder, because the spirit was what counted; you didn't kill anyone's spirit . . . you just sent it to a different place. These were acceptable sacrifices to the eventual greater good.

According to Swann, once an individual's identity has fused with the group, it becomes important to parade the extent of that commitment. "I'll do more for my group than any other group members would do."

October 2016

I once asked Leslie about her reaction when Manson showed up in court with a swastika carved on his forehead. (Originally he had carved an X on his forehead to symbolize his removal from society.) Leslie (along with Pat and Susan) followed suit and seared an X on her forehead with a hot bobby pin. After getting to know Leslie's mother and learning about her upbringing, I wondered what her reaction was to that symbol. It may seem like a trivial question, given that she was being tried at the time for murdering two innocent people. That, too, was against the values her mother had instilled. But to anyone growing up so soon after World War II, the swastika was a powerful and jarring symbol. This man had been a Christ-like figure to her and now he was claiming allegiance to Hitler. How did that square with what she knew about him?

When I asked her about it, she told me she was stunned when she saw him with the swastika on his forehead. She questioned him and he told her it was some kind of Native American symbol. "As usual he was telling me one thing and meaning something else." She doesn't remember anti-Semitic talk before that . . . that language seemed to come with the trial. "When he told me it was a Native American symbol, I held on to that. I saw the media's reaction as yet another example of how he was being misunderstood and persecuted."

chapter fifty-five
YES, SHE WOULD KILL FOR HIM

August 10, 1969, Spahn Ranch

Something big had happened the night before. Leslie didn't know exactly what it was, but she knew it was part of Manson's "Helter Skelter" plan. She concluded from the comments she'd overheard in the morning that unlike previous outings, this one had not been a trial run. In the past they had conducted what they called "creepy crawlies." They would all dress in black and break into people's houses as dress rehearsals. The point was not to be detected. On the previous night's venture, confrontation was the point. She was pretty sure people had died. She knew Pat had been included, along with two others of Charlie's inner circle: Tex and Susan.

Leslie felt terrible at being left out. The fact that Linda Kasabian, a new member of the group, was invited along as the driver was salt in the wound. Mid-morning, Leslie met Charlie on the boardwalk and he stopped her and asked, "Do you believe enough in what I say and who I am to kill?"

She did not hesitate. Yes, she believed in him and yes, she would kill for him. She was desperate for his approval. She would do anything for his approval. She wanted him to know she would be obedient. A good soldier. That she was ready to lay her life on the line for him. She didn't know what the assignment would be. She didn't care. She would do what she was told to do. She would try to live up to Charlie's selection of her. She was, at last, on the inside. She was happy.

chapter fifty-six
INSATIABLE AND WARPED NEED FOR LOVE

From the outset of this inquiry, after meeting Pat and Leslie, I was looking for what I call my "Priscilla Phillips" moment. Because I have often written about subcultures, as well as individuals behaving aberrantly, I've always found it essential to find something in my life that corresponded—no matter how remotely—to the experience of my subjects. The first in-depth magazine article I wrote as a rookie reporter was about a social worker named Priscilla Phillips, a woman who was convicted of intentionally killing her three-year-old daughter by surreptitiously spiking her baby formula with baking soda. The baking soda caused a deadly imbalance in the child's electrolytes and required extended hospitalizations. The little girl was subjected to countless tests, including exploratory surgery, in which surgeons opened up her weakened little body from stem to stern. These repeated assaults accumulated and eventually killed the child.

During the trial, in an effort to establish a motive, the prosecutor's expert psychiatric witness testified that it was a case of Munchausen Syndrome by Proxy—in essence, Priscilla was a mother who made her kid sick in order to garner attention and sympathy for herself. (This was Martin Blinder, the same psychiatrist who devised the "Twinkie defense" for Dan White.)

At the time, my own daughter was three, the same age as Priscilla's when she killed her. One rainy afternoon, stumped and desperate to take a break from my deadline, I escaped from my office that was littered with half-empty coffee cups and crumpled false starts and repaired to the living room to spend time with my daughter. She wanted to dance. She wanted to dance to The Beatles. I put on the *White Album* and watched her dance to "Ob-La-Di, Ob-La-Da" in that unfettered way toddlers dance. I wept. How on earth could a mother want to end the life of such a joyful little creature? I knew I wouldn't be able to write the article if I couldn't tap into the motivation, and I didn't buy the prosecution's theory. (I could understand killing a child impulsively—out of anger, sleep deprivation, frustration—but systematic poisoning?)

And then I remembered the relationship I had with my childhood dog. When I was around six, I started gratuitously scolding her. Randomly and without provocation, I'd shake my finger and say, "Bad girl, bad girl." She'd put her tail between her legs and slump into the corner. Then I would tell her that she was a good girl, a very good girl. She was so relieved that she was forgiven for her non-existent crime, she'd wag her tail furiously and lick my face. (Even now I feel ill when I think about it.)

And then I understood: Priscilla Phillips didn't want to kill her kid, she wanted to make her sick because of her insatiable and warped need for love, for the little girl to cling to her, to be totally dependent on her. I could have been wrong, I don't think I was, but establishing that link to my life experience helped me write the article. Her behavior was still demonic, but I could see it in a human context. Hard as I tried, even after living with this material for years, I could find no such entry point to either Leslie's or Pat's violent behavior. The "Priscilla Phillips" moment continued to elude me, and I realized that I would have to settle for other ways of understanding the women.

chapter fifty-seven
THE ULTIMATUM

Summer of 1961

I left El Cholo and returned to my parents' house in Santa Monica where I told them what happened with Craig's parents. They were as shocked as I had been. We talked and talked and talked until we couldn't talk anymore. Since there wasn't much we could do, eventually talking seemed pointless.

I got up early to take a walk. My first stop was at Pacific Ocean Park, the amusement pier. When I was in high school my dream was to have a summer job there. I applied many times, and on every application I wrote that I'd be willing to take any assignment—even work at the cotton candy counter in spite of the fact that you got spun sugar in your hair, on your eyebrows, and on the fine hairs of your arm. I was never hired.

When I got to the Senior Center on the Venice Beach walk, I felt a rush of affection for the old Jews clustered around the benches and picnic tables playing chess and mah-jongg even at that early hour. The women all looked like versions of my grandmother—leathery faces, wispy gray hair, and babushkas. No matter the season, they all wore threadbare wool coats and carried around shopping bags, and they all looked as though they'd just walked off the steerage compartment of the boat, chicken feathers from the shtetl still in their hair.

They had come in waves, the first in the late 1800s fleeing the sadistic boots of the Cossacks; in the second wave, fleeing the sadistic boots of the Nazis. It was agonizing that they were being forced to flee again, this time by work boots of the construction companies hired by developers who were beginning to tear down the single-occupancy hotels, the only places they could afford to live. The vision the developers had—high-end, high-rise apartment buildings—prevailed and destroyed that community.

When I was younger and walked there with my mother, she always stopped to speak Yiddish to the women, and invariably one or more of them would pinch my cheek until it hurt. *Shayna maidel* (pretty girl) one would say as my mother looked on admiringly. As a kid, I didn't like those pinches on my cheek but today I felt affection for this ragtag remnant of my grandmother's tribe. I also felt a flash of anger. I thought about Craig's parents. How dare they? Maybe they were too young to know about pogroms, or Cossacks, but surely they knew what came later. They knew about Hitler. Craig's father served in the military in World War II. Why would I want to have anything to do with them? Why would I want to attend those goddamn weddings? Why would I want to be involved with their perfect specimen of an Aryan son?

I cut over to the beach. My eyes fixed on a schooner with a billowing red spinnaker tacking close to shore. The horizon was without the usual ribbon of tawny haze—it was so clear I could see the tip of Catalina Island. I followed the shore's scalloped edge to a small jetty, and then I turned back to the beach walk where I stopped at the storefront synagogue. The first summer my parents lived at the beach (they bought the house when I was in junior high and used it as a summer cottage until they retired and moved there permanently), my father was jogging on a Saturday morning when an old rabbi motioned him to stop.

"Please," he said in a thick Yiddish accent and motioned for him to follow. He pointed to the light switch. "Would you turn it on for me?" My father looked at the rabbi's hands to see if they were wet, or dirty, injured or in some condition that would preclude such a straightforward task. My father shrugged, flipped the switch, and was on his way. When he got home and told my mother about the incident, she laughed. "You were his *Shabbos goy*," she said, explaining that it's a gentile who performs work that Jews are forbidden to do on the Sabbath, such as turning on electricity. She kissed him. "You did your part for my people." This story became part of our family lore.

I stopped at a hamburger stand, bought a bad cup of coffee (no Starbucks in those days) and headed back to our house. When I got there I discovered that my parents had a guest for breakfast: Craig. I was worried that this was one of my mother's interfering maneuvers. "What are you doing here?" I asked, trying unsuccessfully to get the accusation out of my voice.

He said he had called to talk to me, and my parents had invited him to come for breakfast. Clearly I couldn't rule out my mother's intrusion. After breakfast, I helped my mother clear the dishes, and in the kitchen I asked her what they talked about before I got there.

"Not much. He said he loves you and he wanted us to know that he hated what his parents are doing. It did make me feel better that he wanted to distance himself from them," she said. She came a little closer to me and swept my bangs away from my forehead.

"Don't," I said, recoiling. This bob-and-weave maneuver between us had been going on my whole life.

"But you're so pretty. I want people to see your face."

"But I don't," I said, pushing my bangs back across my forehead. "Mom, I'm not a baby," sounding very much like one. "I'm in college. I'm allowed to wear my hair the way I want."

Craig brought some dishes into the kitchen and asked if I would take a walk with him on the beach.

As we walked toward the water, he put his arm around me. I pointed out Catalina. The wind was up and there were white caps and several sailboats tacking parallel to the shore. When we got to the water, we turned north toward the Santa Monica Pier. We turned back when we got to the pier. When we got to lifeguard station 25, the one that marks the place where we turn to go to my house, he asked me if I minded if we sat for a bit. We climbed up to the platform and watched the sailboats.

"I didn't tell you this last night. I couldn't bear to. But the situation is even worse than I said."

"What could be worse? They want to hire someone named Carmine to kill me?"

He smiled, but only faintly. "Well, that would be worse. As it is, what they said is pretty shitty for me, for us." His voice wobbled when he said this.

"My mother said they had raised me to have good values and they expected me to honor their wishes. My father was there but he let my mom do the dirty work. She said, 'What happens is completely up to you. You know we love you, but you can't be with that girl.'

"And I said, 'what are you threatening? That you'll disinherit me?' It was mean for me to say it. God knows they don't have much to leave . . . especially divided three ways."

Then I remembered my own family's history. My mother told me that when my grandmother got romantically involved with my gentile, anarchist biological grandfather, her family said they would declare her dead if she married him. The joke was on them. She had no intention of marrying anyone.

"My mother said it was very simple. 'You choose her or you choose us. If you choose her, you will no longer be our son.'"

chapter fifty-eight
THE TRUTH IS, THE TRUTH DOESN'T MATTER

1997–2016

*I*n the first few years of knowing Leslie, I remained distant from the issue of parole. After I had known her for a number of years, she asked me to write a letter on her behalf to the parole board. I agreed. By then I was feeling that the project was so jinxed I'd abandoned the idea of ever publishing anything about the women.

In the time I've known Leslie Van Houten she's been routinely judged by a justice system that is, in her case for the most part, devoid of justice. I'm talking about the California Department of Corrections Parole Board. It's true: by nomenclature, it's corrections, not justice, but I think many people would agree that a measure of justice should be involved when deciding whether an inmate should win her freedom after more than forty years of incarceration. In this context I'm talking about the fundamentals of justice: fairness, impartiality, integrity, and truthfulness. The parole board has routinely struck out on each of these criteria, no matter how broadly or narrowly you apply them. (That is, until 2016. See epilogue.)

Leslie takes these hearings seriously. She always prepares. She always hopes. It reminds me of a friend who had to get MRIs every six months after he was diagnosed with malignant melanoma. The anxiety and anticipation, the waiting for results, was almost worse than the results, which were always bad. In my head I can hear the Steve Kays of the world saying that what Leslie goes through is nothing compared to the horror she put the LaBiancas through. I don't have an easy answer for that. I know, though, that she has been punished extensively, and if there's room in our criminal justice system for rehabilitation and forgiveness, then there is no justification for keeping her in prison. There certainly should be no room for the kind of cruelty the deputy district attorneys routinely subject her to.

When an inmate appears before the parole board, the policy is to consider the following: the seriousness of the original crime, the inmate's remorse over the crime, the inmate's behavior in prison, and the inmate's academic and vocational achievement while in prison. At Leslie's hearings there are two groups who weigh in on these criteria: the people who know Leslie very well and the people who don't know her at all. The unanimous opinion of the people who know her well is that she is ready to be paroled and has been for at least two decades, but the opinion of the people who know her well is disregarded and with every parole hearing, it is more aggressively disregarded. The people who know her not at all (and I do mean not at all) oppose her release, and their opinion carries the weight in the panel's determination of her suitability for release. (The one thing both sides agree on is the number one item: the seriousness of the crime. No one disputes that.)

The fact that the people who know her best, either professionally or personally, are so unwavering in their positive regard for her is actually a problem. It took me awhile to see the pattern, but I am now convinced that the more positive people are in their assessments and the larger that group is, the more likely it is that she will be denied parole and denied it rather viciously. (I'm even apprehensive about writing this chapter. The fact that there are so many people who write letters on her behalf is viewed as sinister by the deputy district attorneys.)

Who are the people who think so highly of her? The positive evaluations she receives include guards and correctional staff who supervise her work daily; psychiatric professionals who are hired by the correctional system to evaluate her; journalists who have interviewed her; teachers who have taught her and others who have overseen her college work, first for her bachelor's degree and then for her master's thesis; volunteers who have worked with her; and many, many friends, some who have known her for decades, others who are newer friends. All of these people have been saying, declaring, writing, pledging—shouting it from the rooftops if they could—that she is not only not a danger to society, she has prodigious gifts as a human being (intelligence, integrity, insight, discipline) that, if she's released, could contribute uniquely to society.

For a minute, though, let's go back to the first item on the list: the seriousness of the crime. There are many people who will maintain that she's been denied repeatedly because of the seriousness of the crime. But the pattern of these hearings belies that. The dreadful nature of the murders has not changed over the years. What has changed is Leslie: her acceptance of responsibility, her remorse, her insight, her maturity. As she has grown into a person her family and friends are proud of, however, the anger against her on the part of the people who oppose her release—the district attorney and relatives of the victims—has grown in intensity and each hearing gets more brutal.

She is a symbol, not a human being. These people claim to be experts on Leslie Van Houten when, in fact, their only exposure to her is a couple of hours at a parole hearing every few years. When these people take the microphone, they describe a nineteen-year-old girl, a girl encased in amber.

Over the years, the lengths to which the representatives of the

DA's office go to demean Leslie are stunning. The assault on her character was started by Steve Kay, who, for three decades hacked away at her character and her accomplishments. When he retired, the next guy, Los Angeles Deputy District Attorney Patrick Sequeira, assumed the mantle. He's not quite as bright as Steve, but the blunt-force trauma he inflicts is just as painful. The person he portrays in the parole hearings bears no resemblance to the woman who is described in the multiple staff reports and letters of support the panel receives at every hearing. Over the years there hasn't been a single positive trait that Leslie possesses that isn't twisted and used against her. It goes like this:

- *If she's slim*, and she is, she must be anorexic and anorexia is aggression turned inward. If she were to be paroled, watch out! There is a very real danger that her inward aggression could be turned outward. She killed before, she'll kill again.
- *If she's intelligent*, and she is, she uses her IQ to plot.
- *If she's personable*, and she is, she uses her congenial personality to manipulate everyone around her.
- *If many people write letters of support*, and they do, it's because she's a sociopath and has conned them into thinking well of her. (None of the psychiatric professionals have diagnosed her as having a personality disorder.)
- *If she expresses remorse for the horrible damage she inflicted on the LaBianca family*, and she does, she's only expressing it so she can be released. She's not sincere.
- *If she's done well in prison*, and she has, it's because she's so adaptable. She adapted to Manson and now she's adapted to prison. That she's an ideal inmate, pursuing almost every avenue of self-improvement available to her proves how adaptable she is.

Some of the accusations are either absurd or totally contradictory. Leslie has had a sustained interest in philosophy and psychology, specifically in the moral development of children; and more recently, in her master's thesis, she explores the factors that enable inmates to transition from irrational behavior, the kinds of behavior that caused them to commit their crimes, to concluding that "determining actions based on sound reason, it is necessary for the individual to be able to articulate and account for who she is and why she makes the choices she does." To Los Angeles Deputy District Attorney Patrick Sequeira, Leslie's interest in examining factors that enable inmates to transition from irrational behavior to rational decision making is suspect. To him it's proof that she hasn't fundamentally changed since she was with Manson.

In the past two hearings, it was difficult to figure out if he's ignorant or desperate or both. For example: when considering suitability for parole, psychological insight is one of the criteria that the board looks for. Sequeira declares she has none. The only way he can claim that she has no insight into her behavior is to totally ignore her psychiatric evaluations and simply repeat the horrible details of the crime and the shocking lack of remorse and insight she had when she committed the crime forty-five years ago. Apparently he's all for psychological insight, but he's against psychology.

She's been offered a job in the Department of Psychology at Chaffey College, if she's paroled. The job was arranged by a professor from whom she took a class. He was obviously impressed with her performance, but this offer earns her a black mark in the eyes of the deputy district attorney. "Again, this fascination with philosophy and psychology continues with this inmate," Sequeira said to the parole panel. He then reminded them that when she first met Manson, she was attracted to his philosophy promoting peace and love. "You would think that at some point in her life, maybe she would turn away from these areas that have caused her problems in the past, but she doesn't seem to do that."

> ***Then:*** Leslie has said there was a spiritual aspect to her
> initial attraction to Manson.
> ***Now:*** Leslie is sometimes invited to join American
> Indian inmates in their sweat lodge ritual. Also, Leslie
> practices a Zen form of meditation.
> ***Conclusion:*** There is still a spiritual aspect to her inter-
> ests; therefore Leslie hasn't changed.

Depending on the day, the hearing, perhaps the phase of the moon, Leslie has either changed not at all since the day of the murders or she's changed so much, it's cause for suspicion. When Deputy DA Steve Kay was arguing the latter, he said, on more than one occasion, that he had more respect for Charles Manson because he hasn't changed his tune at all. He's still spouting the same nonsense (my word) that he was spouting decades ago.

Another job offer, another strike against her. A defense attorney has said that she could work in his office if paroled. According to Mr. Sequeira, this job offer proves that Leslie still gravitates toward the criminal element because, of course, she would be exposed to criminals in the law offices of a criminal defense attorney.

Remorse. Leslie has expressed remorse many, many, many times but Sequeira claims she has none. To support that claim he quotes her psychiatric evaluation from 1971, two years after the murders when her brain was still saturated by Manson's poison.

"Her character structure and value system is so at odds with society and appears so deeply ingrained in her that it is difficult to see a true change as ever occurring. She views herself as now even more capable of committing a similar offense than in the past, and this is probably not just bravado." Keep in mind, this is from a report written more than forty years ago.

Sequeira acknowledges that she no longer spews that rhetoric but claims that she only started expressing remorse after there was no threat of the death penalty. "I find it interesting to note that her remorse only starts after the death penalty has been overturned in her case."

This doesn't even make sense. According to Sequeira, when she was facing death she continued to say she'd murder again. When she was no longer facing death, she expressed remorse.

That isn't the only thing that doesn't make sense. In Leslie's 2002 parole hearing, the parole panel praised her for her excellent disciplinary record and for taking self-help classes at Frontera. But they denied her parole because, according to Sharon Lawin, the chairwoman at the time, Leslie's accomplishments were outweighed by other factors—the main "other factor" was her need for "continued therapy to further understand the enormity of the crime and its impacts on the victims." Sounds reasonable, perhaps, except that psychotherapy was no longer available in the prison. "You just recommended something that they don't offer," Leslie responded. But then, clearly worried that she might appear uncooperative, she added plaintively, "But I will do what I can."

After the hearing, Leslie's attorney, Christie Webb, said she had no idea how to advise her client. "What can she do? They are asking her, again, to do therapy that is not available."

Webb wasn't the only one who was at a loss. This parole denial came just weeks after San Bernardino County Superior Court Judge Bob Krug harshly rebuked the parole board for ignoring Leslie's exemplary prison record, repeatedly rejecting parole for Van Houten in an "arbitrary and capricious" manner in deciding that she remains a threat to public safety based solely on the severity of her crime.

"I cannot find any indication where Miss Van Houten has done anything wrong in prison. They can't keep using the crime forever and ever. That turns her sentence into life without parole." Recognizing her outstanding achievements, the judge wrote, "If I was Miss Van Houten, I wouldn't have a clue what to do at the next hearing."

This decision provided a glimmer of hope but in March 2004, the Fourth District Court of Appeal reversed his decision, ruling that Judge Krug had applied the wrong standard when he held that the parole board had failed to balance the heinousness of Van Houten's crimes against her subsequent efforts at rehabilitation.

Presiding Justice Manuel Ramirez, writing for the Court of Appeal, said that the courts must uphold the board's exercise of its discretion to find an inmate unsuitable for parole as long as there is "some evidence" to support it. And that evidence can come solely from a review of the circumstances of the crime, Ramirez said. On June 23, 2004, the California Supreme Court declined to review the Court of Appeal's ruling upholding the denial of parole to Van Houten.

One of the more insidious trends started after 9/11 when the issue of terrorism started to creep into the argument against her release. In Leslie's 2006 parole hearing, Sequeira said, "We see examples in society now. People will blow themselves up for a cause. People will be so immersed in an ideology, whether it be a religious or social or political ideology, that they will do unbelievable things. And they will do them because they are committed to the cause. And there's absolutely no question that this inmate was committed to the cause and that she has a proclivity for following causes, for following bad influences in her life."

The relatives of the victims have picked up the theme. In Leslie's 2010 parole hearing, Louis Smaldino, a nephew of Mr. LaBianca, said, "Miss Van Houten is a murdering terrorist, and her character does not change," adding that she should have been executed.

Over the years, Leslie has tried to parse what factors contributed to her attraction to Manson as well as the factors that contributed to her willingness to murder for him. She has mentioned, among other things, her alienation from her parents, the abortion her mother arranged, and her drug use. Of course, these were the very things the shrinks encouraged her to talk about, and when she answered their questions, the shrinks put what she said in her evaluations. This, to the Deputy DA, is proof that Leslie refuses to take responsibility for her behavior. "Blame Charlie, blame LSD . . . and more recently it's blame the abortion," Sequeira said in Leslie's last parole hearing. "It's blame all of these other factors. This inmate has always portrayed herself as being the victim, as being subject to these forces outside of her control that have forced her to become one of the most notorious murderers in U.S. history."

Examining one's life and what influenced it in the context of a therapeutic relationship is very different from blaming others for your behavior. Since I have known Leslie, she has assumed total responsibility and has never tried to rationalize what she did; in fact, this is the only reason I was interested in getting to know her.

In 1978, Steve Kay announced that Leslie was the only one of the Manson group that he could see being paroled one day. What changed that?

There's an incident in Leslie's history that is held against her with the same frequency and almost the same intensity as are the murders. It's her marriage in 1982. She was in her early thirties when she started corresponding with Bill Cywin, an inmate in the nearby men's prison. When he was paroled, he started visiting her and they eventually married in a small prison ceremony. They were subsequently allowed to have a conjugal visit.

The man had bigger plans for Leslie. He devised a nutty scheme to break her out of prison, a plan she knew nothing about. A prison matron's uniform was discovered by the police in his apartment. As soon as Leslie learned of this, she cut off all contact with him, divorced him, and never saw him again. Steve Kay acknowledged that she knew nothing of this plan, but he continued to use it as a reason, decades later, for her unsuitability for parole. Mr. Sequeira continues the tradition. In her last parole hearing, he used the marriage as evidence of her lack of judgment.

Leslie says Cywin was the last man in a series of bad choices she made but ultimately learned from. "I was lonely. He was a grifter, but I didn't know it until later."

"How many in this room can say they haven't made bad marriage choices thirty years ago?" asked Brandie Devall, Leslie's lawyer at her 2010 parole hearing.

The truth is: the truth doesn't matter. Year after year, as Leslie has gotten better as a human being—more mature, better educated, wiser—the case *against* her has mounted correspondingly.

At each hearing, the parole panel goes through the motions of making a fair decision. The panel enters the positive reports and letters of support into the record, discusses their conclusions, but then proceeds to ignore them.

The exercise is a charade. It doesn't matter how accomplished, insightful, or remorseful she is. No one has the courage to say the decision is political. That the case has too high a profile for fairness to apply.

In 2006, the board once again denied parole but said she could come back in one year. This seemed reason to celebrate. Leslie was hopeful but guarded. Debra Tate, Sharon's youngest sister, was outraged at the one-year interval. To her, this was evidence that the board was ignoring the spirit in which the crimes were committed. "The perpetrators get to dance their prison victories before the board, but [the board] doesn't hear from the people who were murdered."

Historically, Debra Tate was prohibited from speaking at Leslie's parole hearings because she was unrelated to the LaBiancas and Leslie didn't have anything to do with killing Sharon. But in recent years, she has appeared regularly as a spokesperson for the LaBianca relatives at Leslie's parole hearings, arguing against her release.

The one-year date was a hopeful sign. After that, Leslie got two-year intervals until 2013 when she was given a five-year date. That hearing was the most brutal one yet. The transcript reads more like a character assassination than an honest assessment of the pros and cons of release.

Since the advent of DNA testing and the growth of innocence clinics across the country, increasing numbers of people care about injustice. But Leslie isn't innocent. Her best friends can pay for attorneys, but it's hard to get the public to care. The Manson murders have embedded themselves in the national psyche in a way that's impossible to shake loose. Even young people who weren't alive at the time, have strong opinions.

In addition to the horror of the murders, I have another theory about why Leslie is treated so harshly. I believe that her normality, along with her intelligence, her empathy, her warmth, is far more threatening than an inmate who seems creepy. If someone with her gifts is capable of murder, if someone with her upbringing and her basic humanity is capable of killing someone like Mrs. LaBianca, anyone is capable, and that means we can never be safe. I believe that everyone in the district attorney's office, every person on those parole panels, and every relative of Mr. and Mrs. LaBianca is aware that we are safe from Leslie now, but they still worry. The more she is Every Woman, the more dangerous the world seems even if *she* isn't.

(Note: in 2016 both truth and justice prevailed when the parole board recommended parole. See the epilogue for the outcome.)

chapter fifty-nine
NOT THAT KIND OF GIRL

Spring of 1962

*W*e were talking about God. It was spring break and we had just left my parents' house in Silver Lake and were on Sunset Boulevard headed to downtown L.A. I was feeling expansive. Not because we were talking about God but because the day before I had mastered a stick shift for the first time. My newly acquired skill meant that we were able to take my mother's new car, a fire-engine red VW Bug that I'd been wanting to drive, and I was excited about our destination. Craig had never been to Olvera Street, the tree-shaded Mexican marketplace—part of the original Pueblo de Los Angeles—and I wanted to share it with him. I didn't care that its shops were crammed with kitsch and crowded with tourists. The aroma of perfumed candle wax, the pastel piñatas, the cactus lollypops, and the Mexican jumping beans were all a joyful part of my childhood.

God entered the picture when I took a little detour around Echo Park to show him Angelus Temple, the church founded by evangelical preacher Aimee Semple McPherson. In addition to being the first woman to preach on the radio, in the 1920s, '30s, and '40s, she was known for faith healing and for whipping up enormous crowds by speaking in tongues. Craig was religious—

Lutheran or Methodist or one of those Protestant denominations I can never distinguish from each other—and I knew he harbored evangelical fantasies. Before he decided on politics, he had planned to be a minister, and he once confided that his goal had been to reach thousands, if not millions, of people with his oratory. Since I was an atheist, born and raised, we'd had a few conversations about religion, some of them testy.

"Too bad Preacher Aimee isn't still alive," I said. "She could have healed your knee." We'd been in an accident six months before, and Craig was still hobbling on his injured knee. As soon as I said it I worried that he'd take offense, but I looked over at him and he was smiling. We were on safe ground.

"Did I ever tell you about my month as a Christian?" I said.

"You? A Christian?" I looked over. Still smiling.

I told him that in high school many of my friends were members of the Hollywood First Presbyterian Church, and I often tagged along to functions in the teen program. Unlike other high school parties, these were the opposite of hip and, I guess, so was I. No drinking, no sex, no dancing. Instead, they had taffy pulls, ice cream socials, and they played parlor games. At one of the parties, a counselor in the teen program introduced herself and invited me to join my friends the following weekend at a retreat in the San Bernardino Mountains.

This experience combined all that was great about camp with a religious dimension that, to me, translated as emotion, topped off with a bonus of just enough heterosexuality in the mix to make it interesting. Those folks knew what they were doing. The teen boys were in a club called the Crusaders . . . they were all good looking, athletic, and looked trustworthy. Think Mitt Romney. No longer my cup of tea, but in those days that type was my ideal 1950s cute guy. I loved every minute of that retreat—flirting, swimming, singing, and, occasionally, praying. After two days of that, I buckled under the pressure to accept Christ as my savior. I think that's what's called born-again, though, for me, it was born-again for the first time.

I was having fun dredging up the details for Craig, and my tone got increasingly jocular. "My parents were tolerant of my deviant behavior. I didn't yet have my license, so they cheerfully drove me to Sunday school every week and every night, when they came into my bedroom to kiss me good night and found me reading the Bible, they said nothing. If they worried about me or laughed at my newfound religious zeal, they waited until they closed the door of their bedroom. In a way, it made sense. They always said they wanted me to be happy, and I was a happy Presbyterian. For one month, it was a match made in heaven. And then it wasn't."

"What happened?" Craig asked.

"It all started in the beginning," I said, laughing. "You know, Genesis. That's where it all started." I remember liking my little joke—the double meaning of the beginning—but my audience wasn't so appreciative.

"What do you mean?"

"The Sunday school teacher told me to start reading the Bible at Genesis and being the good little student that I was, I did. But Genesis was a problem for me. A big problem and I brought that problem to Sunday school. I talked about the obvious . . . you know, all the stuff the Bible says about creation doesn't make any sense . . . take evolu—" Before I could finish the word, Craig jumped in.

"Sounds like you're proud of being a smart ass."

"Come on, Craig," I said, "are you telling me that you don't have a little trouble with the time table in Genesis? I'm a little hazy on it now, but doesn't the Bible tell us that God created the universe in seven days? Or was it six? Either way, it's not logical."

"That's not the point," he said. "The point is that religion provides comfort to people. It's about faith; logic doesn't matter."

"Of course it matters. We're talking about young, impressionable kids." I was into the volley so it took a while for me to become aware of how angry he was. Finally I noticed the scowl on his face.

"Why are you getting so worked up about this?"

"Because you have no way of knowing how important that church or that religion was to the other kids in that Sunday school class. Maybe there was a kid whose parents were getting a divorce. What if his faith was helping him get through it? And what about poor kids? Religion provides solace to them."

"Come on, Craig," I said, "these were not poor kids . . . we're talking about some of the most privileged kids in L.A."

"That snide remark about my knee shows . . . well, your . . . ignorance. Faith healing gives people hope."

"What about talking in tongues?" I asked. "Does that give you hope? Do you even know what's being said?"

"You are so fucking cocky." Now he was yelling.

I had to admit I was feeling a little cocky, but it had to do with mastering a clutch and a gearshift. I didn't think my views on evolution and talking in tongues reflected arrogance, just common sense. "Why can't we talk about this calmly? I can't believe how seriously you're taking this."

"Stop!" he yelled.

"Jesus, what is going on with you? This is crazy."

"Let me out of the car," he bellowed.

"You're being ridiculous."

"Stop!"

I kept driving.

He suddenly reached his leg over my leg and jammed his foot on the brake. The car came to a screeching halt and both of us lurched forward. If there had been a car behind us, it would have sailed into the back of the car, launching the VW engine into our backs.

Shaking, I pulled over to the curb. I was only seventeen, but I was certain the adrenaline surge was going to give me a heart attack. I looked at him, expecting an apology. He was defiant. "I asked you to stop!"

He got out of the car and walked about a half block up Sunset Boulevard. I had no idea what to do. Now, of course, I wonder why I didn't just leave him there, but I don't think it occurred to me. I hate to admit it, but I pleaded with him to get back in the car and, eventually, he did. We didn't go to Olvera Street and we didn't talk. I took him back to his brother's car that was parked at my parents' house.

We had argued before, but outbursts like this started after we had the accident. We'd been on a lonely stretch of Highway 99, somewhere around Turlock in the San Joaquin Valley, on our way home for Christmas vacation. A sixteen-year-old kid who'd only had his license a couple of weeks moved into our lane without signaling. We crashed into him and Craig's right knee slammed into the car keys that were in the ignition, damaging the tendons in his knee. I hit my face on the dashboard, but, according to the paramedic, I avoided serious injury because I'd been asleep. We were in Craig's 1949 Chevy—no bucket seats, no seat belts—so I was sleeping with my head in his lap. I was bruised and my nose and my lips were so swollen they joined together, comprising a single facial feature.

It was a bad night for me and Craig but perhaps a worse night for the kid who'd been driving the car that hit us. When we were all in the emergency room at Turlock (it was, literally, one small room) the kid kept saying his father was going to kill him when he got home. He was standing, slightly rocking and trying to steady himself against the wall, and then he fainted, falling face-first into a crash cart. The clatter of the metal on the tile floor was terrifying. The nurses revived him with some mixture, I assume of smelling salts, and he seemed okay, but he was so scared I think he might have preferred remaining unconscious.

For some reason the accident seemed to have unleashed anger at me. Craig hadn't hit his head, so I didn't understand his new belligerence.

Even though he couldn't walk without a crutch and my face was so grotesque people stared at me, we kept telling ourselves that we were lucky that more damage wasn't done. But something had changed. As I said, we had always argued a bit, but now our fights were more frequent and fiercer.

The first time he hurt me was one morning when we were eating breakfast in the dining room of our dorm complex after school started in January. Two days before, I'd confessed a flirtation I'd had with a guy who also lived in the same complex. I don't know why I confessed it. I told myself that my motive was honorable . . . I didn't want us to have secrets between us. It's quite possible, however, that it was retribution for Craig's policy of not acknowledging me as his girlfriend when we were on the Cal campus as part of his political calculations. As I said before, he planned to run for student body president some day and believed that girls would be more likely to vote for him if he was unattached romantically. I laughed it off, but it hurt my feelings.

He insisted on calling the flirtation an "extra-marital affair." When I pointed out that we weren't married and it was not an affair but a flirtation that involved some kissing, it made him angry. When I realized that he was also hurt, even tearful, I felt terrible. I promised to cut off contact with the guy. I thought it was settled, but the next morning it became clear that it wasn't. I was sitting next to Craig at a long, communal table, and Craig's crutch was propped up against the table. The guy, I'll call him Michael, walked by with some friends, and just as he did, Craig's crutch slid down to the floor. Before I or Craig had a chance to retrieve it, Michael picked it up and propped it up again in the same place.

I said, "Thank you." Michael nodded at me and kept walking. Craig didn't say a word, but he took my hand, which was in my lap twitching nervously, and smashed it forcefully against the underside of the table, bruising my knuckles. I was stunned. It hurt like hell, but I was embarrassed so I said nothing. I massaged my hand and watched it turn blue. We never talked about it.

The next outburst was a couple of weeks later. We'd been to see *Westside Story*, which was playing at the Shattuck Theater. As we were walking back to the car in the underground garage after the movie, we started fighting about Natalie Wood. One of us said her singing voice had been dubbed and the other said it wasn't. I don't even remember which of us took which position, but I do remember the nightmarishly dim light in the garage, the dead echo to his voice as he yelled at me, and my fear as he started to wave his crutch overhead—not close enough to hit me but close enough to make me think he was going to. I felt the breeze as it passed near my head. I don't know if he intended to strike me, but I think the possibility even scared him because he immediately cooled off. We got in the car and he drove me back to my dorm. We didn't talk.

I remember telling my kids about this relationship years later and how puzzled they were. It wasn't consistent with how they saw me. My son, who was then a teenager, was especially surprised. He and I were going through a tumultuous time in our relationship, but he was protective of me and couldn't fathom a guy hitting me.

I told them it was long before there were general discussions of battered women. There was no talk of syndromes. No talk of "no one is immune." No talk of partner abuse being an equal opportunity phenomenon. In those days it was straightforward: he was a guy, I was a girl, and every once in a while boys hit girls.

Now it's possible to look back with relief and see that it wasn't the beginning of a pattern of relationships. It was a departure from my life's trajectory, not the norm. Nonetheless, it could have been a dangerous one.

One of the reasons I tolerated the physical abuse was that I thought it was my fault. I now know this is a common perception of abused women the world over, but I didn't know it then. Here's how my thinking went: because of my family's education, I was better with words, so when we got into verbal sparring I had the upper hand. Therefore, it was unfair of me to keep arguing once he got angry. As my arguments sharpened, his frustration would build and build. By the time I recognized how angry and out of control he was, it was too late. I'd see the impotence in his face and I'd feel terrible. I had no right to hurt him, to unman him in that way. He couldn't help his feelings, but I could've worked harder to control myself. I pushed him too far. I was supposed to be making him feel big and powerful, and instead I was making him feel small and helpless—perpetuating the inequality of our upbringings. He had to fight for everything he had achieved, and it had all come to me easily. Instead of violent boy against articulate girl, it was a war between the classes, at a particularly sensitive time in our country's history, especially at Cal where we were supposed to be overturning society's inequalities.

In recounting this, I think about Leslie telling me how the women felt terrible for Manson, for his rejection, for his institutionalizations. It was their parents' generation that did that to him, and knowing that made them feel guilty. Whereas they had come from middle-class neighborhoods with loving families, he'd been abandoned to fend for himself. He used that guilt to manipulate their sympathy.

As Manson pointed to Leslie's and Pat's families of origin as their biggest problems, Craig, too, blamed my parents. He said my parents had been too lenient when I was growing up and had not set enough limits, so he was redressing the balance. This was ridiculous on several fronts. My parents were liberal politically, but in terms of setting limits, they were the strictest parents I knew. But even if they had been lenient, what kind of twisted excuse is that to hit someone? I knew that at the time, but I was too preoccupied with my own guilt to even argue with him about it.

What else did we fight about? We fought about sex. We fought about sex all the time. (This, I did not include in my talk with my kids.) My official position was that I wanted to be a virgin when I got married, but the truth was that I didn't feel ready. (I may have been the last holdout among girls of my generation—I certainly was among my friends.) I was seventeen. He was twenty-one and he'd already had several girlfriends with whom he'd had sex. We did sleep together—on weekends we'd take little road trips and stay in motels—but I held firm to my position. He lobbied constantly. He said if I loved him, I would have sex with him. That's what people did who loved each other, he said. Though I held my ground, I felt guilty about that, too. It didn't seem fair to him. I would propose that we stop sleeping together. He said we shouldn't stop sleeping together, we should keep sleeping together but we should have sex when we slept with each other. And around and around and around we'd go.

So, we argued about sex, we argued about religion, we argued about politics. I was more liberal. There was a new group of young turks on campus who raised issues that I cared about—free speech and academic freedom as well as the right of students to take positions on off-campus public issues such as civil rights and capital punishment. The group was called Slate and it was a precursor to the Free Speech Movement, which came along a few years later. Craig was more aligned with student leaders whose platforms had to do with campus issues. Want a jukebox in the Bear's Lair (the café in the student union), Craig's your guy.

And we fought about his hands-off policy toward me in public when we were on campus. I no longer even pretended to buy his reason. As I pointed out to him, John Kennedy married Jackie and women still voted for him.

And then there was the issue of his parents. We didn't fight about them; we didn't talk about them at all. He'd always been close to his parents, and we both knew that if he stayed with me he'd have to give up his relationship with them. It didn't seem fair.

The worst fight we had happened in early June, right before I left school for the summer. I don't remember what it was about, but I do remember that it fit the pattern. It started as a tiff, built to an argument, and by the time I was aware of his intensity, it was too late. He punched me in the stomach, knocking the wind out of me.

Why did I put up with it? For one thing, and this now seems weird, each time it happened it felt like an isolated incident. My boyfriend hit me . . . not my boyfriend hits me. As I say, no one was talking syndrome.

I never, not once, considered breaking up with him because he hit me. I loved much about him. I loved his husky voice and his wide, hazel-eyed gaze, his athletic good looks. I loved his relationship with his sister and his brother and how proud he was of his parents' strong marriage. Unlike the frat boys I had dated, he didn't have even a whiff of entitlement about him. He had every reason to be anti-Semitic and wasn't. But most of all, I loved that he had chosen me. I was astonished when he asked me out. That's why his disavowal of me as a girlfriend on campus was especially hurtful. It confirmed my belief that I wasn't quite good enough.

The night he hit me in the stomach, I ran up to my dorm room. I was crying, so my roommate demanded to know what happened. She was so upset that later, after I'd gone to sleep, she called her mother in Southern California to talk about it. The next morning, her mother called to talk to me. She said I should break up with Craig. She'd had a dream that he killed me. It felt like a pre-monition.

I thanked her for being concerned, but I told her not to worry. "He's not going to kill me. It was my fault. I push him too hard. I have to learn when to stop arguing."

My memory about how my own parents reacted is hazy. I don't remember that they were particularly upset. Actually, I don't re-member that they were upset at all. Now it seems out of character that parents, especially a father who thought his daughter should have her own career and was a version of an early feminist, would tolerate such a thing. I think maybe there was still a feeling that the rules of engagement were different with couples. Either that or my parents also bought into my belief that I was lucky to have landed him. I also don't know how much I revealed. I think I told them that he hit me, but I also think that I would have down-played it. I was reluctant to reveal problems because I didn't want them, especially my mother, to intercede. All of this is confusing to me now. If our daughter were ever in a relationship with a man who hit her, at any time in her life, my husband and I would not have held back. Maybe I didn't tell them all of it.

I was never again involved with a man who hit me. Strangely, however, for the rest of my life I've thought of myself as the kind of person who couldn't be with a man who would hit me. I'm pretty sure the people who know me best would assume that too. I'm not suggesting that this relationship became a repressed memory—I was aware that it happened—I just somehow didn't think it counted. It wasn't until I started to recall the details through the lens of my inquiries about the Manson women that I wondered if some of my assumptions about myself (and other women) were accurate.

Without articulating it, I've believed that women like Pat and Leslie are on a (metaphorical) list of women who could get involved with men who would mistreat them, while I was on a different list—a list of women who would never be involved with such men. Or if a woman on my list did find herself with such a man and he struck her once, she would immediately leave him.

Given my history, and given what I know of Pat's and Leslie's, I've had to rethink that list. Each of them has such a strong sense of herself as a woman now, it's difficult to comprehend that either could have ever been so categorically dominated by a man.

Considering the similarities in our histories, the categories are not nearly as clear as I once thought they were. The two factors that kept me from bolting—believing that it was my fault and the honor of being chosen by him—blended together to produce the glue that caused me to stick, and also prevented me from having a clear-eyed look at our relationship. Both Pat and Leslie talk about variations of these same themes preventing them from seeing Manson clearly before it was too late.

So, am I really on a different list after all? Are any of us? I know, or think I know, that, other than protecting my children, there are no circumstances that would cause me to murder. But my experience with Craig shows that I might have been more vulnerable to some of the steps that led up to that horror than I'd like to admit. The issue, I think, is the question of departures—departures from what one could predict about one's life, given family history, genetics, and a whole lot of other variables.

In my case, the departure didn't define me. I can chalk it up to youthful naïveté and turn it into a deeper understanding of what causes abused women to stay in dangerous relationships. For Leslie and Pat, however, their paths crossed with Charlie, not Craig, and the departure defined the rest of their lives.

chapter sixty
WE ARE ALL RWANDAN

July 2007

*I*n 2007, my family traveled to East Africa to visit our daughter who had just finished an assignment for Doctors Without Borders in the Democratic Republic of the Congo. The first leg of our trip was to Rwanda, where we hiked to see the mountain gorillas. In describing that experience, it's impossible for me to avoid hackneyed superlatives—joy, awe, magical—and my sense of wonder extended beyond an appreciation of those magnificent animals. I was filled with appreciation for the humans who made the experience possible.

Among those was the ranger who led with his machete, clearing a path for us by cutting down dense bamboo and giant lobelia and tracking the location of our little tribe of gorillas with a system of walkie-talkies. Our ranger was a shortish, stocky, very dark-skinned man—a classically built Hutu. He could not be identified as such in Rwanda where, because of the genocide, it is now against the law to identify ethnic differences. The country's motto: "There is no ethnicity here. We are all Rwandan."

But I'm not Rwandan and our guide's ethnicity did distract me. I found myself wondering who in his family or among his friends slaughtered Tutsis in the summer of 1994, when the majority

Hutus murdered an estimated eight hundred thousand Tutsis and other Hutus considered "moderate." "Murdered" is putting it mildly. Those people were butchered, day after day after day for three months. When you walk through the streets of Kigali, you see many amputees. They were the lucky ones who escaped with only limbs missing.

On that hike, I didn't yet understand the story behind those labels. It later occurred to me that my discomfort was not unlike my mother's with the German woman in Pisa.

Because this country is trying to face its history, there are hundreds of genocide memorials scattered throughout. The main one is in the capital, the Kigali Memorial Centre—a burial ground for some 250,000 victims of the genocide, and also a museum.

As I walked through the museum, an exhaustive display, I realized that this was Manson's "Helter Skelter" scheme. So many of the elements were there—the labeling, the propaganda aimed at vilifying the Tutsis. (When the Germans and then the Belgians controlled Rwanda, they exploited the ethnic prejudices. The Europeans preferred the Tutsis, claiming their lighter skin and slimmer bodies were aristocratic and more like Europeans'. The Hutus were characterized as subhuman.

Consequently, the Hutus lived under the thumb of the Tutsis for decades, building up toxic resentment. When that bubble burst, the tables were turned and the Tutsis were labeled cockroaches. Glass cases displayed the weapons used—machetes, clubs, and knives. The killings were all horrific and at close range. The next collection included personal accounts by the killers, so many of them expressing the same chilling disconnection, the absence of humanity that both Pat and Leslie had talked about.

"We no longer saw a human being when we turned up a Tutsi in the swamps. I mean a person like us, sharing similar thoughts and feelings," wrote one man. He described a chilling kind of twinning, writing that it had been as if he had allowed another person to take on his appearance. He knew the killer was himself but the ferocity of that self was a stranger to him. He acknowledged that it was his fault, that the victims were his, he acknowledged his obedience to the directions to kill but he failed to recognize the wickedness of the one who raced through the marshes on "my legs, carrying my machete."

The Rwandan government puts the number of dead at one million, the estimated number of killers at eight hundred thousand. Were all eight hundred thousand of them monsters? I felt overwhelmed by the enormity of the bloodbath. Once again, as with 9/11, it dwarfed the number of perpetrators I was trying to understand. But there were so many parallels. If I could understand Leslie and Pat, maybe I could understand brutality on such a massive scale. And if I could understand brutality on such a massive scale, maybe I could understand Leslie and Pat.

Summer of 1962

*C*raig and I spent the summer apart—he stayed in Berkeley to work as a research assistant, and I went south to work as a counselor at a camp for blind kids in Malibu. As far as I was concerned, the fact that he hit me in the stomach was a footnote; it didn't change anything. I was as committed to the relationship as ever. At camp, I taped his photo in a prominent place at the end of my bunk. It embarrasses me to recall that my motivation was so the other counselors would know how good looking my boyfriend was. I don't know if I was in love with him. I do know that I was in love with us as a couple.

It was a hard summer for me. For one thing, the camp had an abundant supply of rattlesnakes. The combination of blind campers and lots of poisonous snakes made for jumpy days and restless nights. On mornings that I'd forgotten to turn our shoes upside down before bed, there'd be a good chance of finding a baby rattler curled up in a shoe. (The babies are more dangerous than adults because they strike wildly and don't regulate the poison. Later they learn to be judicious with their bites.) So as not to alarm the kids, when we spotted a rattler, we'd yell the code word "jeep" and someone would run to get the maintenance crew to come and kill the snake.

The hardest part of the summer had to do with Natalie, a nine-year-old camper with silky chestnut hair, warm brown eyes, and a malignant brain tumor. After she was diagnosed the surgeons removed as much of the tumor as they could, and in the process severed her optic nerve. In the notes her mother sent along in her duffel bag, she wrote that Natalie had been lethargic at home. For the first few days at camp she was both lethargic and withdrawn, but by the fourth day she was a radiant little girl.

The philosophy of the camp director was to treat the kids as though they could do anything and everything, and Natalie wanted to do anything and everything. In those days, parents of most blind kids tended to be overprotective; it was understandable that Natalie's parents had even more reason to be worried about her. On family day when I met Natalie's parents, it was clear they saw her as fragile. But at camp where she had the freedom to make mistakes, she was excited about every milestone, from pouring milk without spilling to learning to swim. Because I knew how few milestones she had left in her life, I had a chronic lump in my throat. As she got happier, I got sadder.

I wrote to Craig frequently, describing camp, the kids, the snakes, but I mostly wrote about Natalie. I was desperate for his support. I wanted to be buoyed emotionally—what I got in return were descriptions of summer weather in Berkeley, restaurants he'd been to, the friends he had seen. That was as intimate as it got, and even those letters were few and far between. Finally I wrote telling him that I was tired of reading between the lines. If he wanted to break up with me, I wished he would come right out and say it.

One week later I got a one-sentence letter: "Consider it said." No salutation, no sign-off. I still have the letter. I saved it because

I thought that someday I would have trouble believing that someone who once said he loved me could be so cruel. But in terms of cruel, he had just gotten started.

That letter was in early August. I didn't hear from him again until the end of September when we were back at school. He called on my birthday. My roommate told him I was at the library studying for a test. He knew that I always sat at the same table in the main library, and he showed up there arm-in-arm with a girl, a girl I knew, a girl he had dated before me. They sat across from me. As I quickly collected my things, he passed me a note with a stick figure holding a birthday cake, big smile on his stick figure face: "Happy 18th Birthday!"

I managed to get out of there before the tears started and, as fast as I could, pedaled my bike back to the house where I was living that semester—a big drafty Victorian on the south side of campus. On the way home, I came up with a way to make myself feel better. Craig's maneuver was infantile, mine was perhaps even more so, but enormously satisfying.

Everyone who was in the house at the time pitched in to make it a party. My roommate served the chocolate cake she had baked that day, a couple of guys bought six-packs of beer, someone brought wine, a girl who was into health made herbal tea, one guy played his guitar. After the party was under way, I brought out two expensive wool sweaters Craig had given me—one for my birthday the year before and one for Christmas. We took turns unraveling them. At first the partygoers were apprehensive. "Are you sure you want to do this?"

"I'm sure."

When we were finished we had many balls of pretty wool yarn: half were periwinkle blue, and the other half were camel colored. We divided into two teams and created a game using badminton racquets.

I loved those sweaters—Craig had good taste—but the satis-

faction I felt tossing around those balls of yarn was worth the sacrifice. I wasn't, however, quite done with him.

His "consider it said" letter was hurtful and confusing, but his
birthday stunt was so transparently mean, I wanted an explanation. I called him and suggested coffee. He wanted to take a walk.
We compromised and met in front of Sproul Hall, the administration building. He was waiting when I got there. "Why don't we
find a place on the grass?" he said. The grass would have been
pleasant—it was a warm, fall day—but I had an agenda. I shook
my head and told him I was on a fact-finding mission, and I didn't
need or want to take the scenic route.

I sat down on the steps. He sat down next to me. I turned to
face him: "Why are you so angry at me?"

On my walk to campus, I realized that my biggest fear was that
he would deny his anger. If he did that, there would be nothing to
talk about. Sure enough, he shrugged and gave me a "Who me?"
look.

"You really need evidence? First there was your letter . . . then
your stunt on my birthday—"

"I surrender," he said, throwing his arms up dramatically, the
way someone would in a hold-up in an old fashioned Western.
"You've caught me. I was angry."

"Was? Your birthday stunt was two days ago."

He smiled, a not pleasant smile. "Okay," he said, taking a deep
breath. "Give me a minute to think about this."

We sat on the steps watching students stream through Sather
Gate onto campus. I wasn't sure what I expected but something
along the lines of, "You're a bitch when you argue," or "You
don't give me time to respond before you come back at me," or "I
can't catch my breath." This is how I would have answered my
question.

Finally, in almost a whisper, he said. "You took everything
away from me." He looked tearful. "Everything I cared about."

This, I didn't expect. "What did I take away from you?"

"You really don't know?"

"I really don't know."

"You took God away from me."

"I . . . what?"

"You hammered away, questioning me relentlessly . . . questioning what shouldn't be questioned because the answers are about faith, my faith . . . day in and day out you worked on me."

At first I was too shocked to respond, but then I said I thought he was exaggerating. We argued about religion but I didn't think I hammered away. I started to say more, and then I realized he wasn't finished with his list.

"My politics . . . you mocked my ambition . . . you belittled my strategy."

I couldn't stop myself. "You mean your hands-off policy? Treating me like a stranger to get votes? That strategy? That's not a strategy, that's a—"

"Hold on, I'm not done," he said. "I know this isn't your fault but . . . the situation with my family . . . my parents . . . because of you I—"

I erupted. "You're angry at *me* because your parents hate Jews?" I stood up, grabbed my book bag, and took off toward Telegraph Avenue. As I threaded my way against the stream of students on their way to classes, I looked back at him and yelled, "You're crazy."

His reaction finished it for me, finished *him* for me. These days it's called closure. It was the complaint of a little boy. I was hurt, but I knew I couldn't revive the respect I once had for him.

After that I started dating other guys. Self-made atheists. Life was good.

In November, the weekend before Thanksgiving, the doorbell rang. When I answered it, I found Craig standing on the porch.

"Look," he said, holding up car keys. "I rented a car . . ." he pointed to a Mustang convertible that was parked in front of the house. "I know you love convertibles."

I figured he had another sadistic ploy in mind. A new girlfriend would pop up from the backseat. I said nothing. I waited. The man did indeed have a plan: he wanted us to get married.

"It's only a four-hour drive to Reno. We can get married and make a weekend out of it. I called the wedding chapel and they're open until midnight."

"Craig. This is nuts."

"I want you to be my wife."

I told him, in the nicest way possible, that I thought he was insane. He lobbied. I listened politely. Finally, I told him I had laundry to wash. He said he'd check with me later to see if I changed my mind.

I didn't run off to Reno with him, but his grand gesture did have an effect. I agreed to go out with him when I got back from Thanksgiving vacation. He stayed in Berkeley over the holiday but wrote letters and called me long distance every day. He sent flowers. When I got back to school, we started going out again. Things were calmer. We didn't argue and he didn't hit me. He applied to a PhD program in economics instead of law school. He graduated in December and signed up for the Coast Guard Reserve. He was required to do six months active duty, but he'd be stationed nearby at Treasure Island. We didn't talk about his parents.

chapter sixty-two

UNFORGETTING, UNFORGIVING

*I*n late 2016 I got a letter from Pat asking that I write to the parole board recommending her release. I was surprised by the request. In the twenty years that I'd known her, she had appeared before the board thirteen times but had never before asked. When I first knew her, she told me that she'd requested that people not write to the parole board on her behalf because she felt there was no chance she would be paroled and didn't want them to go to the trouble. This letter, which was addressed to "dear friend," was, as far as I knew, the first time she was organizing support for her release.

The letter presented a problem for me. My book was finished and being shown to publishers. One of the people on whom I rely for publishing advice suggested that it would be better for me to abstain because writing it would place me in the category of advocate and detract from my credibility as a journalist. Though I had already crossed that line with Leslie a few years before, the circumstances had been different. As I explain earlier in the book, Leslie asked at a time when I had given up the idea of publishing anything about the women so I wasn't worried about blurring the lines. Now I was.

I agonized about the decision. Didn't I owe this to Pat? The two of us had spent many hours together, and she had helped me understand the hold Manson had on her and the other women. Also, she was the one who talked Leslie into meeting with me in the first place. Ultimately, though, I decided to decline. Since her letter was not directed to me alone, I was able to reassure myself that she would have enough people writing on her behalf. I didn't think the absence of a letter from me would present a problem. I wrote to her explaining all of the above.

One of the reasons I was surprised at her request: because of the extent of her involvement in the murders, the chances for parole didn't seem much better than when we first met. She had taken an active role in both nights of bloodshed. She had confessed to chasing down Abigail Folger before stabbing her twenty-eight times on the first night; on the second night, she was found guilty of stabbing both of the LaBiancas. After Leno LaBianca had been killed, she had plunged a fork into his abdomen and in his blood, wrote "Death to pigs," "Arise," and "Healter [sic] Skelter" on the walls. Because she had participated both nights, she'd been convicted of murdering seven people. And though the courts had recently ruled that the nature of the crime could not be the sole criterion for refusing parole, the details of those murders were going to be very difficult for members of parole panels to extinguish from their brains.

If parole had been a tough sell for Leslie who was convicted of killing the LaBiancas, getting the parole board to recommend release for Pat and then getting the governor to approve it seemed like a bridge too far. I didn't know anyone who thought Pat had a chance. Why was she putting herself through the ordeal? If the past was any indication, she would be subjected to terrible verbal abuse by the deputy district attorney as well as the relatives of the victims. But maybe none of the above was the point. Perhaps she was simply looking for support from her friends. I didn't think of it that way at the time. If I had, the outcome might have been different and Pat and I might still be friends.

Weeks went by. I didn't hear from her. Christmas came—I had always received warm holiday greetings from her—and Christmas went. *Nada* from Pat. I was worried.

In spite of my anguish, the earth continued to turn on its axis and on December 29, 2016, Pat's parole board convened. After an all-day hearing, the members of the panel voted to postpone a decision. According to a statement released by the California Department of Corrections and Rehabilitation, the decision to postpone was made after Pat's attorney, Keith Wattley, claimed that she had been a victim of intimate partner battery while she was with Manson. The panel concluded that the information warranted further investigation.

Relatives of the victims were outraged by the reason given for the postponement. Debra Tate, Sharon Tate's surviving sister, called it "absurd"; Anthony DiMaria, the nephew of Jay Sebring, said an investigation of this nature at this late date was "mind-boggling."

I saw the postponement as a chance to redeem myself. I called Pat's lawyer's office and found out that there was still time for me to write a letter on Pat's behalf. I wrote her again, telling her that I'd been having second thoughts about my initial decision. Would she consider meeting with me so we could talk about it? Would she give me a chance to explain more fully what my pushes and pulls had been? I suggested a couple of dates. I didn't hear from her. I wrote again expressing sadness about the breach. Once again, I asked for the chance to discuss what happened in person. "If, after we talk, you decide you don't want anything to do with me, fair enough, I'll leave you alone." I told her I would hold every weekend free the following month until I heard from her. In closing, I wrote that given the politics in Washington, it seemed more important than ever for kindred spirits to stick together. I didn't hear from her. Clearly, she no longer considered us kindred spirits.

Was she hurt? Was she angry? Was she both? Whatever her reaction, I was bewildered that her feelings were so extreme that she was foreclosing even the possibility of discussing what had happened. Looking at it in the framework of crime, she was treating me as though I had committed a serious felony while I believed I had committed the equivalent of a misdemeanor. She was asking society for a measure of forgiveness for brutally murdering people. I was asking for a measure of forgiveness for initially declining to write a letter to the parole board. I not only wanted the chance to explain my decision, I wanted to hear what it had meant to her. Her unyielding refusal made me doubt how well I actually did know her.

Maybe I shouldn't have been surprised that she was not interested in trying to understand what had happened. I'd been aware that she had unexamined areas of her psyche, but it seemed that there had been enough good stuff between us to try to salvage a relationship of twenty years. And I was the most puzzled by the abrupt way she slammed the door on the possibility.

I remembered that once, when Pat and I were talking about movies, books, and articles about the so-called Manson Family, she had said: "All those people have gotten rich on our backs." At the time I assumed she was referring to people who requested interviews, feigned interest in her, and after completing their projects, moved on. Did she think I was one of those people? Did she think I feigned interest in her for a couple of decades so I could achieve fame and fortune at her expense?

My daughter wondered whether being a high-profile criminal (she used the term "celebrity criminal") is a bit like being any kind of celebrity. (It is an apt characterization. Both Pat and Leslie have gotten requests from high school students for dona-

tions of their running shoes for school auctions—an idea that re-
pulses both of them.) There must be times when you wonder
whether people are interested in you for yourself or just want to
be close to fame, even this kind of fame.

If that was the case with Pat, maybe my refusal was proof to
her that I was never interested in her in the first place. It seemed
like a plausible explanation, but we'd known each other for
twenty years, and even when I had abandoned the idea of writing
about her, I continued to visit and to write. I thought about what
Bill Sessa, a spokesman for the California Department of Corrections, who, in discussing Pat with an *L.A. Times* reporter, listed
the qualities the parole board would be seeking: "They are looking for insight from the inmate and a sense of true taking responsibility, contrition, accountability."

Wasn't I doing that? If she was asking a parole board to judge
her on those issues, why couldn't she extend that consideration
to me?

Now I had another problem. Could I, in good conscience, write
a letter of recommendation to the parole board based on knowing
Pat? When she first asked me to write the letter and I declined, it
was all about *my* issues—my concern about my boundaries, my
role. Now it had to do with my concern about *hers*. But was it fair
of me to think that the way she cut off our relationship had anything to do with her suitability to be paroled? Did I think she
would be a danger to society if released? No I didn't but, on the
other hand, I no longer believed I could claim that I knew her well
enough to predict much about her at all. Once again, I struggled
with the decision. I wanted to make sure that I wasn't declining to
write the letter out of anger that she had "ghosted" me. Then I realized that I wasn't angry at all—I was sad and confused. I had
believed that we would know each other for the rest of our lives.

But was I confused enough to believe that she should be
deemed unsuitable? On paper, she can check most of the criteria

for suitability: she's expressed remorse for the murders; she's served many more years than required for her offense; she had no prior criminal history. She's made rehabilitative efforts and she's free of disciplinary action. It is also true that she harbors a well of bitterness—but isn't that understandable in someone who has been incarcerated for so many years? Was her anger relevant to her parole? I hadn't thought so before but now I wasn't so sure.

After a few turbulent dreams, I woke up in the middle of the night and realized I couldn't possibly answer those questions. My only responsibility was to answer one question: Did I know her well enough to recommend *anything* to the parole panel?

In my life I have written three letters to parole boards. One was for my brother when I was in college and the other two were for inmates more recently incarcerated in California's correctional system. In all three cases, if I had been asked whether I knew the person well enough to be comfortable inviting him or her to live with me and my family, the answer would have been an unqualified "yes." In Pat's case it would be a question mark. Writing a letter containing a question mark would not be doing her a favor.

In many ways, convicted murderers, at least those asking for parole, have to be better than everyone else: kinder, more forgiving, more able to turn the other cheek. With every movement, gesture, decision, they need to telegraph "I am safe . . . I am above the fray of ordinary life." In normal life, one has the luxury of snubbing a friend or acquaintance, no matter how trivial the reason. When one is applying for parole, the rules are different. It must, at times, seem unfair to be scrutinized this way. Fair or not, it is the reality. Pat's refusal to explore the feelings in a relationship of long-standing is a refusal to play by those rules. My hunch is that there are other people in her life she's decided to treat that way. I don't know what to make of those decisions; I suspect I never will.

chapter sixty-three

"I'D BE NICE TO A STRAY DOG IF IT NEEDED HELP"

December 1962

There was a holiday party at the prison. My parents couldn't go because my mother had planned some sort of celebration for foster parents at the Coconut Grove in L.A. that night. Craig offered to come to the prison party with me. I picked him up at a Denny's a couple blocks from his home.

Nothing had changed with his parents since the summer except that we had stopped talking about "it" or them. The ultimatum just sat there on the virtual table, avoided by everyone. Every once in a while, Craig would start to say something about what had happened at one of the weddings, and then he'd catch himself. I never said it, but I thought he should have boycotted them on my behalf. I knew that wouldn't have been fair to his siblings. But I also wished that his siblings had insisted that I be allowed to come. But how could I expect that kind of loyalty from people who didn't know me? On the other hand, what about loyalty to the principle of standing up against anti-Semitism? Craig and I tried to talk about this once right after my invitations were withdrawn, but it was clear we couldn't.

Craig couldn't talk to his own parents about it, but I had to give him credit—he talked to mine. The summer his parents had issued their ultimatum, he stopped to talk to my parents on his drive back to Berkeley. He told my parents once again that he loved me but he also loved his parents and he didn't know what to do. He reiterated that he didn't share any of his parents' prejudices and he was hoping that someday they would change. But he couldn't predict.

I don't think my parents knew how to handle it. Or maybe they handled it perfectly by doing nothing. My mother had a history of taking on my battles even when I didn't want her to, *especially* when I didn't want her to. But she didn't this time. Occasionally she'd ask if anything had changed and when I said no, she'd say, "I wish you didn't have to go through this." Before that, she'd instilled in me the policy of dumping before getting dumped though she never said it quite that way. This time was different. I'm not sure why. I had assumed she'd be outraged by his parents, but then she probably wasn't surprised given her "scratch the surface of a gentile" philosophy.

The Christmas party at Don Lugo was fun. There was a talent show and an abundance of talent among the men. The abortion doctor was a classical pianist, and the warden managed to locate a piano for the party; someone else provided a marimba for a kid named Carlos who had a band on the outside made up of his cousins. Cousins figured prominently in Carlos's life. An older cousin had talked him into robbing a gas station; during the robbery, the cousin and the attendant exchanged gunfire and the cousin was killed. Carlos was serving a ten-year sentence for murder. In California if someone dies in the course of committing a felony, you go to prison for murder even if the guy killed was one of the perps—even if you didn't kill him. My brother's contribution to the talent show: he and a buddy sang a long, bawdy ballad that was cleaned up enough for the G-rated audience.

By the time Craig and I left the party to go home, the tule fog had rolled in and was so dense that we had trouble finding the

VW in the parking lot. I had never seen it that bad. It made pea soup look like consommé. I avoided the freeway and crawled along surface streets to the Denny's where I was to deliver Craig. The only way I could see well enough to drive was to turn my headlights off, but then no one could see us. (In low-hanging dense fog, headlights make visibility worse. The fog no longer appears vaporous; it looks like a solid wall.)

It took what felt like an hour just to drive the few miles to the Denny's. When I pulled up, Craig said, "I can't let you drive home. It's too dangerous."

Neither of us had credit cards for a motel. In those days, college kids usually didn't. "Do you have some cash at home? I would pay you back."

"Wait here. I'll be right back."

He walked over to the phone booth in the Denny's parking lot. I assumed he was calling a friend. I looked at my watch; it was 11:30. He got back in the car.

"My parents are inviting you to spend the night at their house."

"I can't do that."

"You don't have a choice. Besides, they were very nice about it. They agreed that it's too risky for you to drive. They have a friend who was killed in one of those chain reaction accidents on I-5 . . . they've never quite gotten over it."

"You have got to be kidding, Craig. I cannot sleep in the house of people who hate me."

"They don't hate you, they hate . . . oh, please, let's not do this now. My mother is making up the bed in the guest room right now."

"I don't know what to do." I looked at my watch again. Maybe they would be asleep by the time I got there and I could get up early and be out of there before they woke up and I wouldn't have to see them.

"Really, honey," he said, "you don't have a choice here."

When we got to his house, his parents had gone to bed. Craig showed me to the guest room. Someone had made an effort. On the dresser burned a lavender candle, and there was a bowl of small lavender soaps. The double bed was turned down, a sprig of lavender on the pillow and a stack of snowy white bath towels at the end of the bed. The room was so welcoming, I couldn't help feeling a little hopeful. This was not the bare minimum.

"Do you have an alarm clock I can borrow?" I asked Craig. "I should get going early."

"I'm sorry. Mine is in Berkeley."

"Will you please come get me as soon as you wake up? I want to get an early start." He said he would.

When I woke up I could smell bacon frying and thought about camping. I remembered that before the shit hit the fan, Craig told me his family camped in Yosemite for two weeks every year. He talked about how some day he wanted me to join them. And then my little disappointed heart sank because I remembered that the people in the kitchen cooking breakfast were never going to take a Jewish girl, quarter breed or not, camping. For a minute I wondered if I could escape through the sliding glass window. I got dressed and joined the happy threesome in the kitchen.

Both of his parents greeted me warmly. It was an exact repeat of the other time I had breakfast there before they knew about my tainted blood. His dad, who had the same brush cut, was wearing the same plaid flannel shirt and jeans. His mom, a slightly plump woman with smooth olive skin and a perm that was a little too permed, was wearing the same apron. The fabric was decorated with the same cupcakes and it had the same lace trim. As before, there was a platter of scrambled eggs with cheese, a platter of bacon and grilled tomatoes, a platter of silver dollar pancakes. Somehow we came up with enough topics to discuss, though I was the one doing the heavy lifting. (Your apron is so pretty. Did you make it?) And then I was out of there. But not before his mother gave me a raft of crisp bacon wrapped in foil. "Maybe you can make BLTs for your lunch."

The fog had lifted, revealing a stunning, clear day. The San Bernardino Mountains, snow-capped and towering beyond the freeway, reminded me of how much I love Southern California when it's clear. On the drive back to my parents' house, I composed the thank-you note I would write. "Without a doubt you saved my life last night, and then this morning to present me with such a beautiful breakfast was beyond generous. Thank you for your hospitality."

Driving my mother's little red VW, a sure sign that hatred didn't have to be forever, and looking at my foil pack of bacon I thought about Anne Frank's quote: "In spite of everything I still believe that people are really good at heart."

Buoyant. I was utterly buoyant.

I was glad my parents weren't home. I didn't want the grilling. I rummaged through my mother's desk and found some expensive, cream-colored stationery and I wrote the thank-you note. I took a bath and then went for a walk.

When Craig called that night, I took the phone into my bedroom. "It was really sweet of your parents to have me there."

He said nothing.

"I just wrote your mother a thank-you note."

"That's nice," he said. Silence. Then: "After you left, I walked in the kitchen where my mother was washing dishes. I put my arm around her and kissed her cheek. I thanked her for being so gracious. I told her I was happy that she had a chance to get to know you. The smile left her face and the hateful look returned.

"'You don't understand,' she said. 'Just because I was nice to her doesn't mean a thing. I'd be nice to a stray dog if it needed help. Nothing has changed, Craig, and it's time you accepted it. Way past time.'"

chapter sixty-four
THE MOTHERS WHO POISONED THEIR
BABIES AT JONESTOWN HAUNT HER

July 2012

I was driving home to California from Arizona on Highway 58 through the Mojave Desert. I make this trek every summer after six weeks in the high desert south of Tucson. It was hot—the outside reading on my car thermometer read 115 degrees—and desolate. When I saw the Highway 395 turn-off to Death Valley I started thinking about my trip to Barker Ranch (see chapter 45). At that very moment the NPR program *To the Best of My Knowledge* came on the radio. The topic: "Why do people join religious cults?" Like so much that's happened since I started researching this topic, I thought, "Synchrony!" Or maybe it was the primeval ambience of the desert. Or maybe the heat was getting to me.

In any event, the host Jim Fleming was interviewing Diane Benscoter, a former member of the Unification Church. When the focus turned to dangerous cults, Fleming asked why some cult members commit violence. Benscoter said that in 1974 when she was recruited by the Moonies she was an idealistic seventeen-year-old who wanted to make a difference in the world. She was invited to join a peace walk from Omaha to Des Moines.

Two young people accompanied her, and the three attended lectures along the way. There was much talk of the Messiah and making the world a better place—"creating the Kingdom of Heaven on Earth." Her companions told her that God was choosing her to be part of this grand project. They told her it was not necessary to wait for the Second Coming. It had already occurred in 1920 in Korea in the form of Sun Myung Moon, and they were on their way to meet him in Des Moines, Iowa.

With every mile she walked, her excitement built. When they arrived and she met said Messiah, she was a convert. She cut off her hair, started to fast, and committed the rest of her life to Sun Myung Moon. She spent the next five years selling candy and flowers on the street to raise money for him. Her family was not willing to lose her permanently to the Moonies, so her parents hired a deprogrammer. Eventually, it worked.

Part of her deprogramming was to read a book by Robert Jay Lifton about idealistic totalistic communities. Point by point, she realized that the Unification Church qualified: the church manipulated people, both personally and spiritually; the church promoted black-and-white thinking; the church forbade criticism of the leader or the principles of the group; the world was divided into good (everyone in the group) and evil (everyone outside the group). The scales fell from her eyes. She was free from the church's grip.

Jim Fleming asked her if it was a relief to reach the end of the deprogramming. Did she feel free at that point?

Benscoter replied that she felt free in some ways but that freedom came with a price. It left her feeling extremely empty. She said she didn't know anything about herself. She didn't know what she believed in, she didn't even know what music she actually liked—it had all been fed to her. She didn't know what to do with her life.

(As I've mentioned, Pat and Leslie told me that they, too, had "no self" when they were with Manson.)

When Benscoter hears about people in cults committing violence, either toward themselves or to others, she understands. The mothers who poisoned their babies with Kool-Aid at Jonestown haunt her. Suicide bombers who kill themselves and innocent people haunt her. She knows that she would have been capable of doing such things when she was a Moonie. "I was so dedicated to my Messiah, it had taken over my thought processes, my rational thought, such that I would have done anything and so I empathize with those people greatly."

November 10, 2012

After missing each other for weeks Diane Benscoter and I finally talked, and when I got off the phone I felt as though the lock I'd been trying to pick for so long gave way. In an attempt to understand the women's psyches under Manson's influence, I had tried every combination of numbers, turned the dial both ways, held up the lock to my ear, listening to the vibrations of the pins, each time clicking impotently. Finally the numbers, the tumblers, the whatevers, slipped into place and something unlocked. Our conversation didn't supply me with all of the answers, but it gave me a context that made their behavior if not totally understandable, at least not as alien as it had been.

Here is a summary of our conversation:

I told her what I had told so many. I described what Pat and Leslie were like growing up and how they changed when they were with Manson. I told her that the women were not only removed from any civilized idea of right and wrong, they were detached from any sort of feeling for their victims. Not an ounce of empathy for their suffering, not a fraction of an ounce.

She told me that because of her experience as a Moonie, she understands. She repeated what she'd said on the radio. She not only understands, she identifies. She identifies with suicide bombers and with the mothers who poisoned their babies with Kool-Aid at Jonestown. They were all part of totalistic communities as described by Lifton—the book that helped her get free from the church.

"Because you think of the leader as God and God is above the law, you have permission to spurn the laws of society, too. You start believing that the laws that you grew up believing in are wrong because they are man-made. The leader spouts the same stuff over and over, and everyone in the group keeps reinforcing it. There's no countervailing force. There are no checks and balances. The instructions come from above. You start to feel special. We're in on the secret. No one else is."

"But," I asked, "what accounts for the brutality?"

"In a situation like that there's a chemical reaction," she said. "Adrenaline is released . . . you're euphoric in that moment because you believe that what you're doing is exactly right. You have what feels like super-human energy." She likens this state of mind to a mother who is able to gather enough strength to lift a car off her child. "You're in a bubble of righteousness. Everything else disappears. You're above the law of physics. There is nothing you can't or won't do."

She said the bubble is impenetrable, so impenetrable that it can override the most basic human instinct, a mother protecting her young. When the Jonestown mothers watched their babies foaming at the mouth from the poison Kool-Aid, it still wasn't enough to shake them out of it. "You believe the world is evil and now you have the ticket to heaven. You are so special. You have special permission to do anything."

She talked about how someone's mind can become so distorted that it makes sense to try to save the world by any means necessary, even if it's brutal and ugly. In fact, she said, when your brain is working like that, you think it would be wrong if you didn't participate. "Something happened to my brain when I was in the church. I know my brain changed."

"But, Diane," I said, "five years. It took Pat and Leslie five years of being away from Manson and the other cult members to get out of that bubble."

This did not surprise her. She said it's precisely because the behavior was so extreme, so brutal, they couldn't let it in. The brain has a way of protecting itself when someone has done something so horrific. "What they did was so enormous. How could they comprehend that?"

Diane never did anything as extreme as Pat and Leslie when she was in the Unification Church, not even close, but she acted in ways that, for her, were so out of character that she later had difficulty believing accounts of her behavior. "At one point I got a call from my brother telling me that my mother had breast cancer. He asked me to come home and I refused. I felt that what I was doing was more important than being with my mother. Before that it would have been inconceivable for me to turn my back on my mother when she was sick with cancer, so once I made the decision not to go home, I was even more dedicated to the church because I had to justify that decision."

"In for a dollar, in for a dime?" I asked.

"Exactly," she replied.

"But," I said, "it's one thing to believe that you're above the law because of divine intervention, but it's quite another to cause terrible suffering and feel nothing for your victims."

"Once you've crossed the line," she explained, "you shut down the part of you where empathy resides. Your survival depends on being able to shut it down. The cognitive dissonance between who you were and who you are is so great, you wouldn't be able to tolerate it otherwise. And it isn't just empathy that you shut down. It's your values, it's everything you believed in. It takes a long time before your original, primary version of what's right and wrong returns."

chapter sixty-five
STARLIGHT BALLROOM

June 2012

I was roaming the periphery of the Starlight Ballroom, trying, with all of my visual might, to make out the faces of former classmates hanging in clusters around the room. All attendees of the reunion at the Hollywood Renaissance Hotel had their high school yearbook photos pinned in prominent places on their persons, and thank God for that. Father Time, with his habit of multiplying chins, subtracting hair from the top of heads while adding adipose to midsections, had been of no use in helping me recognize old friends. Most of us had not seen each other since 1960 when we'd marched across the stage of the Hollywood Bowl to Pomp and Circumstance to receive our diplomas.

At the Starlight Ballroom on reunion night, the music was provided by a homegrown group, The Four Preps, one of our claims to fame. I didn't know the guys; they were in my brother's class and first got together to perform in the 1956 Hollywood High talent show. They sounded great, even without the deep voice of tall Eddie Cobb or the high tenor of Marv Ingram—both of whom had been replaced by younger men after they died in 1999.

My eyes landed on one face that looked almost exactly the same as his yearbook photo: Stephen Kay. No extra chins or adipose on Steve. He was the same tall, lean, erect guy—if anything, more erect—that he'd been in high school but, as I'd discovered in our more recent contact, he now wore an armor of righteousness that hadn't been there when we were teenagers.

When I first talked to him after embarking on my Leslie and Pat journey, I'd assumed he could help me flesh out the women, help me understand who they'd been and who they'd become. I didn't yet know about his laser focus on only one part of that: who they'd been. He not only had no interest in who they'd become, he was hostile to the very idea that they had changed in any way.

The more time I spent at the prison the less contact I had with Steve, and I knew that once I decided to write a letter to the parole board supporting Leslie's release I was sure he'd believe that I had been naive, seduced by her dangerous charm. I also assumed he would see it as a betrayal of him. As a result, I'd been apprehensive about encountering him at the reunion.

But there he was and there I was and there we were talking courteously. He introduced me to his wife, who was lovely and cordial. I knew he had officially retired and that he no longer attended parole hearings. He told me that he was now working on cold cases. I'd read that one of those cases was the 1947 Black Dahlia murder. Steve Hodel, a former LAPD homicide detective turned private investigator, had asked Steve for help after his own investigation into the grisly unsolved crime convinced him that his own father, psychiatrist George Hodel, had murdered the victim, twenty-two-year-old Elizabeth Short, whose tortured and mutilated body was found in a vacant lot in Los Angeles. An account of this is detailed in Hodel's book, *The Black Dahlia Avenger*, including his relationship with Stephen Kay.

We chatted about cold cases and then about the mutual friends we had seen that night, and then there was a lull in the conversation.

"So . . . you've spent time with Leslie."

"Yes," I said. "I've gotten to know her pretty well."

I couldn't think of anything more to say. Apparently, neither could he. Another silence.

Before I realized it, I was enveloped by some sort of altered state. Perhaps it was the romantic lighting that created a dreamy atmosphere. The soft light erased the harshness in Steve's face and relaxed his bearing. He looked like the affable, sweet boy I'd known in high school. Or maybe it was the music. The Four Preps had just finished singing "26 Miles" ("Twenty-six miles across the sea, Santa Catalina is a-waitin' for me"), a song about love and hope, and now they were singing "Big Man" ("You were a big man yesterday, but boy, you ought to see me now"), a song about regret.

I felt expansive and sentimental and in that moment I believed anything was possible.

"Steve," I said, "I have an idea."

He said nothing. He simply stared at me, waiting. I was waiting, too—waiting for the idea to fully hatch. I thought about how Steve Hodel had described Steve Kay: "a stand-up guy." And I thought about how every once in a while *60 Minutes* has a segment on a district attorney who, years after prosecuting a criminal, advocates for him or her, either because of new evidence pointing to the individual's innocence or because of a dramatic transformation.

"Now that you don't have any official role," I said, "you could get to know Leslie. You wouldn't have to tell anyone. You could just go and visit." I knew Leslie well enough to know that she wouldn't exploit such a visit for her own gain. I truly believed that.

"Why in the world would I want to do that?" he said. The soft lighting wasn't soft enough to disguise the look of horror on his face.

"If nothing else, wouldn't it be interesting? In all these years you've only talked to her in front of the parole panel. It's adversarial . . . you can't get to know someone that way." I reminded him that he once said that of the three women, Leslie was the one he thought could someday be released.

"That was before she married that guy. It showed how bad her judgment is."

"Steve, that was in 1981." I swept my arm across the aging crowd in the ballroom—the paunches, the gray hair, the wrinkles. "Don't you think we've all changed in the past thirty years?"

He smiled, a tight and not particularly friendly smile. I realized that approach would never work. He was suspicious of change. He views all of Leslie's progress as one long manipulation; the more people in the outside world, no matter how distinguished, who vouch for her, the more entrenched his opposition. In Steve's world, it's all a ruse, a veneer.

As I searched my brain to come up with another argument, he pulled out what he considered his heaviest artillery. "You have to remember," he said, "they wanted to start a race war."

I don't know if my mouth flew open, but I was surprised enough that it might have. The obsessive, nonsensical fixation of this remark astonished me. Not because I hadn't heard it before. I had. But not for a few years so I had assumed he'd dropped that argument. For decades he'd been quoted as saying that he would never let up on these people because they wanted to destroy society in a race war and have hundreds of thousands of innocent people murdered. But somehow, I thought that his fury about Leslie's short, bad marriage, which seemed to intensify every decade, had supplanted it.

Steve is a nice guy, a decent person, a smart man, but there's lunacy to this. The race war was part of Manson's delusional system, a psychosis one psychiatrist at the first trial characterized as a *folie a famille* because it engulfed the whole group. Remember the grand plan? They would leave a wallet from the LaBianca house in a gas station in a black neighborhood, the blacks would be blamed for the murder of the LaBiancas, and years and years of repressed rage would explode and result in a massive race war. The Manson group would escape the bedlam by driving their dune buggies into the hole in the earth in Death Valley to wait it out. A golden rope would lower them, dune buggies and all, into the bottomless pit, a kind of Shangri-la where none of them would age. They would wait out the race war in this paradise and then re-emerge after the troubles were over. The blacks, now victorious, would immediately see them as allies, and because Manson believed that blacks were inferior and incapable of governing, they would enlist him and his band of loonies, with their superior knowledge and wisdom, to lead the country. The Family would move from Shangri-la to the White House.

My expression must have communicated my incredulity.

"Sure, it might have been unrealistic," he said, "but that doesn't matter. What counts is that they wanted to."

In Steve's static world consistency is the premier virtue, and from that vantage point, Manson is the one worthy of trust. The first time he said this to me, I thought he was kidding because he had a smile on his face. But then he said it again. This time he wasn't smiling, but I got the feeling that he was pleased by the surprise on my face. Like the race war argument, this was a position he had held for a very long time. I came across a May 14, 1989, article in the *Los Angeles Times* where, in talking about the three women and Tex, Steve explained to the reporter why, of all of the former members of the Manson Family, it was Charles Manson who earned his respect.

"Charlie has changed so little over the years," Steve said to me with, though faint, an unmistakable look of fondness on his face. "He's basically the same old Charlie."

EPILOGUE

Spring/Summer of 2016

On April 14, 2016, a panel of the California Parole board recommended parole for Leslie Van Houten. Before that, she had been denied parole nineteen times. Near the end of the five-hour hearing, Commissioner Ali Zarrinnam cited her decades of favorable psychological evaluations and her exemplary prison record. He said they had looked for even a single indication to demonstrate evidence of current dangerousness. "After these forty-six years . . . there just isn't one anymore." He told Leslie she deserved to be released. She was sixty-six. She'd been in prison since she was nineteen.

Word of the parole panel's decision quickly spread throughout the prison. As Leslie, in a stunned state, left the hearing room to walk back to her unit, the inmates she walked past in the yard stopped what they were doing and started to applaud. The younger women knew her as a mentor; the older women knew her as a friend. They all knew how hard she had worked on herself and how much, year after year, she had given to their community.

The decision was a shock to both sides of the Leslie divide, but the journey wasn't over. The ruling had yet to be reviewed by the parole board's legal team and, if upheld by that body, then for-

warded to Governor Jerry Brown, who would either affirm or reject the recommendation.

The battle lines were drawn.

Leslie's allies—her lawyer, friends, and family—were optimistic. Her best friend since childhood said she believed, truly
believed, that the governor would do the right thing. "For the first
time in more than forty years, I'm not worried about her. I know
she's going to be released." A self-proclaimed "friend of Leslie"
established a Facebook page devoted to gaining support for her
parole.

The other side was fired up and immediately launched an effort
to reverse the recommendation. Debra Tate, Sharon Tate's youngest sister, though she had no connection to the LaBianca killings,
led the charge to keep Leslie behind bars, by launching a
change.org petition. To the anti-Leslie forces, rehabilitation is beside the point. "Maybe Leslie Van Houten has been a model prisoner," Cory LaBianca, Mr. LaBianca's daughter told reporters,
"but you know what? We still suffer our loss. My father will never
be paroled. My stepmother will never get her life back."

Jackie Lacey, the L.A. district attorney, wouldn't even concede
that Leslie is rehabilitated. In an open letter to the governor she
claimed that Leslie is a threat to public safety because she continues to maintain "a disturbingly distorted view of Charles Manson." When I first read the letter, her accusations were so extreme
and off base, I wondered if she had the wrong file. Her conclusions were shockingly inaccurate and had no bearing on any psychological evaluation or report that had been done on Leslie
during the past four decades. Lacey declared that Leslie "clearly
lacks insight, genuine remorse, and an understanding of the mag-
nitude of her crimes." The woman she described was unrecogniz-
able to anyone who knew Leslie.

It was difficult to predict what Jerry Brown would do. When I
worked for California Public Radio in the late 1970s, I covered

his campaign for re-election. (He served two four-year terms starting in 1975 and was re-elected in 2011. He's now serving his fourth term, which will end in 2018.) On two campaign swings through the state I traveled on the press bus with him, and there was ample opportunity to talk to him about a range of issues. He was unapologetically in favor of punishment as a guiding principle. He saw no reason to spend money on rehabilitation because he said there was no evidence that it worked.

I also knew this from a personal angle. My brother had applied to him for a pardon. When he was interviewing criminal lawyers to represent him, they all said, to a person, that it was a hopeless endeavor: Brown was a more strident law-and-order governor than Ronald Reagan. But since that time he'd served two terms as mayor of Oakland, a city with a large African American population, and he saw firsthand how the punitive approach was ruining lives and destroying communities. There was reason to believe Brown would be sympathetic to Leslie's release.

On July 22, 2016, three and a half months after the parole board's decision, Brown overturned the recommendation. While he acknowledged the progress Leslie has made, he declared that she posed an unreasonable danger to society "because it remains unclear how she had transformed herself from a smart, driven young woman to 'a member of one of the most notorious cults in history and an eager participant in the cold-blooded and gory murder of innocent victims.'"

Within days of Brown's decision, Leslie's attorney, Richard Pfeiffer, filed a writ of habeas corpus in San Bernardino Superior Court. In October 2016 Superior Court Judge William C. Ryan issued an eighteen-page ruling upholding Brown's reversal, claiming that there is "some evidence" that Leslie still presents an unreasonable threat to society and adding that he respected Brown's broad discretion in such decisions.

Leslie's parole decision came at a critical turning point in the state's criminal justice system. From a political angle, there is no one more central to this than Jerry Brown and no inmate more central to the issues of rehabilitation and parole than Leslie Van Houten.

In 1976 Brown signed into law the Uniform Determinate Sentencing Act, which greatly reduced opportunities for parole, and stated directly that the purpose of imprisonment is punishment. The result has been catastrophic, not only for California but, because the state led the way legislatively for the whole country. We've lost a couple of generations of young people who lived large portions of their lives behind bars where they didn't receive necessary education, adequate vocational training, or effective therapeutic intervention.

Brown, who now acknowledges the problem, is determined to reverse the damage. He sponsored the Public Safety and Rehabilitation Act of 2016, which appeared on the state's November ballot and passed. The bill reinstates rehabilitation as a goal for the prison system and will vastly expand parole opportunities, shifting power to make parole decisions away from prosecutors and back to parole boards.

It was Leslie's bad luck that at the very moment Brown was gaining support for his initiative, the decision about her parole landed on his desk. If her crime had not been so notorious, she could have been an exemplar of his goals: a prisoner rewarded for good behavior, for taking an active role in her rehabilitation, for taking advantage of educational opportunities. Done, done, and done.

At the end of July, about a week after Brown reversed the parole board's decision, I visited Leslie at Frontera. She said she understood the governor's dilemma. She knew it would have been difficult for him to be associated with the release of a member of the Manson Family while trying to gain support for the bill.

"He was in a tough spot," she said. "Opponents of his initiative would use my release against him."

She said she was in agreement with what he was trying to accomplish. Over the years she has witnessed so many young women come to Frontera with no education, no skills, and no hope of acquiring either while they serve extraordinarily long sentences. Many of them are young mothers with young children. "They don't have a chance and neither do their kids.

"This initiative needs to pass. It's important. And I know it would have been harder to pass if I was in any way associated with it.

"Of course I'm torn," she said. She looked at me with a bittersweet smile. "I'm torn between my desire to get out of prison after more than forty-five years and what I know is best for the community."

Meanwhile, the saga continues. In December 2016, the California Supreme Court denied a petition that Leslie's attorney, Rich Pfeiffer, had filed seeking a review of her case. In the petition, Pfeiffer contended that the governor did not focus on Van Houten's "current dangerousness" but instead focused on "a crime committed by a youthful offender almost 47 years ago, and a factor that can never change regardless of any amount of rehabilitation that is accomplished." He asserted that the governor did not have evidence to support his finding that Leslie remains an unreasonable risk to public safety.

After the Court ruled, Pfeiffer announced that he's not giving up.

In their response, attorneys from the California Attorney General's office countered that the governor "properly considered the aggravated nature of Van Houten's crimes" to assess her "current dangerousness," and that the governor's findings are "reasonably supported by ample evidence in the record."

Furthermore, according to the attorney general's office, "Van Houten eagerly carried out some of the most infamous crimes in history with her fellow Manson Family members and she continues to downplay her participation in the murders."

Once again, Leslie appeared before the parole board on September 6, 2017.

Fall 2017

On September 6, 2017, Leslie appeared at her twenty-first parole hearing. The predictable parade of folks opposing her release showed up: LaBianca family members, Debra Tate, representing Louis Smaldino, the LaBianca's nephew (though he also attended and testified), and Deputy D.A. Donna Lebowitz. For the second time in a little over a year, their objections didn't prevail. In spite of their claims that Leslie was not rehabilitated, that she was still a danger to society, that she was a "narcissist who doesn't care about anyone but herself," the parole panel, once again, chose to believe the testimony of people who actually know her—prison staff who had worked with her, professors who had taught her, psychiatric professionals who had evaluated her, and friends who had known her for decades. The consensus of those people was that she was not a danger to society and had the character and experience to be an asset to the community.

Presiding Commissioner Brian Roberts and Deputy Commissioner Dale Pomerantz said that in addition to Leslie's stellar disciplinary record, they were influenced by her accomplishments, pointing out that she had earned her bachelor's degree as well as a master's degree in counseling, had been certified as a counselor, and had headed numerous programs to help inmates.

"You've been a facilitator, you've been a tutor, and you've been giving back for quite a number of years," Roberts said to Leslie. Taking into account her entire time of incarceration, they concluded that she no longer poses an "unreasonable risk of danger or a threat to public safety."

Before closing, however, Roberts sounded a cautionary note. He told Leslie that parole officials had heard from "tens of thousands" of people who didn't want her released, and he warned her that living in society "will not be easy."

"So, with that," he said, "we'd like to wish you good luck."

After their recommendation on September 6, the Board of Parole Hearings had 120 days to review the panel's decision, and Governor Jerry Brown had 30 days after that to confirm, reverse, or modify the decision.

"If he rejects it, we'll go back to court," Van Houten's attorney, Rich Pfeiffer, told *Vice News*. "I'm not going away, and she's going home."

As of this writing, the governor has not made his decision.

Acknowledgments

Much of my gratitude goes to my friends who have been so good to me during this book's long, difficult, and sometimes painful gestation period. If I had been in a twenty-year, on-and-off relationship with a demanding man—a man who often scared me, made me weep, a man who frequently caused sleepless nights and from whom I learned some of life's most painful lessons, I trust they would have told me to dump the guy years ago. Not one of my friends ever told me to abandon this project—instead, they often told me they thought it was a valuable endeavor and perhaps even worth the suffering.

Unlike other writers I know, I generally don't talk about what I'm writing while I'm writing it, and I don't send pages, chapters, or, with a few exceptions, even final manuscripts to friends. Maybe it's the introvert in me. Or maybe I'm afraid if I share too early someone else's voice will be in my head making it difficult for me to hear my own with any confidence. At the other end of the journey, if I share too late, I'll be too exhausted to welcome input. This is not to say I've been without editorial help, especially in the later stages of the book.

First on that list is my daughter, Caitlin Meredith. Having a daughter who is also a writer and a litigation consultant with a similar worldview (though different enough to provide a much-needed perspective) has been invaluable. She has helped me with various aspects of this book, from a foray into the badlands of the Mojave Desert, to the final stages of the manuscript. In addition to her critical feedback she is a natural-born problem-solver and the most resourceful person I know.

I am indebted to Christopher Noel for editing my almost-final manuscript and to Annette Brehmer, my friend since the seventh grade, whose eleventh-hour proofing of the final manuscript was a lifesaver. I'm grateful to Melinda Worth Popham, my *in case of* (*writing*) *emergency* friend, for her assorted and useful remedies. She's always been available when I most need her.

To Carole Marcus for her loyalty and support through the many chapters of our long friendship. To Anne Taylor, whose friendship helped me keep my head above water when full immersion in this project threatened to drown me. To Elizabeth Spinner, my English usage genius; to Joann Ruskin for her diagnostic expertise in the early stages of this project.

To Michael Krasny, my treasured friend and liaison with the established literary world. Without Michael my work might have remained safely tucked away in my sock drawer.

Just as I've had my own editorial department in the form of a daughter, I've had the help of my own IT team in the form of a son, Ben Holbert. In spite of putting in a full day as the director of technology of a school district, he always answered his mother's panicky calls and within a matter of minutes solved the problem and saved the day. (When I was writing the chapter on Haight-Ashbury, I realized that I had been pushing him, my new baby boy, in his stroller on the same blocks in the same year that the newly paroled Charles Manson was prowling the streets for young girls. My joy with my infant, a peace symbol embroidered on his onesie, symbolized what the Haight had been; Manson's particular kind of menace symbolized what the Haight was becoming.)

I want to thank my agent, Suzy Evans, with the Dijkstra Literary Agency. Her early enthusiasm for this book mattered more than she probably knows. I have to thank two of my former editors—Linda Xiques and Wendy Lapides—who nurtured me when I was still green and instilled confidence in me that persisted long after I stopped writing for them. I lost Wendy to Cornwall, England, but Linda has been a valuable sounding board in the later stages of this book. I'm grateful to my Kensington editor Michaela Hamilton whose belief in the value of asking "why" launched this book.

I am indebted to Leslie Van Houten and Patricia Krenwinkel for helping me understand the treacherous process by which the Charles Mansons of this world lure young people who are at vulnerable times in their lives.

I'm grateful to Stephen Kay for generously giving his time when I was learning the criminal justice aspects of this case.

Finally, infinite gratitude to my husband, Dr. Larry Meredith, a man who, in his professional life, is committed to evidence-based approaches to public health but in his personal life, at least when it involves his wife, a man who consistently relies on blind faith as a guiding principle.

Connect with

U S

Visit us online at
KensingtonBooks.com
to read more from your favorite authors, see books
by series, view reading group guides, and more.

Join us on social media

for sneak peeks, chances to win books and prize packs,
and to share your thoughts with other readers.

facebook.com/kensingtonpublishing
twitter.com/kensingtonbooks

Tell us what you think!

To share your thoughts, submit a review,
or sign up for our eNewsletters, please visit:
KensingtonBooks.com/TellUs.